Studies in Intelligence

I0113484

Studies
in
Intelligence

A collection of articles on the historical, operational,
doctrinal, and theoretical aspects of intelligence

GOVERNMENT REPRINTS PRESS
Washington, D.C.

© Ross & Perry, Inc. 2001 All rights reserved.

No claim to U.S. government work contained throughout this book.

Protected under the Berne Convention. Published 2001

Printed in The United States of America
Ross & Perry, Inc. Publishers
717 Second St., N.E., Suite 200
Washington, D.C. 20002
Telephone (202) 675-8300
Facsimile (202) 675-8400
info@RossPerry.com

SAN 253-8555

Government Reprints Press Edition 2001

Government Reprints Press is an Imprint of Ross & Perry, Inc.

Library of Congress Control Number: 2001092606

http://www.GPOreprints.com

ISBN 1-931641-26-9

♾ The paper used in this publication meets the requirements for permanence established by the American National Standard for Information Sciences "Permanence of Paper for Printed Library Materials" (ANSI Z39.48-1984).

All rights reserved. No copyrighted part of this publication may be reproduced, stored in a retrieval system, or transmitted, in any form or by any means, electronic, photocopying,
recording, or otherwise, without the prior written permission of the publisher.

Center *for the* Study *of* Intelligence
Washington, DC 20505

EDITORIAL POLICY

Articles for *Studies in Intelligence* may be written on any historical, operational, doctrinal, or theoretical aspect of intelligence.

The final responsibility for accepting or rejecting an article rests with the Editorial Board.

The criterion for publication is whether, in the opinion of the Board, the article makes a contribution to the literature of intelligence.

EDITORIAL BOARD

Lloyd D. Salvetti, Chairman
Thomas Behling
Joseph B. Castillo, Jr.
Peter A. Clement
A. Denis Clift
Dawn R. Eilenberger
Dolores D. Greene
Joseph Hayes
Joanne O. Isham
William C. Liles
William Nolte
Maj. Gen. Richard J. O'Lear,
    USAF (Ret.)
Barry G. Royden
Julie M. Savell
L. Britt Snider
Michael Warner
Jon A. Wiant

Members of the Board are drawn from the Central Intelligence Agency and other components of the Intelligence Community.

EDITORS

Henry Appelbaum
Wendy Hilton-Jones

CONTENTS
45th Anniversary Special Edition
SELECTED UNCLASSIFIED AND DECLASSIFIED ARTICLES, 1955-1999

Foreword   vii
Lloyd D. Salvetti

The Framework
The Need for an Intelligence Literature   1
Spring 1955
Sherman Kent

1955-1959
William J. Donovan and the National Security   13
Summer 1959
Allen W. Dulles

1960-1964
The Defections of Dr. John   27
Fall 1960
Delmege Trimble

1965-1969
On the Soviet Nuclear Scent   53
Fall 1967
Henry S. Lowenhaupt

1970-1974
Soviet Deception in the Czechoslovak Crisis   71
Spring 1970
Cynthia M. Grabo

1975-1979
The Holocaust Revisited: A Retrospective Analysis   87
of the Auschwitz-Birkenau Extermination Complex
Winter 1978
Dino A. Brugioni and Robert G. Poirier

1980-1984
An Interview with Richard Helms   107
Fall 1981
David Frost

1985-1989
A Stone for Willy Fisher   137
Winter 1986
Richard Friedman

1990-1994
The San Cristobal Trapezoid   149
Winter 1992
John T. Hughes and A. Denis Clift

1995-1999
A First Tour Like No Other   167
Spring 1998 unclassified edition
William J. Daugherty

List of Contributors

Sherman Kent, the "founding father" of *Studies in Intelligence*, headed the Office of National Estimates and was a pioneer in the then-emerging field of intelligence analysis.

Allen W. Dulles was Director of Central Intelligence from 1953 to 1961—the longest anyone has served in that post.

Delmege Trimble was a CIA intelligence officer.

Henry S. Lowenhaupt was a CIA specialist on nuclear matters.

Cynthia M. Grabo was an intelligence officer at the National Indications Center.

Dino A. Brugioni was an intelligence officer at the National Photographic Interpretation Center and has long been a frequent contributor to *Studies in Intelligence*.

Robert G. Poirier was a CIA imagery analyst whose work included seeking ways to broaden the applications of imagery analysis beyond purely military concerns.

David Frost is an internationally acclaimed broadcast journalist.

Richard Friedman worked for the National Intelligence Council.

John T. Hughes was a Department of Defense imagery analyst.

A. Denis Clift is President of the Joint Military Intelligence College.

William J. Daugherty, who served in the Directorate of Operations, is now a faculty member at a university in the southern United States.

Sherman Kent

45th Anniversary Special Edition

Foreword

The first issue of the Intelligence Community journal *Studies in Intelligence* was published in 1955. It featured an article by Sherman Kent, a legendary figure in CIA called the "father of intelligence analysis," who served with great distinction from 1952-1967 as chairman of the Board of National Estimates and as director of the Office of National Estimates. Kent laid out the arguments for studying and treating the analysis of intelligence information as a defined, rigorous discipline with its own criteria and standards. Kent's 1955 article, reproduced in this Special Edition, eloquently argued "The Need for an Intelligence Literature" by proposing regular production of a journal such as *Studies* to build a body of professional intelligence literature to keep it a "robust and growing discipline."

Kent's call was heeded, and *Studies* has endured and prospered for 45 years. Intelligence officers, current and retired, as well as scholars of intelligence—both teachers and students—have been the journal's lifeblood, writing articles that encompass the entire craft of intelligence—historical, operational, doctrinal, and theoretical.

Studies was a quarterly classified journal until 1992, when an annual unclassified edition—composed largely of unclassified articles from previous classified issues—was added to reach a wider audience beyond the Intelligence Community. Hundreds of scholars in the United States and abroad, as well as CIA Officers in Residence and Faculty Representatives at American colleges and universities, now rely on the journal's wider publication for thoughtful and thought-provoking articles on topics that are otherwise scarcely covered in regular academic literature.

This Special Edition consists of a noteworthy article from each five-year period in the 45 years that *Studies* has been published. Because of the wealth and quality of material available, we have not labeled these articles as "the best," although we have tried to represent each major component of intelligence activity—science and technology, analysis, operations, and support. The scope of this collection ranges from broad, policy-relevant topics to more narrowly focused, highly specialized subjects.

Most of these articles were published in the original classified edition, but along with many other articles, are now available in declassified format at the National Archives. Declassified articles from *Studies in Intelligence* are available to researchers at the National Archives as part of the Records of the Central Intelligence Agency (Record Group 263). Contact the Archives II Reference Branch, National Archives, 8601 Adelphi Road, College Park, MD 20740 or call (301) 713-7250.

The Center for the Study of Intelligence seeks to maintain *Studies* as the premier journal of the Intelligence Community well into the new century. The Editors and Editorial Board welcome comments and opinions as well as scholarship in producing new editions of *Studies*. Contact me, any member of the *Studies* Editorial Board, or the Editorial Staff, for comments, questions, or contributions.

Lloyd D. Salvetti,
Chairman, Editorial Board
Studies in Intelligence
November 2000

~~FOR OFFICIAL USE ONLY~~

THE NEED FOR AN INTELLIGENCE LITERATURE
by Sherman Kent

IN most respects the intelligence calling has come of age. What has happened to it in the last fourteen years is extraordinary. Maybe our present high is not so extraordinary as our low of 1941. In that day the totality of government's intelligence resources was trifling. We knew almost nothing about the tens of thousands of things we were going to have to learn about in a hurry. As emergencies developed we found ourselves all too reliant upon British intelligence. Many of us recall important studies issued by US intelligence organizations which were little more than verbatim transcripts of the British ISIS reports.

In 1941, the number of people who had had prior intelligence experience and who at the same time were available for new government assignments in intelligence was very small. There were few in Washington who could give any guidance as to how to go about the business in hand. What intelligence techniques there were, ready and available, were in their infancy. Intelligence was to us at that period really nothing in itself; it was, at best, the sum of what we, from our outside experience, could contribute to a job to be done. It did not have the attributes of a profession or a discipline or a calling. Today things are quite different.

Let me briefly note the principal assets of today's intelligence community. To begin with, we are at strength. Per-

~~FOR OFFICIAL USE ONLY~~

haps we are not as strong as the present volume of work requires, but by and large we have the staff to do the man-sized job before us.

Again, we are not novices at our business; we have a lot of experience behind us. We are officered and manned by a large number of people with more than a decade of continuous experience in intelligence, and who regard it as a career to be followed to retirement. By now we have orderly file rooms of our findings going back to the war, and we have methods of improving the usefulness of such files. We have orderly and standardized ways of doing things. We do most things the right way almost automatically. We have developed a host of new and powerful overt and covert techniques which have increased the number of things we can and do find out about. Most important of all, we have within us a feeling of common enterprise, and a good sense of mission.

With these assets, material and experiential, intelligence is more than an occupation, more than a livelihood, more than just another phase of government work. Intelligence has become, in our own recent memory, an exacting, highly skilled profession, and an honorable one. Before you can enter this profession you must prove yourself possessed of native talent and you must bring to it some fairly rigorous pre-training. Our profession like older ones has its own rigid entrance requirements and, like others, offers areas of general competence and areas of very intense specialization. People work at it until they are numb, because they love it, because it is their life, and because the rewards are the rewards of professional accomplishment.

~~FOR OFFICIAL USE ONLY~~ **3**

Intelligence today is not merely a profession, but like most professions it has taken on the aspects of a discipline: it has developed a recognized methodology; it has developed a vocabulary; it has developed a body of theory and doctrine; it has elaborate and refined techniques. It now has a large professional following. What it lacks is a literature. From my point of view this is a matter of greatest importance.

As long as this discipline lacks a literature, its method, its vocabulary, its body of doctrine, and even its fundamental theory run the risk of never reaching full maturity. I will not say that you cannot have a discipline without a literature, but I will assert that you are unlikely to have a robust and growing discipline without one.

Let me be clear about this literature that we lack. First, let me say what I do *not* mean that we are lacking. I do not mean the substantive findings of intelligence. Manifestly, I do not mean those thousands of words we disseminate each day about past, present, and probable future goings on all over the world. I do not refer to the end product of all of our labors. We produce a great deal of this sort of literature and possibly we produce too much of it. It is not that literature that I am talking about. What I am talking about is a literature dedicated to the analysis of our many-sided calling, and produced by its most knowledgeable devotees. The sort of literature I am talking about is of the nature of house organ literature, but much more. You might call it the institutional mind and memory of our discipline. When such a literature is produced, it does many things to advance the task.

~~FOR OFFICIAL USE ONLY~~

~~FOR OFFICIAL USE ONLY~~

The most important service that such a literature performs is the permanent recording of our new ideas and experiences. When we record we not only make possible easier and wider communication of thought, we also take a rudimentary step towards making our findings cumulative. We create a stock of relatively imperishable thinking which one man can absorb without coming into personal contact with its originator and against which he can weigh and measure his own original ideas. His large or small addition to the stock enriches it. The point is reached where an individual mind, capable of using the stock, can in a day encompass the accumulated wisdom of man-decades of reflection and action.

Consider such disciplines as chemistry or medicine or economics and ask yourself where they would be today if their master practitioners had committed no more to paper than ours. Where would we be if each new conscript to medicine had to start from scratch with no more to guide him than the advice of fellow doctors and his own experience? Where would we be in medicine if there was nothing to read and nothing to study, no text books, no monographs, no specialized journals, no photographs, no charts, no illustrations, no association meetings with papers read and discussed and circulated in written form? Where would we be if no one aspired to the honor of publishing an original thought or concept or discovery in the trade journals of his profession? It is not impossible that blood letting would still be considered a valuable panacea and exposure to night swamp air the specific for syphilis.

The point is that in the last few centuries we have accumulated an enormous amount of knowledge. And the fact that this accumulation has taken place since the discovery of

~~FOR OFFICIAL USE ONLY~~

~~FOR OFFICIAL USE ONLY~~ 5

printing from movable type is by no means merely coincidental. The translation of new thought into words, and the commission of words to the permanence of print, more than anything else has made possible a progressive and orderly advance in all disciplines and all areas of learning.

In our calling, I am saying, we do not do enough of it. To be sure we do do some writing. We have produced a good many Training Manuals of one sort or another. We have done a good bit of chronicling of interesting case studies with an educational end in view. We have made transcripts of oral presentations at training centers. If you ransacked the "libraries" of intelligence schools you would find quite an amount of written material. Even so there is a very considerable difference between this volume of written material and the systematic professional literature I am talking about.

It is hard to define such a literature, and I will not try to do it in a sentence or two. As a starter I will note what I think to be three important aspects of it. To begin with, *the literature I have in mind will deal with first principles.* A portion of it will certainly have to deal with the fundamental problem of what we are trying to do. What is our mission? And as soon as that question is submitted to careful analysis, there is no telling what will emerge. One thing I think is certain: that is, that we have many more than a single mission and that many of us have been confused not only about the number and character of the many missions, but also how each of the many relates to the others.

Another first principle that will have to be elaborated is how we are going about our mission — what is our method? Here again we will find out, when the question is systemat-

~~FOR OFFICIAL USE ONLY~~

ically answered, that there is not a single method, but that there are dozens of methods; and from further examination or discussion we will confront a good many new concepts which will speed our task and enrich our product.

Let no one feel either that we are necessarily sure of the nature of our first principles or that dispassionate examination of them would be a waste of time. In recent months the intelligence community has had to wrestle with such fundamental concepts as "national intelligence objectives" and the criteria for the selection of such objectives; the nature of "warning"; the role of "indications" and so on. The results of these discussions have been generally praiseworthy, but the amount of time consumed and the consequent delay of important decisions quite otherwise. An analogous situation might be a consultation of surgeons deadlocked on a discussion of the nature of blood, preliminary to handling the emergency case presently on the operating table.

This takes me to a second thing which I would expect from a systematic literature of intelligence: *a definition of terms.* Hastily let me add that I am not proposing that we write a dictionary. Words which stand for complicated concepts cannot be defined by a dictionary. Words like "liberalism" and "democracy" require the equivalent of scores of dictionaries, or scores of shelves of dictionaries. You cannot define those as you define "paper" and "ink." So with our own words that stand for complicated concepts — such as "evaluation," "indicator," "capability," "estimates," and so on. As of today we use these words easily and often — yet one wonders if they are always understood in exactly the way intended. For example, we would be almost tongue-tied without the word "capability"; we use it perhaps more often than

~~FOR OFFICIAL USE ONLY~~ 7

any other of our semi-technical words. Yet a little reflection on the matter shows that we use it indiscriminately to mean one of three quite different things: a feasible course of action, a raw strength, and a talent or ability. Can we be sure that we are always conveying an intended sense?*

If we do not rigorously define our terms we are likely to find ourselves talking at cross purposes; and such discussion, we all realize, risks being more of a fruitless dispute than an elevated debate. This takes me to a third point.

The literature I have in mind will, among other things, be an *elevated debate*. For example, I see a Major X write an essay on the theory of indicators and print it and have it circulated. I see a Mr. B brood over this essay and write a review of it. I see a Commander C reading both the preceding documents and review them both. I then see a revitalized discussion among the people of the indicator business. I hope that they now, more than ever before, discuss indicators within the terms of a common conceptual frame and in a common vocabulary. From the debate in the literature and from the oral discussion I see another man coming forward to produce an original synthesis of all that has gone before. His summary findings will be a kind of intellectual platform upon which the new debate can start. His platform will be a thing of orderly and functional construction and it will stand above the bushes and trees that once obscured the view. It will be solid enough to have much more built upon it and durable enough so that no one need get back in the bushes and earth to examine its foundations.

---

* Editor's Note: In our next monograph, one of Mr. Kent's colleagues, Abbot Smith, takes up precisely this problem in his article *Capabilities in National Estimates.*

~~FOR OFFICIAL USE ONLY~~

FOR OFFICIAL USE ONLY

Now if all this sounds ponderous and a drain on time, I can only suggest that, so far, we of the Western tradition have found no faster or more economical way of advancing our understanding. This is the way by which the Western world has achieved the knowledge of nature and humanity that we now possess.

These are only three things that I would expect from this literature. There are many others. It could and should record such things as new techniques and methods, the history of significant intelligence problems and accomplishments, the nature of intelligence services of other countries, and so on. But the three items that I have singled out remain the most important.

There are perils of going forward in our profession without laying down such a literature. First, there are the obvious perils of denying our calling the advantages I have discussed above. There is, however, another peril and one we should heed for strictly utilitarian reasons. As things now stand, we of the intelligence profession possess practically no permanent institutional memory. Our principal fund of knowledge rests pretty largely in our heads; other funds of knowledge are scattered in bits through cubic miles of files. What happens to our profession if we are demobilized as we were after the two world wars? What happens to it if our heads and files find themselves in the middle of a nuclear explosion? The answer, I fear, is that a new beginning will have to be made virtually from scratch. Most of what we know will go when we go; only a very small part will be left behind. A literature of intelligence is a reasonable insurance policy against repetition of two demobilizations of intelligence that have occurred within our memory.

FOR OFFICIAL USE ONLY

In highlighting the desirability of producing a literature of intelligence and stressing the perils of not producing one, I do not wish to seem to close my eyes to problems and difficulties.

The first of these is probably the matter of security. One can expect the question: "Do you want to put all the secrets of the profession in writing and bind them up in one great book so that your enemy's success with a single target will at once put him abreast of you?" The answer comes in two parts. In the first place, many of the most important contributions to this literature need not be classified at all. They could be run in the daily press and our enemies would get no more good from them than from the usual run of articles published in our professional journals. Surely the enemy would benefit in some degree; he would benefit as he presently does from his reading of *The Infantry Journal* or *Foreign Affairs*. On the other hand, another type of contribution would deal with delicate trade secrets and would have to be classified. But is this reason not to write or circulate it? Every day we have to decide on the correct security procedure with respect to sensitive materials. Why should the literature at instance be necessarily more delicate or sensitive than the last cable from Paris, and why should its proper handling be more difficult or dangerous? In this case, as in the more familiar one of the sensitive report, we must again equate the value of exposing many minds to a problem with the increasing danger of disclosure. The plain fact is that "security" and the advance of knowledge are in fundamental conflict. The only reason we get anywhere is because we do not demand either perfect security or unlimited debate about secrets of state. We do get somewhere because the necessity for compromise at both ends is well and fully understood.

There is another difficulty and a very practical one. How is such a literature to be written if most or all of the potential authors are practicing members of the profession, already burdened with seemingly higher priority tasks? I know of no magic formula by which a man can do two things at once. The question that we face is the familiar one of priorities. Surely one of the guiding principles to a solution is the desirability of investing for the future. Taking Mr. X off the current task and giving him the time to sort out his thoughts and commit them to paper will more than repay the sacrifice if what Mr. X puts down turns out to be an original and permanent contribution. If it buttons up a controversial matter and precludes thousands of hours of subsequent discussion, the cause has been well served. It has been well served even though one of Mr. X's would-be consumers had to get along without his advice on another matter. What we are faced with in this case is nothing more complicated than the value and pain of capital formation.

A third problem. How may the Mr. X's be paid for work-time spent in the creation of this literature? If what has gone before is the fact and the Mr. X's of the calling are really creating intelligence capital, then it seems to me that they are entitled to their wage exactly as if engaged upon their regular assignments. Indeed, in logic, if what Mr. X produces contributes to the solution of the next hundred problems, he should be paid more than if he spent his time merely solving the single assigned problem before him.

~~FOR OFFICIAL USE ONLY~~ 11

Beyond these rather fundamental matters, there are hundreds of other problems. If a large proportion of the Mr. X's are sure to come from intelligence staffs, where do they work? Are they to have secretarial help? Will they keep regular hours? Must they be in residence? How will their findings be reproduced? How circulated? What editorial controls will be exercised over their output? These are really easy questions. The hard ones are to find the Mr. X's in the first place, and to induce them to undertake the most difficult job of all: original creative writing.

~~FOR OFFICIAL USE ONLY~~

Adaptation from an address delivered in tribute to the father of central intelligence.

WILLIAM J. DONOVAN AND THE NATIONAL SECURITY

Allen W. Dulles

It was my privilege to be associated with William J. Donovan both as a lawyer between the wars and then during World War II, when I served under his command in the Office of Strategic Services. His courage and leadership made a profound impression on me. I should like to convey to you something of that impression, and some idea of what his pioneering has meant to all of us.

His interest in our national defense and security started early. In 1912, as the war clouds gathered in the Balkans, he helped organize Troop I of the New York National Guard. In 1915 he went to Poland as a member of a Rockefeller commission charged with relieving the great shortage of food there, and particularly of milk for the children. When the National Guard was mobilized in 1916, he came home to join his Troop I on the Mexican border.

War Service

Then came his fabulous career in World War I with the 165th Infantry of the 42nd Division—the renowned "Fighting 69th" of the Rainbow Division. Here he got his nickname Wild Bill. The legend goes that after the regiment landed in France he ran them five miles with full packs to limber them up. As the men were grumbling with exhaustion, Donovan pointed out that he was ten years older and carrying the same 50-pound pack. One of the men replied, "But we ain't as wild as you, Bill!" Another story has it that the honorary title was transferred to him from a professional baseball pitcher of the same name whose control left something to be desired. Whatever its origin, the title stuck.

The citations Colonel Donovan received in France tell the military story: On July 28, 1918, a Distinguished Service Cross: "He was in advance of the division for four days, all the while under shell and machine gun fire from the enemy, who were on three sides of him, and he was repeatedly and persistently

71

counterattacked, being wounded twice." Three days later the Distinguished Service Medal: "He displayed conspicuous energy and most efficient leadership in the advance of his battalion across the Ourcq River and the capture of strong enemy positions. . . . His devotion to duty, heroism, and pronounced qualities of a Commander enabled him to successfully accomplish all missions assigned to him in this important operation."

And then, for action in combat in the Meuse-Argonne on October 14, the highest of all awards, the Congressional Medal of Honor: ". . . Colonel Donovan personally led the assaulting wave in an attack upon a very strongly organized position, and when our troops were suffering heavy casualties he encouraged all near him by his example, moving among his men in exposed positions, reorganizing decimated platoons and accompanying them forward in attacks. When he was wounded in the leg by a machine gun bullet, he refused to be evacuated and continued with his unit until it withdrew to a less exposed position." "No man ever deserved it more," said General Douglas MacArthur, who had seen this action.

Three aids were killed at Donovan's side in the course of these actions. Reverend Francis P. Duffy, the chaplain of the 69th, said, "His men would have cheerfully gone to hell with him, and as a priest, I mean what I say." Several years ago General Frank McCoy, describing his close association with Bill Donovan during World War I, said he was one of the finest soldiers he ever saw in his life-long service in the Army, that he had the qualities of the ideal soldier, judgment and courage and the respect and affection of his men.

Law Career

In 1922 Donovan was appointed U.S. Attorney in Buffalo, N.Y., and shortly thereafter he entered a new phase of his career. In 1924 President Coolidge reorganized the Department of Justice and called Bill to Washington to be assistant to the Attorney General, heading the Antitrust Division. Here he showed both his fearlessness in law enforcement and his intense interest in making law a practical vehicle to promote the economic welfare.

72

William J. Donovan

He was firmly convinced that individual freedom is vitally linked to our system of free enterprise. He attacked restraints and monopoly with effective enthusiasm. In the Trenton Potteries case he won Supreme Court agreement that price fixing among dominant competitors is of itself illegal. He brought under legal attack such diverse industries as oil, sugar, harvesting machinery, motion pictures, water transportation, and labor unions. Yet he recognized that the uncertainties of our antitrust laws pose serious business problems, and accordingly instituted the practice of giving advance opinion on the legality of proposed mergers and other business activities that might be questioned under the law.

Offered the Governor Generalship of the Philippines when President Hoover entered the White House in 1929, Bill turned it down and went into law practice in New York City. He was soon appointed counsel to several of the New York bar associations in connection with a general overhauling of the bankruptcy laws. During this period he also served as counsel to a committee for review of the laws governing the State's Public Service Commission. In 1932 he unsuccessfully ran for Governor of the State.

As a corporation attorney he won in 1935 the important Humphrey case, in which the U.S. Supreme Court held that the President could not arbitrarily remove a chairman of the Federal Trade Commission. He also won an important decision in the Appalachian coal case, upholding the right of coal producers to organize a joint selling agency in economic self-defense. This agency is still in existence.

During this period of corporate law practice, Bill never lost his interest in world affairs. He took time off to visit Ethiopia during the 1935 Italian invasion. He was in Spain during its Civil War, carefully observing the Axis efforts to test their new equipment in these foreign adventures.

Presidential Emissary

In the early days of World War II Donovan was called into action by President Roosevelt. In 1940 he was sent on a fact-finding mission to England and in 1941 to the Balkans and the Middle East. Anthony Eden told Washington that the Balkan

73

mission had been most helpful to the British assessment of the situation there.

From the first trip, the one to Britain not long after Dunkirk, Bill had brought back to Washington a very important report. You will recall there was skepticism at that time in some quarters as to whether the British could effectively carry out Churchill's thrilling promise, "We shall defend our island, whatever the cost may be, we shall fight on the beaches, we shall fight on the landing-grounds, we shall fight in the fields and in the streets, we shall fight in the hills; we shall never surrender." Donovan reported to Roosevelt that the British could and would do just that. This had a direct effect on American policy. He also warned Harry Hopkins that the Germans might strike toward Suez through French North Africa—a prophecy that soon became a reality.

Donovan also recommended to the President that the United States start preparing immediately for a global war. He particularly stressed the need of a service to wage unorthodox warfare and to gather information through every means available. He discussed this idea at length with his close friends in the Cabinet, Secretaries Knox and Stimson, and with Attorney General Jackson.

The seeds which Bill planted bore fruit. In July 1941 the President established the Office of the Coordinator of Information and called Donovan to Washington to head it. In original concept this Office was to combine the information and intelligence programs with psychological and guerrilla warfare. This proved to be too big a package for one basket and in 1942 the organization was split. That portion of it coordinating wartime information services became the Office of War Information, and the intelligence and unorthodox warfare work, where Bill's greatest interest lay, was put under an Office of Strategic Services.

The O.S.S.

Truly one of the remarkable accomplishments in World War II was the organization and activity of the O.S.S.—feats which would never have been achieved without Bill Donovan's leadership and his vast interest in the unorthodox, the novel and the dangerous. Starting from scratch in 1941, he built

74

William J. Donovan

an organization of about 25,000 people that made a real contribution to the victory. Many of the deeds of O.S.S. will have to remain secret, but with the passage of time many have been disclosed.

Bill conceived the O.S.S. as a world-wide intelligence organization that could collect the facts necessary to develop our policy and war strategy. He was convinced that Axis secrets were to be found not only in Berlin, Rome, and Tokyo, but in other capitals and outposts around the world. So he immediately set about dispatching officers to key spots in Europe, Asia, and later Africa. The pay-off justified the effort. He was able to obtain information of great value from carefully established agents with contacts in Berlin, in the German High Command, and in the Abwehr, the German military intelligence service. The work of these agents gave us advance information about the development of German jet aircraft, about German work with heavy water in the effort to develop a nuclear weapon, about the V–1's and V–2's, and about the plot against Hitler.

In addition to his organization for the collection of strategic intelligence, Donovan provided means to help gather tactical information in the combat areas, forming teams of parachutists—Americans as well as indigenous—to drop behind enemy lines. But not content with passive intelligence, he also wanted action. He knew that well-organized guerrillas operating behind enemy lines in areas where the local population was friendly could wreak havoc on enemy lines of communication and tie down troops that could otherwise be used in combat. Working with our allies, he built up teams of leaders and communicators to organize resistance in the countries occupied by the Nazis, Fascists, and Japanese. There were also air drops of supplies and equipment deep behind the Axis lines in France and Italy, in Burma and elsewhere.

These action teams were well supported by a headquarters technical group, which under Donovan's guiding hand was imaginatively developing new ways to sabotage the enemy war effort and new gadgets either to harass the enemy or help our own cause—equipment ranging from the most sophisticated communications systems to a repellent used by personnel forced to bail out in shark-infested waters. Not all of the products were so practical as these. Ambassador David

75

Bruce, one of Bill Donovan's closest associates, in a recent tribute to the General's qualities of leadership, vividly described his excitement over ideas. Ambassador Bruce wrote, and I subscribe to every word of it:

> His imagination was unlimited. Ideas were his plaything. Excitement made him snort like a race horse. Woe to the officer who turned down a project, because, on its face, it seemed ridiculous, or at least unusual. For painful weeks under his command I tested the possibility of using bats taken from concentrations in Western caves to destroy Tokyo [with delayed action incendiary bombs]. The General, backed by the intrigued President Roosevelt, was only dissuaded from further experiments in this field when it appeared probable that the cave bats would not survive a trans-Pacific flight at high altitudes.

Many ingenious ideas to work on the nerves of the enemy were born in another part of the O.S.S.—the Morale Operations Branch. This was the undercover psychological warfare branch of the war effort. While the Office of War Information was telling the enemy about the magnitude of the U.S. war effort and getting the facts and figures well circulated, this Branch was dedicated to confusing the enemy and breaking their will to resist.

General Donovan was convinced that there were great untapped reservoirs of information in this country about foreign areas which had become of vital interest in the war effort—data in the archives of business organizations, information acquired abroad by American scientists, academicians, and tourists, and also that held by foreign experts residing here. He set about to collect this information and data and a mass of photographs of foreign areas. As the war reached more and more areas of the globe, this information came to have great importance.

He also realized the importance of analyzing and presenting information to the policy makers in readily usable form—one of the most difficult tasks of intelligence. He established in the O.S.S. a major branch for research and analysis, assembling in Washington the best academic and analytic brains he could beg, borrow, or steal from the universities; laboratories, libraries, museums, the business world, and other agencies of government. Theirs was the task of probing the political and economic aspects of the war, assessing both our

William J. Donovan

allies and our enemies, both neutrals and the occupied lands. Theirs also was the task of estimating Axis vulnerability and war potential and the staying power of the Russians, who even then told us almost nothing about themselves.

Bill Donovan had the qualities a great intelligence officer must have. He took nothing for granted and at the same time was insatiably curious. He had a good nose for the news: a faint whiff of something unusual would speed his mind into a dozen possible explanations, generally as ingenious as the wiles of the enemy. He wanted to see things on the spot and judge for himself. He was constantly on the move and drove his staff wild trying to keep him from places they thought too exposed. He also put them into a state of near exhaustion trying to keep up with the pace he set himself. One of his great qualities was his dedication to the men who served under him, and his ever-readiness to give them his full support. He, in turn, had their complete loyalty, respect and affection. I vividly recall a personal instance.

For about two years, from November 1942 to September 1944, I was working for Donovan in Switzerland, then entirely encircled by the Nazi-Fascist forces. In September 1944 the American Seventh Army, coming up from Southern France, broke through to the Swiss border near Geneva. Under orders to return to Washington to report, I had joined a group of the French underground in a secret hideout in the Rhone Valley between Geneva and Lyon to await a clandestine flight to take me to London. As far as I knew, General Donovan was in Washington and had not the slightest idea where I was hidden. After weather had held up my plane for several days, there was a knock on the door of my hideout in the middle of the night. It was one of General Donovan's aides, telling me that the General was waiting for me at the nearest available airstrip south of Lyon, which had just been evacuated by the Nazis. He had been searching the area for some twenty-four hours before he discovered where I was.

Together we flew back to London, arriving, I well remember, on that day in September 1944 when the Germans launched the first of their ballistic missiles on the British capital. It descended near the center of London after a flight of nearly two hundred miles. Both the American and the British intelligence services had been closely following the development of this

77

missile. I have often wondered why, in this country, our technicians and strategists failed to see earlier the full implications of the success of the V–2, as I believe the Soviet did, and to realize much earlier in the game that the combination of the ballistic missile with the atomic bomb, which was then about to be unveiled, could change the nature of war and the security position of this country.

Few men of his time were more alert than Donovan to the new threats that might develop. In late 1944, sending a man to Cairo to take over the direction of activities at that post, he gave oral instructions to the effect that the main target for intelligence operations should now be what the Soviets were doing in the Balkans rather than German activities in the Middle East. The German threat was receding. The Soviet danger was already looming. Operations were to be adjusted accordingly, although such instructions could not be put into official writing.

Also, while the war was still in progress, General Donovan was looking forward to the peace. He foresaw the need for a permanent organization not only to collect intelligence but, perhaps even more important, to coordinate the whole government intelligence effort and see that the President and policy makers get comprehensive and consolidated analyses to guide their decisions as to our course of action.

The Father of Central Intelligence

In the fall of 1944 Donovan presented to the President a paper proposing an intelligence organization operating on a world-wide scale and having direct responsibility to the President. While it was not to take upon itself the responsibilities of the departmental intelligence services, it would act as a coordinating mechanism for all intelligence. The paper stressed that the proposed organization would have no police or subpoena powers and would not operate in the United States. President Roosevelt expressed considerable interest in this proposal, and a week before his death in April 1945 asked Donovan to poll the Cabinet and the heads of agencies concerned for comment on it. These comments, ranging from the opinion that there was no need for such a peacetime organization to the belief that it was vital to national security, make interesting reading today.

78

William J. Donovan

18 November 1944

MEMORANDUM FOR THE PRESIDENT

Pursuant to your note of 31 October 1944 I have given consideration to the organization of an intelligence service for the
post-war period.

In the early days of the war, when the demands upon intelligence services were mainly in and for military operations, the
OSS was placed under the direction of the JCS.

Once our enemies are defeated the demand will be equally
pressing for information that will aid us in solving the problems
of peace.

This will require two things:

1. That intelligence control be returned to the supervision
of the President.

2. The establishment of a central authority reporting
directly to you, with responsibility to frame intelligence objectives and to collect and coordinate the intelligence material required by the Executive Branch in planning and carrying out
national policy and strategy.

I attach in the form of a draft directive (Tab A) the means
by which I think this could be realized without difficulty or
loss of time. You will note that coordination and centralization
are placed at the policy level but operational intelligence (that
pertaining primarily to Department action) remains within the
existing agencies concerned. The creation of a central authority
thus would not conflict with or limit necessary intelligence functions within the Army, Navy, Department of State and other agencies.

In accordance with your wish, this is set up as a permanent
long-range plan. But you may want to consider whether this (or
part of it) should be done now, by executive or legislative action.
There are common-sense reasons why you may desire to lay the keel of
the ship at once.

The immediate revision and coordination of our present intelligence system would effect substantial economies and aid in the
more efficient and speedy termination of the war.

Information important to the national defense, being gathered
now by certain Departments and agencies, is not being used to full
advantage in the war. Coordination at the strategy level would
prevent waste, and avoid the present confusion that leads to waste
and unnecessary duplication.

Though in the midst of war, we are also in a period of transi-
tion which, before we are aware, will take us into the tumult of
rehabilitation. An adequate and orderly intelligence system will
contribute to informed decisions.

We have now in the Government the trained and specialized
personnel needed for the task. This talent should not be dispersed.

William J. Donovan
Director

79

William J. Donovan

THE WHITE HOUSE
WASHINGTON

April 5, 1945

MEMORANDUM

TO: MAJOR GENERAL DONOVAN

Apropos of your memorandum of November 8, 1944, relative to the establishment of a central intelligence service, I should appreciate your calling together the chiefs of the foreign intelligence and internal security units in the various executive agencies, so that a consensus of opinion can be secured.

It appears to me that all of the ten executive departments, as well as the Foreign Economic Administration, and the Federal Communications Commission have a direct interest in the proposed venture. They should all be asked to contribute their suggestions to the proposed centralized intelligence service.

F.D.R.

80

William J. Donovan

Donovan received an Oak Leaf Cluster to his Distinguished Service Medal for his wartime work, but his plan to develop the O.S.S. into a peacetime intelligence organization was beset with conflicting views. Some would have the new organization, like the O.S.S., report to the Joint Chiefs of Staff, while others preferred that it be put under the Department of State. And there was controversy as to whether one individual could or should be responsible for presenting a consolidated view of the intelligence picture to the policy makers, rather than leave this the collective responsibility of the chiefs of all the intelligence services. No agreement had been reached by the time the war ended in August 1945, and the O.S.S. was soon ordered disbanded.

A proposal for a central intelligence organization such as Donovan had conceived was contained in the first draft of the so-called unification act submitted by Ferdinand Eberstadt to Secretary Forrestal in October 1945. And in January 1946, to preserve assets while the issue was being settled, President Truman issued the order creating the Central Intelligence Group, which later picked up some of the functions and personnel still remaining from the O.S.S. and other scattered independent intelligence activities.

Bill Donovan's dream was not yet completely realized. Congress still had to act. After extensive hearings to which General Donovan contributed important testimony, the provisions for a Central Intelligence Agency were incorporated into the National Security Act of 1947, which created a Department of Defense and set up the National Security Council to advise the President and oversee the new intelligence agency. In July 1947 final executive and legislative endorsement was thus given to the views which Donovan had been striving to have accepted. I have always felt that the decision to place the C.I.A. under the President, as Donovan recommended, was wise and necessary.

Bill Donovan's restless energy had turned elsewhere with the disbanding of O.S.S., although he never gave up his interest in the organization or stopped hammering home to the public the necessity for providing adequate and accurate information to the policy makers of the government in order to protect the national security. His varied talents were being called on for other important services. His legal ability and

81

vast knowledge of German wartime activities were used to help prepare the Nuremburg trials for the Nazi war criminals. He went to Greece to investigate the murder of newsman George Polk, a clear effort of the Communists to prevent the truth about the extent of their activities in the Greek civil war from seeping out.

The more General Donovan saw of the Soviets in action the more concerned he was with alerting the American people to the dangers. He co-authored an article in the Yale Law Journal for July 1949 presenting a "Program for a Democratic Counter Attack to Communist Penetration of Government Service." The article said:

> The Communist Fifth Column . . . seeks to identify itself with every social grievance. Russian espionage and subversive operations are made up of trained and skilled spy technicians and intelligence officers, propaganda specialists, experts in spreading rumors. Instruction is planned so that the agent will find it as easy for a minority to operate a labor union, or a pacifist league, or any other such movement, as it is for a minority group to control a large corporation when most of the stockholders take no active interest in the management.

In 1950 President Eisenhower, then President of Columbia University, presided on the occasion of the award to Bill Donovan of the Alexander Hamilton Medal, given by the Columbia Alumni Association for distinguished service and accomplishment in any of the great fields of human endeavor. In 1953 the President named him Ambassador to Thailand. At this time the ancient kingdom of Siam was a main target for Communist subversion. With a vigor that belied his years, this remarkable man of 70 threw himself into the job of helping the Thais bolster their defenses against the Communists so that this keystone of anti-Communism in Southeast Asia could continue free.

Upon his return to the United States one might have expected him to seek retirement, but nothing was further from his mind. He became National Chairman of the International Refugee Committee and the director of that group's fight against the Soviet program to induce Russians who escaped from Communism to return home. At the time of the Hungarian Revolution he turned his energies to aiding the refugees of this unsuccessful effort to win freedom from Soviet tyranny.

82

William J. Donovan

He was Chairman of the American Committee on United Europe from its inception in 1949, and through this organization he continued to further the efforts of our major allies in Western Europe to achieve a greater unity in the face of Communist danger.

Even after ill health forced his retirement to Walter Reed Hospital, General Donovan continued his interest in the fight against Communism and the development of our intelligence work. In recognition of his role in the intelligence field, President Eisenhower in 1957 awarded him the National Security Medal. The citation reads:

> Through his foresight, wisdom, and experience, he foresaw, during the course of World War II, the problems which would face the postwar world and the urgent need for a permanent, centralized intelligence function. Thus his wartime work contributed to the establishment of the Central Intelligence Agency and a coordinated national intelligence structure.

In February 1959 he passed away at Walter Reed among the men he had led. As soldier, public prosecutor, leader of the bar, director of the Strategic Services in wartime, public servant in time of peace, he had left his record with the nation he served so well. He was a rare combination of physical courage, intellectual ability, and political acumen. He was a mild-mannered man, with an insatiable curiosity, an unflagging imagination, and the energy to turn his ideas into action.

The heritage of Bill Donovan is written in the national security. He woke the American people to the need of a permanent peacetime intelligence service. He bestirred Washington into creating a mechanism whereby all the government components which receive information on what is going on anywhere in the world pool their knowledge, share their interpretations, and work together to make one unified estimate of what it means. He helped place intelligence in its proper perspective and stimulated the policy makers to recognize its role in determining American policy abroad. He was one of the architects of an organization that should keep our government the best informed of any in the world.

History's epitaph for William J. Donovan will be:

> *He made his nation more secure.*

83

A once sensational and mysterious intelligence betrayal is examined in the perspective of time for motivation and key circumstances.

THE DEFECTIONS OF DR. JOHN
Delmege Trimble

Rain streaked the streets of Berlin, splashed on darkened houses, glistened in the light from an East-West border checkpoint. A sedan rolled up, its tires singing on the wet pavement. A customs guard sauntered out. For a moment there was only the throb of the engine, a murmur of conversation, the rhythmic click of the windshield wipers. Then the wave of a hand, and the car rolled across the Sandkrug Bridge into the darkness of East Berlin.

A simple incident on this warm, wet night of 20 July 1954, the decennial of a more famous 20 July. Simple, but so fraught with significance for Germany and the West that Chancellor Adenauer called it "terrifying." Dr. Otto John, president of the Office for the Protection of the Constitution, had defected. He was the most important Westerner fallen into Communist hands since the two British diplomats, Guy Burgess and Donald MacLean, had vanished from London in 1951, and far more important than they in point of implications for intelligence.

The puzzle was—and to some still is—the reason why, the causes behind the eastward flight of the Federal Republic's internal security chief in the company of a trumpet-playing gynecologist, a Dr. Wolfgang Wohlgemuth. The contemporary explanations ranged the spectrum. The easiest one, that Wohlgemuth was a Soviet agent who had drugged John and abducted him, foundered on facts that gradually came to light. Some said that John, a mixed-up idealist, had been spurred across the border by a misguided concept of political morality. Some regarded him as a victim of machinations on the part of the neo-Nazis and clerical and other reactionary circles around Chancellor Adenauer. His flight was pictured by

1

others as that of a desperate man whose past was about to catch up with him. Yet others called him a long-time traitor and informer, even a secret Communist fanatic.

There were prejudicial grounds for some of the least pretty interpretations. John's weaknesses for alcohol and the opposite sex were well known, his favorite sport when pixilated being to snap the elastic of women's brassieres. It was persistently rumored that he was a double agent or a homosexual, and he certainly had an affinity for too many characters with one or both of these qualifications. Aside from his companion Wohlgemuth, who had connections with the East Berlin Charité Hospital and made no secret of his Communist sympathies, John was on good terms with Soviet agent Max Wonsig, blown at the Willi Kucher spy trial, and more notably with one Baron Wolfgang Gans Edler Herr von und zu Putlitz. Von und zu Putlitz had been a prewar British agent in the Nazi Foreign Office, whisked to the safety of England in 1938; subsequently he worked in the United States for OWI until he was fired and his valet had to support him by tending bar; later he returned to British employ in Germany; and in 1950 he started working for the Communists in East Berlin.

Yet the stereotype of the weak man made vulnerable by his lusts or corrupted by bad company is not one that fits the Otto John picture. And all the other theses, each arguable, strike only tangentially at the truth. Erich Ollenhauer may have come closer when he remarked, after John redefected and began to show increasing signs of a persecution and Messiah complex, "This is a case for the psychiatrists rather than the politicians." We cannot even now arrive at anything like a tidy analysis of the case, but we can achieve some understanding of it by tracing John's propensities during the Nazi and Nuremberg eras, reviewing the circumstances of his unlikely appointment and ineffectual tenure as president of the Bundesamt fuer Verfassungsschutz, and examining in detail his behavior just before and after his defection on that 1954 anniversary of the unsuccessful 20 July anti-Hitler coup.[1]

---

[1] Except as otherwise indicated, the authority for factual statements in the following account rests in classified documents in U.S., ~~███████████████~~ intelligence files.

~~SECRET~~

Dr. John

Role in the Anti-Nazi Underground

Otto John was born in 1909. Two friendships from his early life remained of importance in his adult career and were to play a part in the events of July 1954. During his school days at Wiesbaden in the mid-twenties he became a close chum of Wolfgang Hoefer, son of the school principal. The intensity of German schoolboy friendships is reflected in the eventual tragedy that flowered from this early acquaintance. Hoefer, whose mother was Jewish, emigrated to the United States in the late 1930's. He changed his name to Hoffer, became a U.S. citizen and a soldier. In 1945 he was sent to Germany and renewed his friendship with Otto John. In 1954, upon John's defection, he committed suicide.

An emotionally more important relationship for Otto was that with his brother Hans, another marked for tragedy. Hans, the younger, brighter, and sturdier, was the extrovert doer, Otto the troubled dreamer. Otto felt no fraternal jealousy; he adored the younger brother who, as long as he lived, supplied the balance Otto needed. Hans was to be tortured to death in the aftermath of the abortive July 1944 coup.

Otto studied for a career in the foreign service, mastering Spanish, French, and English. But when Hitler came to power membership in the Nazi Party became a prerequisite for aspirants to the foreign service, and he shifted to international law. Never a member of any political party (though after the war he once referred to himself as a quondam Socialist), he said his convictions were a blend of monarchism, old-fashioned liberalism, and anti-Nazism. He received the doctorate in law from Frankfurt University in 1935.

By 1936 both John brothers were in Berlin. Hans was studying law at Berlin University. Otto served for two years without pay at Tempelhof Airdrome to qualify for final state law examinations in the service of Lufthansa. In 1937 he became assistant legal counsel, under Klaus Bonhoeffer, of the rapidly expanding civil airline. He was now in a position to do something positive about his anti-Nazi convictions. Through Klaus and his brother Dietrich, a Lutheran minister, he entered one of the circles that later were to band in the conspiracy against Hitler. An airline with routine flights into foreign countries was a convenient front for a conspiracy against a

3

totalitarian regime.[2] Klaus Bonhoeffer assigned Otto to several courier runs.

When World War II broke in September 1939 Hans John went into the Luftwaffe as a lieutenant, but Otto remained with Lufthansa. That autumn he established connections with such anti-Nazis as the Social Democrat Wilhelm Leuschner and Col. General von Beck. Prince Louis Ferdinand, grandson of the Kaiser, had quit his job in a Ford plant in the United States to work for Lufthansa, and Otto John, along with Johannes Popitz, the Prussian Finance Minister, became a chief promoter of the Prince's pretensions to the throne in Carl Goerdeler's early schemes for a Hohenzollern restoration.[3] Louis Lochner, former chief of the Berlin Bureau of the Associated Press, said that on several occasions he accompanied John to meetings in Berlin of the Goerdeler and Louis Ferdinand groups.

Death was to sluff most of Otto's co-conspirators off the stage long before his own desertion, whether through natural causes, official executions, or the goon squads rampant at Germany's last gasp. But Louis Ferdinand remained a member of the cast through the last act. John cultivated him not only because he and his wife Kira, a former Grand Duchess of Russia, were very pleasant social companions but also because John, with his royalist inclinations, was flattered at being allowed to address the Prince by his intimate family nickname, "Lulu."

Beyond these contacts with conspiracy and his flights to neutral countries, Otto's specific resistance activities during this early period are unknown. In 1941 he passed considerable classified information about the Luftwaffe to U.S. correspondent Lochner. Strained attempts have been made to link him a little later with Rote Kapelle, the Communist radio-espionage group active in Berlin in 1941–42. No evidence is avail-

---

[2] Many clandestine interests capitalized on the advantages of this airline's international flights: Admiral Wilhelm Canaris' Abwehr faction, carrying on its own intrigues against the Nazis, had planted agents in it; Himmler's SS and the Gestapo had both infiltrated it; and the Soviets are believed to have recruited a pilot on the Berlin-Moscow run, a man named Radunsk.

[3] Gerhard Ritter, *The German Resistance,* pp. 191–2.

4   ~~SECRET~~

able to support any such connection, although it has been taken for granted that his brother Hans had Communist affiliations.

When eyebrows were raised over the appearance of the healthy Otto in mufti, he entered the Abwehr, likely on Goerdeler's suggestion and through the good offices of General Oster, the activist conspirator under Admiral Canaris. He was assigned to Abwehrstelle Stettin but told that his primary mission was to seek better surrender terms for Germany once Hitler was removed, using his Abwehr commission simply as cover. Threads linking the various opposition groups were now being slowly knit, and John probably provided liaison among those in the Abwehr, in the Army High Command, around Leuschner and Julius Leber, Louis Ferdinand, etc., whose heretofore diffuse activity was manifest in the ineffectual half-dozen different attempts to remove Hitler between 1939 and 1943.

The year 1942 was eventful for him. He was using business trips to Madrid and Lisbon, ostensibly for the purpose of acquiring more Lufthansa runways, to re-establish resistance contacts with the British and try to activate the acquaintance between Prince Louis Ferdinand and President Roosevelt, who had once put the Prince up at Blair House. During this year he was turned in to the Gestapo by an aging and jealous pre-war mistress, Frau Ameliess Pabst, and was rescued by his Abwehr connections. Also in 1942 Hans returned from the Russian front badly wounded and was taken to the famous surgeon Dr. Sauerbruch, who numbered among his assistants at the Charité Hospital the fateful Wolfgang Wohlgemuth. Otto soon learned to know the comrade of his future eastward flight by his pet name, Wowo.

John's peace feelers were received with considerable suspicion by the Allies, especially since he was unwilling at this time to name any conspirators. On 20 February 1943 the British intelligence service issued from London a statement to the effect that the Abwehr or the Gestapo was possibly inspiring his activities as a deception. He persisted, however, using as intermediary Juan Terraza, one of the principal diplomatic secretaries in the Spanish Foreign Office and a close friend of Louis Ferdinand. His attentions were directed toward Graham of the British Embassy in Lisbon and Willard L. Beaulac of the American Embassy in Madrid. Beaulac, on instructions from Assistant Secretary of State Acheson, saw John at his home but made no commitments. He, too, was dubious of his sincerity.

John's sincerity as a representative of the military element of the resistance, a role he was soon to assume, is in fact questionable. He was a dissenter among dissenters, thoroughly disliking the generals and never believing they would act against Hitler. He considered the military component of the 20 July group very weak and continually warned against it.

As 1943 wore along, his approaches became more definite. In December he told his British contact in Madrid that he represented an internal opposition group consisting of industrialists, trade union leaders, churchmen, and generals, all strongly anti-Nazi and anti-USSR. He ticked off names and disclosed details of another plot to murder Hitler.[4] In February 1944 he again came to Madrid ostensibly on Abwehr business. This time he said he was remaining in Spain as a representative of the anti-Nazi generals. As cover he assumed the directorship of the sister Lufthansa company there.

He later told the British that he performed no Abwehr missions on his trips to Spain. In early June 1944, however, the British ascertained that he had transmitted information concerning Allied military intentions to Berlin. The nature of this information is not known; it was probably innocuous. In any case the British and American embassies in Madrid, for their part, got valuable data from him—on the results of Allied bombings of Berlin, the German V-bomb and its launching bases, and the experimental station at Peenemuende.

The current of events leading to the ill-fated Generals' Coup was now quickening. Shortly after the Allied invasion of Normandy in June, John consulted in Madrid with Col. Georg Hansen, who as Canaris' successor at the head of the Abwehr was prospectively a chief negotiator with the Allies, specifi-

[4] At about this time the report that John was a British agent being handled by Major F. Landsdale and Cmdr. A. Fuller of the British Embassy in Lisbon was conveyed from the Portuguese General Staff to a German Lt. Col. von Auenrode (alias Karschof), who in turn informed Admiral Canaris. Canaris, of course, took no action.

Dr. John ~~SECRET~~

cally General Eisenhower at SHAEF, once the revolt had succeeded. In early July he made arrangements that any message from the conspirators would be passed immediately from the American Embassy in Madrid to General Eisenhower. At the same time he learned, to the dismay of the conspirators, that the Western Allies would not consider negotiating a separate peace, and that the British and Americans would probably make no effort to get to Berlin ahead of the Russians.[5]

There is conflicting evidence about his activities at the time of the attempted coup itself. According to his own story, he was called to Berlin to confirm in person his bad news of the unresponsiveness of the Western Allies, and arrived at Tempelhof Airdrome on 19 July. He was at OKW Headquarters in the Bendlerstrasse on the afternoon of 20 July when Col. Klaus von Stauffenberg arrived from East Prussia to report that the bomb had gone off and Hitler could be assumed dead. He worked with the conspirators there until 9:30 that evening, when it became evident that this attempt on Hitler's life had also failed, pro-Nazi officers were regaining control, and conspirators were being summarily executed in the courtyard. The next morning, according to his account, Johannes Popitz' daughter told him of her father's arrest, and he went into hiding. He escaped to Madrid on 24 July by signing on as a mechanic on a Lufthansa manifest.[6]

John's story, however, is contradicted by the lists of applicants for Spanish visas and travel manifests from Aerodrome del Prat del Llobregat. They show him arriving in Barcelona from Madrid via Lufthansa on 18 July and not departing for Berlin until 22 July. Allied intelligence regarded the variant embellishments of his account as probable fabrications and was inclined to suspect that Otto credited himself with activi-

---

[5] Ritter, *op. cit.*, p. 282. The ultimate source is John himself.

[6] That John was one of the pathetically few rebels to escape has been cited to support a theory that he was a Gestapo agent infiltrated into the conspiracy. We have noted that he was out of sympathy with the generals, and he seems not to have been intimately associated with any resistance circle except Louis Ferdinand's; but the Gestapo theory is untenable. He would hardly have betrayed his beloved brother Hans. Moreover, two SS aids of Walter Schellenberg later testified that the Gestapo had partially penetrated the 20 July group, but not through Otto John.

7

ties rightly belonging to Hans. One MI-6 interrogator re-marked that John seemed to change the story to keep from boring himself.

At any rate he turned up in late July or early August in Madrid, where he lived in a hotel some three weeks. ████████ ██ ████████████████████████ On 25 August they smuggled him to Lisbon and hid him at a safehouse, the Boa Vista, which was also used by Spanish Communists. On 23 October the Portuguese police raided this house and arrested John, the housekeeper Romero, and seven of the Spanish Communists.[7]

John was jailed for several days at Caxias. Then the Portuguese General Staff overruled the police and turned him over to the British. He was flown to the UK on 3 November, accompanied by Cmdr. Fuller, his contact at the British Embassy in Lisbon.

In the British Victor's Service

On John's arrival in the UK there was a wartime snafu as to his identity, and he was interned as a high-ranking Nazi. According to his own story, Churchill at this time called him in for a consultation that lasted half the night. He was re-leased from internment and transferred to the Political Intelligence Department of the Political Warfare Executive on 11 December. He was turned over to Sefton Delmer, a top re-porter for the London *Daily Express* and later for the *Times*, who was wartime director of the Morale Branch of PID. According to Delmer, John lived with him for 10 months. Del-mer is another person who will reappear before this drama is acted out.

In 1945 and 1946 John worked for the British in various capacities—with PID on intelligence matters, on the POW re-orientation program at Wilton Park, and on research for ⬤

---

[7] There are diverse accounts of this episode. One intelligence version has it that John was arrested because of his friendship for Professor Egaz Morriz, frequently referred to in Portugal as the unofficial Soviet ambassador. *Der Spiegel*, ten years later, said that he was arrested as a homosexual. Another section of the German press insisted that he was arrested at a fiesta when he got into a brawl over a woman.

8

~~SECRET~~

Dr. John

A tally of John's fellow-Germans ▮▮▮▮▮—Dr. Honigmann, Eberhard Koebel, Karl von Schnitzler, and Putlitz, the agent-baron discharged by the OWI—is intriguing: all of them, like John, were later to decamp to the East Zone of Germany.

After the surrender in May 1945, John did not return to Germany with the bulk of the political exiles. He was working for the British War and Foreign Offices, interrogating German generals in the Kensington cage, and helping prepare legal documents for the approaching Nuremberg trials. At Nuremberg he worked as an adviser to the UK prosecution staff, a fact omitted in his own curriculum vitae.

Up to this time he could lay valid claim to being a German patriot. The cause which met catastrophe on 20 July had been a worthy one, that of revolt against the Nazis, not treason to the German nation. Its watchword was, "Against Hitler, for Germany." But when he returned for the Nuremberg trials, it was in effect as a German in British battle dress. He revisited with the wrath of a prosecutor the country which he had fled as a political persecutee. He kept aloof from other Germans working at the trials, attempted to conceal his identity and purpose, and spent his free time with his British colleagues, trying unsuccessfully to pose as an Englishman doing historical research in the documents of the Tribunal. The spirit of the trials themselves, in which righteous indignation at the Nazi horrors was not untainted by thirst for political vengeance, may have contributed further to the warping of John's character.

He was already showing psychoneurotic tendencies. In 1946 in London he attended a private War Office showing of a film on the Belzen concentration camp. Shortly after the movie, he told an intelligence officer five years later, the lower part of his face began to discharge a pus-like fluid and he suffered a species of nervous breakdown. His explanation was that the movie brought home to him the terrible failure of the 20 July revolt and all it stood for; he had been condemned to virtual inactivity since his flight to the UK and the accumulated frustration was simply too much for him. John clearly identified himself closely with the failure of the anti-Hitler

SECRET

9

resistance and had a strong guilt complex deriving probably from his brother's painful death. This reinforced his obsession with the July affair and his inability to compromise with anything remotely identifiable with Nazis, right-wing politicians, or German military traditions. His excessive drinking and other manifestations of emotional instability would be symptomatic of such a state of mind.

He may have had woman-trouble, too. In 1949, after practicing law in London for a year, he married Frau Lucy-Marleen Mankiewitz, the *mother* of the girl he had been expected to wed. His new wife, a German Jewess whose father was an old friend and adviser of Dr. Theodor Heuss, taught Wagnerian singing at Hampstead. She has been described as making up in charm and intellect for the greater beauty of her jilted daughter Gisela, with whom John had worked in a wartime British operation.

John's mistress, Frau Elsa Mueller Rudolph in Wiesbaden, the widow of a German pilot killed in action in 1943, was another who stood to be offended by this marriage. John wrote in explanation that he was marrying an older woman because of his need for balance, and moreover his bride had important political connections in the new Germany through her family. He hoped that he and Elsa could remain friends. They did. It was Elsa who, as nearly as can be ascertained, enlarged Otto's circle of acquaintances to include Ian Eland, ██████ ██████ who was later helpful in exposing and eliminating one of John's rivals for the presidency of the Verfassungsschutzamt.

In the fall of 1949, no longer trying to conceal his services to the UK, John became openly the chief German assistant to the British prosecution at the trial of General von Manstein in Hamburg. This time he apparently associated with the German lawyers defending Von Manstein. But he irked the defense, it is said, by deliberately twisting facts and evidence to the advantage of the prosecutors, many of whom relied heavily on him because of their unfamiliarity with the German language and with the organization and practices of the Nazi Reich. Several friends implored him at this time to get out of the business of delivering his countrymen to the Allied hangman, and their warning that he was alienating

10

Dr. John

himself from his fatherland must have increased his emotional stresses.

John was not doing awfully well financially in the UK. He was employed by the London solicitors James Brodie & Company on reparation and restitution cases, but he could not base a career on claims arising out of a past era. He suffered from the lack of the British citizenship that had been extended to Putlitz and certain other Germans. (At times he claimed that he had declined a proferred citizenship.) Germany, on the other hand, was getting back on her feet economically.

During 1949 and 1950 he made several trips to Germany to see friends in the Bonn government about a job. Jakob Kaiser, whom he had known as a leader of the Catholic trade union resistance, offered him one in his Ministry of All-German Affairs, but John declined on the ground that he deserved a higher rank than Ministerialrat. Foreign Affairs had no place for him because, he suspected, of his "anti-German" activities in the UK and his role at the trials. He also tried unsuccessfully for an appointment on the German delegation to the International Ruhr Authority.

The Protector of the Constitution

In 1950 West Germany was passing through the interim stage on the road from occupation to sovereignty, and an important question was that of preserving ideological rectitude in the new state. The French did not want it to have any political police. The British favored an adaptation of Scotland Yard. The United States came up with an emasculated FBI plan. The Germans wanted to return to the pre-Hitler scheme, incorporating the political police as Branch 1A into the national police. The eventual compromise was the watery conception of an Office for the Protection of the Constitution, a police force with no power to arrest. It was supposed to be a silent security service keeping tabs on the lunatic fringes to the right and left.

How was it that Otto John, a man who already showed signs of needing watching himself, almost an expatriate, whom Chancellor Adenauer is said to have disliked from first sight, was named head of the sensitive Bundesamt fuer Verfassungsschutz? Or, as the Germans put it in their rough peasant

11

proverb, "Who put the goat in charge of the garden?" As assets he had an influential friend in Jakob Kaiser, his connections by marriage with President Heuss, and most importantly the gratitude of the British for his work for them during the war and in the Nazi trials.

And it was not an easy job to fill, with its international political implications. The German proposal to appoint a nonpolitical civil servant was vetoed by the Allied High Commissioners. The United States suggested an excellent man in Fabian von Schlabrendorff, but he refused on grounds of ill health. The French nominated Colonel Friedrich Wilhelm Heinz, information chief in the embryo defense ministry, but John disposed of this rival by having Ian Eland, his mistress' agent friend, put the finger on Heinz as the source of his espionage reports ▬▬▬▬▬. Finally, after 15 months, 12 rejected nominees, and 10 wrangling sessions of the High Commission, the British quietly sponsored Otto John, for bad luck the thirteenth man.

The German lawyers who had defended Von Manstein and the Nuremberg accused were shocked. They complained to Minister of the Interior Heinemann that John was unscrupulous and altogether a bad choice. Heinemann replied that the British trusted John, and anyway the job was unimportant: Germany was in no position to keep secrets from the occupation powers.

U.S. approval was another Gordian knot. On 22 November 1950 High Commissioner McCloy cabled the Department of State from Frankfurt that the Federal Republic had requested HICOG to approve John's candidacy with all possible urgency, and that only the results of the Department's name check were needed to clear the way. A week later, at 1800 Washington time, 29 November, a cable over Dean Acheson's signature informed Frankfurt that conflicting information regarding Otto John "necessitates thorough investigation by Army G–2 of other sources. Results follow soonest." But on 1 December, at 0909, McCloy wired back:

> On basis of excellent data available here and in absence of any derogatory information and in view of urgency of making a decision and after approval by British and French, we approved appointment of Otto John on 29 November, prior to receipt of your telegram of 29 November.

12

Dr. John   SECRET

The newly installed BfV president was again the center of discussions by the Allied Directorate when, on 7 March 1951, they took up the appointment of Vera Schwart, formerly a secretary of Admiral Canaris, as John's secretary. The United States and the UK raised no objections. But the French did, on the grounds that Vera, arrested by the Soviets in 1946, had turned informer for them the following year. The glandular dislike of French intelligence for John had been reflected in the comment of a Sureté chief on his appointment: he had exclaimed, in chorus with a Turkish colleague, "C'est impossible!"

Just how impossible a choice John was became increasingly apparent. Aside from his instability and his emotional political outlook, he was a poor administrator and lacked balanced judgment. U.S. intelligence saw him muddling through without the energy, imagination, or administrative ability to put the BfV on its feet. He had no patience with the painstaking detail necessary to effective intelligence operations. He was intrigued by special missions and fanciful projects which usually wound up putting the Office and the government in embarrassing, not to say ridiculous, positions.

One of the score of projects John laid on was Operation Maerchenwald. The good fairy of this Fabulous Wood was a buxom widow named Frau Baumann from Ansbach in Bavaria, confessed guardian of a vast Nazi treasure trove from which she was supposed to make monthly withdrawals to support indigent Nazi leaders in Switzerland and South America. The cache was somewhere in the Bavarian Alps, sometimes at the bottom of a lake, a very deep lake, the Frau said. John, taking her at her word, dispatched six green-jacketed BfV men to escort her to the treasure. She took them up into the Tyrolean mountains, where, according to an official report, she found the right blazed tree and the secret path of white pebbles, but was unable to find the stone slab covering the lever that opened the way to the cache.

While John was waiting in his Cologne command post for his men to report the find, U.S. operatives came to see him and showed him documents proving that his good fairy was a swindler, blackmail artist, public nuisance, and congenital liar, once inmate of an insane asylum. Nevertheless John

SECRET   13

~~SECRET~~   *Dr. John*

summoned Frau Baumann to Cologne to reveal more details. Somewhat drunk, he had a two-hour seance with her.

By mid-1952 Bonn was rocking with gossip about his antics. Report after report reaching Adenauer's desk indicated that in his hatred of the Nazis John was not alert to the Communist danger, that he maintained relations with Communist sympathizers, that he was given to fits of melancholy brooding, and that he was increasingly taking to drink. But the Chancellor had no intention of lowering the boom on him until Germany achieved her sovereignty.

The BfV's serious operations were apparently in the hands of its de facto director, former General Staff officer Albert Radke. He was a close associate of General Reinhard Gehlen, who had headed the wartime General Staff's section for evaluating Eastern intelligence and in postwar Germany bossed a high-powered unofficial offensive espionage group. Gehlen distrusted John because of his record of defection to the British.

John's four years in office were extremely unpleasant. He was resented by senior police officials and other German civil servants as an outsider, as a stooge of his British sponsors, and as one who had deserted Germany in her hour of need. Rumors were growing that his days in the BfV were numbered, that his office would be replaced by Gehlen's organization. He may have brooded most over this prospect of being supplanted by Gehlen, whom he regarded as one of the military group responsible for the failure of the 1944 coup and so for Hans' death by torture.

In May and June of 1954 he enjoyed the pleasant interlude of a trip to the United States. He was brought to Washington and shown the courtesies normally accorded the head of a foreign intelligence service. CIA officials dined him, and on 7 June he was briefed on general intelligence matters.

Details in a Defection

John returned to the Federal Republic in fine fettle. Dr. Wohlgemuth, however, who visited him in Cologne on 9 July, insisted he appeared run down and prescribed pills. John, rather than argue about it, took them without visible effect, though later he tried to use this incident in his defense. On 8 and again on 12 July he was visited by Michael Winch, a

14   ~~SECRET~~

Dr. John   SECRET

discredited British-Soviet double agent. The subject of their conversations is not known. Frau John, who happened to be in Cologne, objected to Winch, probably because he was cadging meals and money.

John's twelve-year-old relationship with Wohlgemuth had been a matter of concern for some time. ▮▮▮▮▮▮▮▮▮▮ is reported to have warned him twice about friend Wowo, first in March 1953 and again in July 1954. After the first warning John is said to have detailed a BfV man, Von Berge, to watch him for a while, and on the second occasion to have given an "embarrassed" and conflicting account of his contacts with him. Before John's visit to the United States, a Berlin shopkeeper, Frau Anneliese Schroeder, showed police notes of a conversation with one Helmut Salewski, a close friend of Wohlgemuth's. Salewski told her Wowo kept a tape recorder hidden in his room and persuaded John to talk about secret matters when he visited him for evenings of women and drinking.

On 15 July the Johns flew to West Berlin for the services commemorating the decennial of the 20 July revolt. Beginning with a reception given by Oberburgmeister Reuter on the evening of 18 July, families and friends of the participants in the plot against the Nazi regime met for the purpose of unveiling a monument to the victims in the courtyard of the former OKW in the Bendlerstrasse. John and his wife took advantage of this opportunity to dine twice with his old school friend of Wiesbaden days, Wolfgang Hoffer, now a captain in the American CIC. Hoffer said that the Americans regarded John as a British agent, and that he himself couldn't stand the CIC any longer and wanted John to help him locate a job in Germany. He wanted nothing more to do with intelligence services.

An intelligence officer who spent considerable time with John during this convocation said he "lamented several times about the bad things people were saying about him and about attacks against him coming from Minister Robert Lehr and Herr Sauer. Shortly before he left Bonn to attend the Berlin festivities, he was called into [State Secretary] Ritter von Lex's office and was told they had just received a complaint from the Federal Chancellery accusing him of secretly join-

SECRET   15

ing the SPD. John said he was sick and tired of these rumors, and if a good opportunity presents itself he would seriously consider rejoining the Deutsche Lufthansa when it starts functioning again." [8]

In this mood he came upon a newspaper account of how Minister of the Interior Schroeder, his superior, planned drastic changes in the BfV as soon as West Germany obtained its sovereignty. He was reported to appear visibly shaken. At the commemorative exercises he made an exhibition of himself, sobbing loudly and denouncing two other mourners as Gestapo agents. Although the memories evoked of Hans' death ten years earlier were undoubtedly depressing, he had always been jovial and friendly at the memorial services of previous years.

Immediately after the ceremonies John declined to dine with his old friend Prince Louis Ferdinand, saying that he was meeting with some East Zone people. ████████████████████ ████████████████████████████████████ When Louis Ferdinand then suggested that Otto drop by his hotel afterwards for a nightcap, he gave a curt "No." This was about 1600 on 20 July.

John kept an engagement, however, with an elderly German couple, in-laws of an American acquaintance, at his hotel. In this interval between the memorial exercises in the Bendlerstrasse and his appointment with Wohlgemuth, he also saw Bonde-Henriksen, correspondent for the Danish paper *Berlingske Tidende,* the man who after eighteen months was to help him return from East Germany, and apparently expected to have a drink with him later in the evening.

A perhaps equivocal indication of his intention to come back that night was the fact that when he changed clothes he left papers and notes from his pockets in his hotel room. But he also had reservations for a return flight from Berlin, and his desk calendar in Cologne showed a future schedule of normal activities. Driving from his hotel, he stopped in at the Maison de France, a restaurant near Wohlgemuth's downtown office, in order, according to Erich Ollenhauer, to pick up there an answer to a proposal he had made Mendes-France that the

---

[8] Lufthansa would not have taken him.

Dr. John

Federal Republic's remilitarization plans be exposed to debate at the forthcoming Geneva Conference. The answer was not there.

For John's meeting and movements with Wohlgemuth the evidence consisted until recently mainly of his own account given after redefection, which begins by omitting these known preliminary activities, emphasizes a suspicious cup of coffee served him at the Wohlgemuth apartment, and ends in a theatrical invented scene wherein he awakens from a drugged sleep in an abandoned house and is threatened by Communists speaking with a Russian accent. But there were three important facts from other sources. Item one, Wohlgemuth telephoned the Charité Hospital in East Berlin that evening and said, "I shall come now with my good friend." Item two, he apparently intended, like John, to come back: he left in West Berlin his 10 suits of clothes, four apartments, five mistresses, and third wife. Later we shall look at other evidence of Wohlgemuth's intent made public in 1958 by the release of testimony given at John's treason trial. Item three, the customs officer on duty at the Sandkrug Bridge that night, Ernst Richard Hanke, who halted Wohlgemuth's sedan at the border, peered inside and saw that both occupants were awake and alert. When Hanke pointed out that the vehicle was about to enter the Soviet sector, a man of John's description replied, "Aber dort wollen wir doch hin—Well, that's where we want to go."

The Bonn Government insisted that John must have been abducted. They offered a reward of DM500,000 for conclusive information. A special Bundestag committee was established to investigate the affair. A variant on the abduction explanation was given by a U.S. intelligence cable:

> John was a damned fool caught in a well-baited trap. . . . He very likely overestimated his own position to the extent of believing that the Soviets would not dare harm him. He took and miscalculated a risk in pursuit of bait set by persons who evaluated correctly his psychology and his desire to score a major personal coup following heavy attacks on his office in recent Bundestag debates.

The suicide on 23 July of Otto's friend Hoffer, who had believed that the German secret police supposedly guarding John had actually been holding him under arrest, made the mystery a double one. John claimed, in a statement broadcast from East Berlin, that his friend had been driven to desperation by the CIC's insistence that he spy on him. Part of the German press said that Hoffer killed himself rather than face an inevitable investigation. The U.S. Army officially denied that he had been detailed to check up on John or on Wohlgemuth. U.S. intelligence had him feeling that the defection of his life-long friend shattered his whole intelligence career.

The British, publicly at any rate, stood by John. They denied on 5 August that any British official had been the source of an Associated Press story to the effect that they had dropped John ten months earlier; they considered such a report to be "skillful sabotage." John continued to have a surprisingly good British press,

At the other extreme were those who believed, on the grounds of John's vulnerability and associations, that he might have long since become a Soviet agent; and these included   . At least there were reports pointing to possible Communist pressures and preparation. Baron Wolfgang von und zu Putlitz, who first boasted and then denied having engineered the defection of Burgess and MacLean and who urged John on 16 March 1953 that he at least confer with a Soviet officer about saving Germany from being caught in an East-West conflict, visited Bonn in the spring of 1954 and again in July, and on at least one of these occasions he met with John. Informed circles in East Berlin were reported in August to consider John's defection and that of the Bundestag deputy Karl Franz Schmidt-Wittmack to have been masterminded by Soviet General Ivan A. Serov and run from KGB headquarters in Karlshorst. [9] And a refugee who had worked

[9] Peter Deriabin says that at the time of his own defection in September 1953 Soviet State Security was building up a file on John's dealings with the Nazis, and he suggests John was blackmailed into defecting by the Soviet threat to expose his pro-Nazi activities! (*The Secret World*, p. 197.)

18

Dr. John

for the East German Security Service claimed later to have heard Colonel Beater of the Service remark that two of his agents, Axel and Peter (the Rittwagens) were preparing in West Berlin for the defection or, if necessary, the abduction of Otto John, and that Beater had met at least once with Wohlgemuth and with Wolfgang Hoffer of the CIC.

Except to doggedly suspicious minds the baited-trap, drug-abduction, long-time-agent, and fleeing-wrongdoer theories were disproved and the main mysteries of the case cleared up by John's public appearance and a private conversation on 11 August. At a conference attended by 400 Western and Communist reporters in the East Berlin press building on Friedrichstrasse, he said that the West German government had become a mere instrument of American European policy, which was using Chancellor Adenauer to renazify and remilitarize Germany as a spearhead against the USSR, that there were secret clauses in the EDC treaty in this connection, that Adenauer and the militarists regarded the EDC as an interim device for restoring German military hegemony in Europe, that the Gehlen organization had stepped up its activities in France to this end, and that the Americans, in their hysterical fear of Communism, were preparing a new Hitler Crusade against the East that would leave Germany a mass of atomic ashes.

These standard theses of the Communist propaganda line were probably consonant with John's own anti-Nazi and anti-military obsession, reinforced in recent months by his growing feeling of being not appreciated in West Germany and not wanted in the government, even deliberately persecuted under the influence of the neo-Nazis. And if he felt guilt over his earlier desertion to the British, he could now choose the anti-Nazi East and still remain on German soil rather than "flee for a second time," as he later told the Danish correspondent Henrik Bonde-Henriksen.

After the press conference John had a 45-minute talk over glasses of beer with Gaston Coblentz of the New York *Herald Tribune* and two London paper correspondents, Karl Robson of the *News Chronicle* and his one-time boss and benefactor Sefton Delmer of the *Daily Express*. They were joined at the table in a private dining room of the press building by four

19

Communist members of the Council for German Unity, but these made no attempt to control the conversation. They did not need to, the three Western correspondents agreed: John was saying of his own volition what they would have sought to have him say. The three gave him many opportunities to indicate by some sign that he was being held against his will, but although the talk around the table was going in several directions and it would have been easy, he did not do so.

John reiterated that he had crossed over voluntarily because of his long-smoldering unhappiness about renazification in West Germany. In reply to a question about Dr. Wohlgemuth's role, he said it was relatively unimportant— "he only established my contact with the Communist regime." John substantiated the theory that he had not intended to remain in the Soviet Zone when he drove across the Sandkrug Bridge with Wowo. Asked whether he had decided in advance to stay, he replied: "No. My decision was made only after my talks with the Communist authorities. I came over to confirm that I would be able to stay on my terms. I was able to do so. I would have been free to return if I had wanted to."

John's motives do at this point seem understandable, and the main course of events clear. But as late as November 1958, perhaps because the picture was again confused by redefection, a senior U.S. intelligence officer in Germany was of the opinion that, "barring an unforeseeable stroke of good fortune, we doubt that we shall ever know the true circumstances which prompted Otto John's appearance in East Berlin."

The Way Back

Shortly after his arrival in East Germany, John was reported to have made contact with Dr. Erich Correns, head of the National Front, and to have prepared for the Ministry of Interior a list of some 50 West German government officials possibly susceptible to defection inducements. On 14 August the West Berlin *Telegraf* reported his suggesting that former Field Marshal Friedrich von Paulus, who surrendered the German Sixth Army at Stalingrad, head a committee to "unveil the aggressive machinations of the National Socialist circles in West Germany."

20

Dr. John   SECRET

A few weeks later, the East German government announced plans for a Ministry for German Unity to be headed by John. Its proposed purpose was to establish contact with persons in West German public life who were opposed to the Bonn government and thus encourage their opposition or provide them with an incentive to defect. The ministry never materialized, although John wrote to a number of prominent West German politicians urging them to take a stand against the U.S.-Adenauer policies.

On 19 September 1954 John was reported to be working on the All-German Committee of the East Zone government and also on the German Committee sponsored by the GDR Press and Information Office. It was learned later that he spent several weeks that fall in the USSR. Reports received in December 1954 indicated that he was planning to establish permanent residence in Leipzig, that he was working with the new East German Lufthansa, and that he was making preparations for a propaganda offensive to re-establish a constitutional monarchy in Germany and would soon make overtures to Prince Louis Ferdinand.

In March 1955 it was learned that he had been appointed permanent adviser to the National Council of the National Front and was touring the Soviet zone in official capacity, attending conferences of regional committees and issuing special directives for conducting anti-West propaganda. Late in October he was reported to be editor of a new publication, the *Berliner Politische Korrespondenz*, directed against the policies of the Bonn government and intended mainly for dissemination in West Berlin and the Federal Republic. He was also reported to be writing memoires.

But there had already been indications that John, disappointed with East Germany and with having been given only the position of "itinerant preacher for reunification," as he wrote his wife, was toying with the idea of returning to the West. This was the implication of a statement he made to Bonde-Henriksen in June 1955 that he was free to leave at any moment but hesitated because of fear of being arrested in West Germany. In a three-hour interview with the Danish correspondent, John said he would not have stayed on in East Germany if he thought the USSR desired war. Henrik-

SECRET

sen remarked, "It is a question of whether you would have been permitted to say 'Goodbye and thanks,'" and John replied, "I guess I would have known ways and means . . ." He concluded the interview by saying: "I am a human being with the shortcomings and virtues of a human being. I can be accused of many things, but I have not failed the ideals of my youth. You may call me naive. Nevertheless, I am realistic and developments will prove me right."

In less than six months, however; perhaps particularly moved by a message from Prince Louis to the effect that if John really believed the things he was saying he could no longer be his friend, John arranged with Bonde-Henriksen to be picked up on Unter den Linden in front of the University at 1650 hours on 12 December 1955. At about 1635 he entered the University from Dorotheenstrasse, telling his two guards to wait at the gate since he had an appointment there. The guards let him go in alone. He walked through the buildings to where Henriksen was parked, waiting. Partially disguised in a muffler and dark glasses, he drove with Henriksen in the car bearing the Danish coat of arms through the Brandenburg Gate to the Victory Column and then to Tempelhof Airdrome. ██

Bonde-Henriksen and Wiechmann from the regional BfV office flew with him to Wahn. From there he was driven to Bonn.

Post Mortem

His fears of being arrested after his redefection were soon confirmed. He was charged on 18 January 1956 with treasonable conspiracy and high treason for his East Zone activities. His defense was that he thought it less damaging to West Germany, once he found himself in Communist hands through the drug-abduction routine, if he pretended to cooperate; if he refused, he would be brainwashed and forced to reveal state secrets of importance. He contended that he had had no chance to speak freely with Sefton Delmer and the other Western correspondents at his 11 August press conference or to convey any hint to anyone during the entire eighteen months that he was acting under compulsion.

Dr. John

The court was unimpressed. After a painstaking review of all the circumstances he was found guilty on two counts of treasonable conspiracy for his services to Eastern propaganda organizations. He was acquitted of betraying state secrets, but judged guilty of treasonable falsifications that would have been secret if true—his allegation of secret clauses in the EDC treaty and of activities of the Gehlen organization aimed at European hegemony. Sentenced to four years' imprisonment, he was released in July 1958 under an amnesty granted by President Heuss.

Wohlgemuth was brought to trial on treason charges but acquitted on 14 December 1958 by the West German Supreme Court. The court proceedings in the Wohlgemuth case have not yet been released, but the publication in 1958 of the official *Urteil* from the trial of Otto John [10] confirms the general outline of both men's motivations and actions drawn above and fills in some details.

The testimony of witnesses established that by the spring of 1954 John had become so apprehensive about attacks on him and his Office that he secured the promise of a legal position with an industrial firm against eventualities. It was clear to the court also that he had been genuinely, if unjustifiably, troubled by the idea that National Socialism might regain political power in Bonn. His political thinking, if somewhat vague, was certainly oriented toward the West and away from totalitarian forms of government. He distrusted military men, opposed remilitarization, and was shocked by the very thought of another war.

Witnesses pictured him as almost pathologically disturbed during his July visit to Berlin. He was convinced that the newspaper story of changes planned by the Interior Minister was aimed at him. At a lunch on 17 July, when someone remarked that only a war could resolve the current tension, he "shot up out of his chair." At the BfV Berlin office that afternoon he went to pieces, complaining with half-drunken vehemence about the lack of confidence in him. On 19 July

---

[10] *Hochverrat und Staatsgefaerdung*, Band II (Karlsruhe: C. F. Mueller, 1958), pp. 77–150. The *Urteil* includes an exhaustive and impartial summary of the evidence and arguments of both prosecution and defense.

at lunch he bemoaned the "growing influence of the Nazis" and went into a long reminiscence of the Third Reich and his own misunderstood role at Nuremberg. The memorial service on 20 July had an extraordinarily shattering effect on him.

With respect to any premeditation of his 20 July defection it was testified that he had booked a return flight to Cologne for 22 July, that he had refused his secretary's request for use of the official car on 21 July on the grounds that he would need it himself, that he told his chauffeur after dinner on 20 July that he was through with the car for the day but would call for it in the morning, and that as he left the hotel for the last time, although a clerk told him his wife was in the lobby, he did not say goodbye to her. His frequent letters to her from the East Zone referred again and again to his "sudden" decision and entreated her for understanding.

There was evidence also that the East German security service was unprepared for John's appearance in the East Zone and uncertain about his motives: a West German woman journalist whom it had imprisoned two years earlier on espionage charges and whom it supposed knew a good deal about John was brought before one of its officers in Halle just after 20 July and questioned as to whether she thought John's defection bona fide. Another West German journalist was told by John himself, in complete privacy on 13 May 1955, that the "number two Russian" in Karlshorst to whom he had offered his collaboration on 20 July was surprised, but made a kind of gentleman's agreement not to demand any secrets from him and to let him move about freely.

The testimony did not touch on the Hoffer mystery except to show that John had been inflating a jest of Hoffer's when he claimed the CIC had made him spy on him. From the bits of evidence available here it appears likely that Hoffer was disillusioned with intelligence intrigues, had made some indiscreet contacts in East Germany, and was afraid that his friend's defection would bring on an interrogation and exposure. John's attempt to blame his suicide on the CIC probably reflected a feeling of guilt for it on his own part.

Wohlgemuth, who did not make himself available as a witness, was pictured in the testimony as politically far to the

24

Dr. John

left, announcing to all and sundry his conviction that Communism would come to power in western Europe within a few years. Nevertheless he had apparently not engaged in any legally actionable activities. With respect to his intentions in driving John across the Sandkrug Bridge, it was testified that when the two men left the office-apartment after the end of the Doctor's office hours that night, he was still wearing his white trousers and carrying only a trench coat, and that in the wee hours of 21 July he came back, alone, very much upset, and dashed to and fro through the house hastily packing a trunk.

He told the night nurse that John, whom he had introduced to some people in the East Zone, had unexpectedly decided to remain there, and that he himself might be suspected of wrongdoing and was therefore going back to stay at the Charité until things quieted down. He left a note for the day nurse to the same effect, and told her to take care of the office and apartment. Between 4 and 5 a.m. he telephoned his attorney, gave him the same excited account, and asked him to take full powers over his property. Then he went to his mistress' house in Lietzenburger street, where he maintained a one-room apartment, and called her down to the street. Telling her what had happened, he suggested that his apartment might be searched and asked her to remove his camera, photographs, films, and books. At about five o'clock he stopped at the Uhland garage for gasoline, where the attendant noticed that he seemed to be in "even a bigger hurry than usual."

None of these people informed the police or Frau John, however, who first got from intelligence sources the news of John's probable defection, confirmed on 23 July by his own announcement over the East German radio:

> . . . I have taken a resolute step and made contact with the East Germans. I have been deprived of any basis for political activity in the Federal Republic. After I had been continually heckled in my office by the Nazis again rampant everywhere in political and even in public life, the Federal Minister of the Interior has now made any further work in my official position impossible for me by declaring to the press that with the coming of sovereignty he would have a free hand and be able "to entrust the protection of the constitution to persons who are truly above suspicion." . . . German policy has run into a

25

> blind alley . . . yet there is still a possibility of reunifica-
> tion. . . . I shall soon present my ideas and plans for German
> reunification to the German public.

Some students of the case are still convinced, in spite of the apparent adequacy of John's personal motivation, that he must nevertheless have defected under Soviet or more likely British control. To them the case can but remain a mystery; for although acquaintances like Winch, Putlitz, and Wohlgemuth may well have encouraged John's own obsessions, no evidence has come to light on how a supposed definitive control was exercised, and it is difficult to arrive even at a persuasive theoretical reconstruction of British or Soviet purposes consistent with the facts.

It seemed evident to the court, as it does to a reader of the intelligence files, that John's decision to approach the Communist authorities in the East Zone, made in a state of heightened neurotic tension and perhaps alcoholic befuddlement, derived from his frustration in what he considered his mission to stem the renazification of Germany and was precipitated by the imminent likelihood of his losing what position and influence he still had in the Federal Republic. When his initial Soviet contacts in Karlshorst led him, it seems probable, to believe he would be free of duress in the East and might be able to accomplish there what he could not in the West, he forthwith made his marriage of convenience with the Communists, in which any real position and influence yet escaped him and from which he eventually opted to return to his Western wife and friends.

26

~~SECRET~~
~~No Foreign Dissem~~

Traces of the borrowed German scientists combine with other scraps of information to throw light on the USSR's early atomic program.

ON THE SOVIET NUCLEAR SCENT
Henry S. Lowenhaupt

As World War II in Europe ended, the German nuclear scientists, handicapped by insufficient coordination and paltry official backing, were nevertheless only just short of achieving a self-sustaining chain reaction in a heavy-water-moderated pile. They had elaborated most aspects of reactor theory; they knew the best arrangement for the lattice of fuel elements; they had gained experience in the production and casting of metallic uranium. They had prepared detailed designs for two pilot plants for the industrial production of heavy water. They had also experimented with several methods of isotope separation for concentrating the fissile U-235, especially the gas centrifuge method, though none of these had by any means reached the production stage. In short, they had a body of know-how, experimental machines, and basic materials unique outside the United States and Britain.

U.S. and UK forces moved aggressively to prevent the proliferation of this nucleus of nuclear capability. They promptly seized the scientists and materials in their own zones of occupation and snatched some from the agreed zones of France and the USSR ahead of their advancing armies. They even destroyed by air attack the Auer Company plant, in the prospective Soviet zone, that had produced the uranium metal for the German program. They interned near London the ten ranking scientists, led by Professors Otto Hahn and Werner Heisenberg, most directly concerned with the program, and only after Hiroshima did they release them under such conditions that they would not want to go to the USSR.[1]

Scientists Eastbound

Yet the sweep could not be clean. In June 1945 British intelligence reported that Dr. Nicolaus Riehl of the Auer Company had left Ger-

---

[1] The story of the German effort and its denouement is well told in David Irving's *The Virus Home* (London, 1967), reviewed on page 103 of this issue.

~~SECRET~~

13

GUSTAV HERTZ

many for the USSR along with six others who had worked with him on the manufacture of uranium metal. Then four days after Hiroshima word came from London that Professor Gustav Hertz had flown to Moscow four weeks previously and Professor Adolf Thiessen was in a Soviet camp with eighteen fellow workers awaiting transportation to Russia. Both Hertz and Thiessen, though not immediately involved in the German atomic program, were prominent and technically competent scientists who could command the loyalty of other scientists. Hertz, a Nobel Prize winner in atomic physics, had been chief of the famous Siemens-Halske Laboratories since 1934 and had discovered the gaseous diffusion method of separating isotopes. Thiessen had directed the Kaiser Wilhelm Institute for Physical Chemistry and had published an impressive string of important research papers.

From this point U.S. and UK intelligence had the task of trying to follow the incipient Soviet atomic effort, and it was largely the early results of this pursuit, as decribed below, that encouraged the U.S. Air Force to mount a watch for the first Soviet test explosion two years before it was expected.[2] G-2, OSS, and their British counterparts, under the direction of the two nations' atomic authorities,[3] began with a vigorous campaign to discover which Germans had been recruited for this effort and which Russians were doing the recruiting. The

[2] See Northrup and Rock, "The Detection of Joe 1," *Studies* X 4, p. 23 ff.

[3] The intelligence analysis and the general direction of the collection effort in the nuclear field were vested, on the U.S. side, in General Groves' "Manhattan Engineering District" until its dissolution in January 1947, when these functions passed to CIA. In Britain they were performed through 1952 by a section of the Ministry of Supply and, after its formation, the British Atomic Energy Authority. The Supply section was staffed in part by Secret Intelligence Service officers under the leadership of Lt. Comdr. Eric Welsh. See *The Virus House*, cited in footnote 1 above, for Welsh's role in atomic intelligence to the end of 1945.

SECRET

task was complicated by the fact that the Russians were recruiting German and Austrian scientists and technicians for all sorts of programs; the numbers ran to many hundreds. By the end of the year, however, it was clear that for atomic work well over a hundred technicians were being grouped around a few rather good scientists as leaders.

In addition to Riehl, Hertz, and Thiessen, the group leaders included: Baron Manfred von Ardenne, Germany's foremost cyclotron constructor; Professor Max Vollmer, an outstanding physical chemist; and Dr. Hans Born of the Kaiser-Wilhelm Institute for Brain Research, who had been working on the biophysics of radiation. As for the Russian recruiters: at Leipzig there was a General "Katchkatchian" aided by a Major "Krassin"; a Colonel "K. K." Kikoin at Karlshorst had persuaded Hertz to go; and a Lt. Colonel "Kargin" had handled negotiations with Vollmer. A General "Ivanov," who had had to do with recruitment in Vienna, turned out to be none other than General Meshik, Lavrentiy Beriya's right-hand man.[4]

Many of the German scientists were well enough known that their specialties and skill could be assessed. The intelligence reporting also tended to sort them into groups under the respective leaders. But this did not tell us what each group was to work on in the USSR and where they were to do the work; and that was what we needed to know.

Russian security was initially well below its subsequent standards. By February 1946 the Strategic Services Unit, successor to OSS, was able to report from an agent in the East Zone of Germany that Baron von Ardenne's presumably cyclotron-centered group went to the Crimea in the summer of 1945 and then in October was established in one of the small communities between Anaklia and Poti on the east shore of the Black Sea, about 120 kilometers north of the Turkish border. Another agent reported that Thiessen, Hertz, and Vollmer, as well as Von Ardenne, were on this stretch of the Black Sea coast between Sukhumi and Poti—in ancient Colchis, where the Argonauts found the Golden Fleece. They had reportedly not done any work up to the beginning of November 1945, as housing and laboratories were still under construction. The biophysicists under Born, as well as Riehl's Auer Company group, were left unaccounted for.

---

[4] P. Ya. Meshik was executed on 23 December 1953. As Minister of Internal Affairs of the Ukrainian SSR, he was charged with being an active participant in the coup attempted by Beriya.

15

Soviet Nuclear Start

The Russians rounded out their atomic recruitment early in 1946 by assembling a group of German scientists under Dr. Heinz Pose, who had worked on nuclear reactor physics at Ronneburg under the German Bureau of Standards. This particular group had been considered inferior by their more renowned fellows, but in fact they had shown Heisenberg an error in his calculations and thus put the program on the right track towards a working reactor. We had no information on where the Russians stationed these reactor specialists.

Letters and Defectors

At about this time U.S. and UK intelligence stumbled onto the interception of letters from the expatriated scientists as a source of information about their locations and activities which in the end proved far more fruitful than the alternative of penetrating institutes in East Germany. An intercepted letter dated 18 March 1946 from Hertz to his son disclosed the identity of the Russian go-between in Germany as Lt. Colonel "Cedenko," 46 Wassersportallee, Berlin-Gruenau. Then in August and September there was a change in Russian personnel and their address, for Lt. Colonel "Yelan" and Lt. Petrochenko at Buntzelstrasse 11, Gruenau, were handling the mail.

In October Riehl wrote from Elektrostal—a small town about 60 kilometers east of Moscow. Later his location there was confirmed by a March 1947 letter postmarked Moscow from Mrs. Blobel, his secretary, which indicated that biophysicists Born and Karl Zimmer, as well as the Auer Company people, were living 60 kilometers from Moscow. The implication was that the processing of uranium ore and the study of biological effects were being organized in or near Elektrostal while theoretical and experimental work was going on down by the Black Sea.

The Russians had always maintained a security wall between themselves and the East Germans; but after four German atomic scientists who had been to the USSR for job interviews returned to East Germany and defected to the West in early 1947 the rules were tightened up. From then on no East German was ever told anything about German atomic scientists in Russia. All letters from the scientists were strictly censored and bore without exception the return address Post Box 1037P Main Post Office, Moscow.

The Russian assessment was correct: these defectors did possess information of value to us. For instance, Dr. Adolf Krebs had first had interviews in Germany with Colonel Professor "Alexandrow" and a Professor Leipunski. The former was clearly Professor Simon Peter

16

Alexandrov, who represented the USSR at the Bikini "Crossroads" tests in 1946 and in UN discussions on atomic energy in 1947; the latter presumably was A. I. Leipunski, a well-known Russian nuclear physicist. When Krebs was then flown to Moscow (without his consent) he learned that the German groups worked as an independent organization under the supervision of General "Sawiniaki," whose staff of several generals included a General "Krawtschenko." Ungarbled, the boss must be Colonel General Avram Pavlovich Zavenyagin, the builder of Magnitogorsk in the Urals and the Norilsk Nickel Combine in far northern Siberia; he was reportedly head of the secret Ninth Chief Directorate of the MVD and had a General Kravchenko as assistant. Thus the MVD continued into 1947 to play a significant role in the Soviet atomic energy program, even though this had been reorganized in late 1945 as the First Chief Directorate attached

A. P. ZAVENYAGIN

to the Council of Ministers under Colonel General Boris Lvovich Vannikov, who had managed Russia's munitions production during the war.

Krebs also reported: that the Hertz group was working on isotope separation problems at Sukhumi; that the Von Ardenne and Thiessen groups were also there, as we had thought; that Dr. Vollmer and several assistants were working at Sukhumi on heavy water production methods, that Dr. Riehl and his group at Elektrostal were turning out uranium metal on a production scale; and that Dr. Patzschke, a former director of the Joachimsthal uranium mine in Czechoslovakia, was head of a group prospecting for uranium ore near Tashkent in Central Asia. The Pose group was presumably somewhere east of the Urals, since in May and June of 1945 this territory had been surveyed, Krebs had heard, as to its suitability for their reactor work.

The news that the Vollmer group was working on heavy water came as a surprise: by this time it was known that a group of Germans under Dr. P. Herold from the former I. G. Farben Leuna plant at

SECRET   17

Merseberg in East Germany were continuing their wartime research
on methods for the industrial production of heavy water at the Karpov
Institute in Moscow. But the Leuna group was administered quite
separately from the Post Box 1037P groups, presumably because the
Karpov Institute was a research and design facility of the Ministry
of Chemical Industry, while the 1037P scientists were administratively
under the MVD.

Uranium Production; Isotopes

The year 1947 brought the first real confirmation of the thin information we had about the manufacture of uranium. The UK had
managed to learn in 1946 that one ten-ton freight car of uranium ore
was being consigned from the Jachymov (Joachimsthal) area of
Czechoslovakia to Elektrostal every ten days. The UK had also learned
that the Russians were requiring the former Bitterfeld plant of I. G.
Farben to set up the production of highly pure metallic calcium at
30 tons per month, enough for the manufacture (by oxide reduction)
of 60 tons of uranium metal. Penetration sources had furnished the
specifications on the amounts of impurities allowable in the calcium;
these conclusively indicated that it was for atomic use somewhere.

It remained for the covert collection arm of CIA to acquire a bill
of lading for three freight-car loads of calcium from Bitterfeld consigned to Post Box 3 Elektrostal, Moscow Oblast. This proved beyond
question that at Elektrostal there was a uranium factory making the
metal in quantity, using methods worked out at least in part by the
Auer group under Riehl. Indeed it also forced the conclusion that
the Russians were at least attempting to build somewhere a large
reactor to produce plutonium for nuclear weapons.

Shadowing the German scientists in Russia, largely through mail
intercept, had thus produced information which could form the basis
for detailed debriefing when one of them came to the West, while
penetration attempts had run squarely into Russian security. It was
decided to make thorough preparations, mainly by mail analysis, for
the day when the nuclear scientists might return to an area from which
they could be defected, even though that day might be years away.
Later, in 1951, this concept was extended to all German scientists in
the USSR under a program called Operation Dragon. The work
settled into a routine in which the (U.S.) Army Security Agency inter-

18 SECRET

cepted most of the letters while the detailed collation of the data was performed by UK analysts.

Meanwhile atomic collection proceeded on a broad front. In 1948 former prisoners of war began to return from the USSR to West Germany, and it was soon learned that a number of them had helped construct two institutes in the Sukhumi area, one under Professor Hertz near the village of Agudzeri, the other near that of Sinop, namesake of the Turkish city. The year 1949, if it surprised us with the Soviets' first atomic test, showing that their plutonium production was much farther along than we had suspected, also brought the first of two *Russian* defections which helped the analytical picture immensely.

The first defector was a scientist nicknamed "Gong" who had worked in 1947 at the Institute of General and Inorganic Chemistry under a Professor Dmitriy A. Petrov on a way to make porous metal membranes for the separation of uranium isotopes by gaseous diffusion. A prize of 100,000 rubles had been promised for the correct solution of this problem. In the course of his work Gong had that summer visited Special Laboratory No. 3, located in west Moscow. Here he had spoken to Professor Isaac Konstantinovich Kikoin, Deputy Director of the Laboratory and a corresponding member of the Academy of Sciences. Gong was positive that Special Laboratory No. 3 worked on the separation of isotopes by the diffusion method and on other physical-chemical processes. He had also heard of a Special Laboratory No. 1, location not known to him, and of Special Laboratory No. 2, under the direction of Academician Alikhanov in Moscow. All three Special Laboratories were intimately tied to the First Chief Directorate with respect to work priorities, supplies, security, etc.

Thus it became clear that the Colonel "K. K." Kikoin who in 1945 had recruited Hertz for work on isotope separation methods was the person responsible in Moscow for gaseous diffusion research for the Soviet atomic energy program.

Research papers had been published by Gong's boss, Professor Petrov, in 1947[5] and 1948 on the subject of "skeleton catalysts." The method of preparing these catalysts was just that reported by Gong for barrier membranes. Interestingly enough, moreover, the pores in the "catalysts" were of a size reasonably correct for a membrane to separate out U-235 by gaseous diffusion.

___

[5] "Investigation of the Structure of the Copper Skeleton Catalyst," with L. U. Kefeli and S. L. Lel'chuk; Dok. An. 57, No. 6, 1947.

SEGRET

Soviet Nuclear Start

Procurement Abroad

In 1950 the second Russian defector, "Icarus," proved of even more value. As a Colonel of the MVD concerned with supplies, first in the Moscow office of the First Chief Directorate and later at Wismut AG in Saxony,[*] he knew personally many of the Russians involved in the atomic energy program in Moscow and in Berlin. He was aware that General Meshik was in charge of personnel and security for the whole program. He knew that Lt. Colonel (fnu) Sidenko (the "Cedenko" who handled the letters intercepted in early 1946) had been the representative of the Ninth Directorate of the MVD in Berlin in 1945 and that he had been replaced (by August 1946, our intercepts had shown) by Lt. Colonel Elyan (not Yelan, as we had it), who eventually had returned to Moscow to work for the First Chief Directorate under one Dorofeyev, chief of its Supply Directorate. Icarus also reported that a man named Panin ran a warehouse under Dorofeyev known as Post Box 200, Moscow.

Now that we had the correct Russian spelling of the names of the atomic representatives in Berlin, as well as their addresses, it seemed useful to investigate their activities in depth. It soon developed that the Berlin atomic office was always in two sections at separate locations: one handled mail, packages, etc., for the German scientists; the other was concerned with special procurement for the Soviet program. Both sections changed personnel and location approximately every year and a half. Through some rather clever intelligence work against these offices, CIA covert collection was to show in 1952-1953 that they expedited the procurement of several million square feet of very fine nickel wire mesh per year and that at least one shipment of this mesh was flown from Tewa/Neustadt to Panin's warehouse at Post Box 200, Moscow. This clearly established by administrative procedures that the ultimate user was the Soviet atomic program. The technical specifications and amounts of the mesh suggested porous barrier for U-235 separation as the only possible use in an atomic program.

An attempt to learn whether the Bitterfeld plant shipped other atomic materials than the calcium revealed that all shipments now bore only the Moscow address of the main offices of GUSIMZ, the Chief Directorate of Soviet Property Abroad of the Ministry of Foreign

---

[*] Wismut AG (Bismuth Inc.) was the cover name for the vast Soviet-run uranium mining operation in East Germany.

20

SEGRET

Soviet Nuclear Start SECRET

Trade. All carried nine- and twelve-digit order numbers and five-digit transport numbers. Surely numbers as complicated as these should have character in the cryptographic sense.

For background purposes, we studied documentation on equipment ordered by the Soviet commercial mission, Amtorg, in New York. Unfortunately, by about the time we understood the ordering system the Russians decided to tighten it up, so that this work was nullified. However, the reporting on Amtorg (by the CIA domestic collection organization) showed that a P. M. Sidenko had had a tour of duty with the mission between December 1946 and June 1948. This man, presumably the same Lt. Colonel Sidenko who was at the Berlin atomic office in 1945 and through July 1946, arrived in the United States during the same month that brought the departure of Anatoli Yakovlev, head of the atomic espionage chain involving Harry Gold and Klaus Fuchs.

Others working with Sidenko on procurement were soon identified: Nikolai L. Artemiev, who visited a plant making geiger counters in November 1946 and who tried in June 1947 to purchase helium leak-detectors used in U.S. U-235 plants; Nikolai S. Sventitsky, co-author of an article on spectroscopy, Artemiev's replacement; and N. N. Izvekov, who was interested in all sorts of manufactures, from heavy construction machinery to fine-woven wire mesh "for electronic equipment." Some three million dollars worth of goods purchased by the Sidenko group was identified as apparently for the Soviet atomic program; it included the machinery for a complete plant for extracting radium from uranium ore wastes. Sventitsky joined Artemiev in London in January 1948 when Sidenko returned to Russia.

Into the Fifties

With respect to the German atomic scientists in Russia the early 1950's was a period of continued information collection and analytical consolidation. Letter intercepts by the hundreds were collected and results collated. Not only the main groupings but interrelationships within groups were studied, with a view to the eventual recruitment of adequate representatives of each group when they were allowed to return to Germany. In trying to determine who was in the Von Ardenne group at Sukhumi, for instance, it was noted that letters (all severely censored and postmarked Post Box 1037P Moscow) mentioning the accidental death of a small child, from playing with matches, came from Becker, Felicitas Jahn, D. Lehmann, Gerhard Mueller,

Liselotte Steenbeck, Frau Wittstadt, and Dr. Froelich; that an out-
break of scarlet fever was referred to by Felicitas Jahn, Liselotte
Steenbeck and Frau Schrottke; that "on Saturday the Bernhardts
visited the Schrottkes and on Sunday the Schrottkes visited the
Bernhardts"; that the "bull in a china shop" complained about by
Bergengruen was identified by Felicitas Jahn as Helmut Hepp.

Such studies had resulted in the identification of the seven distinct
groups. The Hertz group was still located in the Sukhumi area, by
the town of Agudzeri. The Von Ardenne and Thiessen groups were
together at Sinop in the same area. Vollmer's group, no longer with
Hertz's, had moved to Moscow, and a POW returnee who had been
used in the electronics program confirmed that it was working on
heavy water production processes. The Riehl uranium specialists
continued at Elektrostal, and Riehl had been awarded a Stalin Prize
and made a Hero of the Soviet Union after the success of the test
explosion he had helped make possible in August 1949. The location of Pose's reactor group posed a problem; likewise that of the
biophysicists under Dr. Born, for they had left Elektrostal in 1948.

Some rather clever analysis by the Directorate of Scientific Intelligence in the UK in 1951 succeeded in narrowing down the location
of the Born group to within 20 miles of the town of Kyshtym in the
southern Urals. The Kyshtym area was the site of the nuclear reactor which had made the plutonium for the first Soviet atomic device,
and the placing of a biophysics group near a reactor site made good
sense. The British detection was done as follows.

Born Found

The letters from the Born group described topography, scenery,
weather, and temperatures strongly suggesting the hilly country of
the Urals. In fact, the heavily censored letters spent so much time
on the weather that it was decided to see what could be done with
this information. So the weather as described by known members of
the group on a given day was compared with weather charts of the
USSR for that day, and the irregular portions of the USSR having
such weather were highlighted. Once some dozen of these weather
overlays had been compiled, it was clear that only one area was common to them all. This was a stretch of the Urals some 100 to 200
miles north and south of Sverdlovsk, with a very slight balance of
probability toward the north.

Now an analysis was made of a train trip from Sukhumi to the Born group which a man named Rintelen reported in an intercepted letter: "After the first long train journey, we had an opportunity on the 10th of December from morning till evening to buy warm clothes, travel by underground and bus and to sit in good cafes. . . . In the evening we traveled on again and arrived on the 12th of December in the next large town from here [i.e. from the location of the Born group]. The following evening we traveled a further five hours by train and on the 14th of December we arrived here after a two-hour bus journey . . ."

Rintelen's pleasant stop on the 10th of December must have been in Moscow, for it alone of Soviet cities possessed an underground railroad at that time. There were three trains leaving Moscow on the evening of the 10th for Perm (then Molotov), a likely "large town" on the Moscow side of the Urals. Two were scheduled to arrive early in the morning and one in the evening of the 12th. Why would Rintelen lay over a day in Perm? An evening train heading for the north Urals left there at 1620 on the 12th, arriving at Kizel the five prescribed hours later, so if Kizel had been his destination he should have taken it. Similarly he would not have had to lay over had he been going to the eastern side of the Urals north of Sverdlovsk, say to the Nizhniy Tagil area, for he would have taken from Moscow one of the two trains that get to Perm in the morning so as to catch the 1150 for Nizhniy Tagil and arrive there near midnight on the same day, the 12th. Thus the north Urals did not appear a likely destination, and the "large town" of the layover must therefore be Sverdlovsk (Chelyabinsk lying outside the area defined by the weather information).

The three trains leaving Moscow on the evening of the 10th were scheduled to reach Sverdlovsk on the evening of the 12th (at 1520, 1609, and 1702 respectively). Five trains left Sverdlovsk for various destinations after 1800, so all these appeared unlikely to have been Rintelen's. The two trains per day to Kamyshlov, five hours away, left Sverdlovsk at 1300 and 1525 and so would probably have required a layover, but Kamyshlov, well east of even the foothills of the Urals, was quite unlikely on geographic grounds. One last midafternoon train, however, left Sverdlovsk southbound at 1420 and five hours later arrived at Kyshtym. Rintelen would have had to stay in Sverdlovsk overnight to catch this, and in midwinter at latitude 56°N, the ride from 2:30 to 7:30 p.m. might well have seemed to be an evening one. Thus by elimination his destination, and the position of the Born group, lay some 20-30 miles (the two-hour bus ride) from Kyshtym in the south-central Urals.

The Reactor Specialists

The Pose group was located in a similar manner. Evidence from intercepted letters had put it a three-hour bus ride from Moscow. Thus it was not now in the Urals, as Krebs had guessed in 1947. Several U.S. analysts, studying the intercepted mail, gleaned the additional information that it was two and a half hours by train from Moscow, that the members had good swimming in a river, and that there was a great deal of building activity in new suburbs around them. After a study of maps and railroad timetables the Maloyaroslavets area southwest of the capital was suggested as a possibility.

UK analysts, spurred by this hypothesis, surveyed their much larger volume of intercept and were able to add that (a) the return trains from Moscow did not "fit well," (b) there was a local market-town a half-hour bus ride away, and (c) the "nearest big hospital was 15 km. away."

Railroad timetables showed that Obnino station, 15 km. northeast of Maloyaroslavets, was 2 hours and 30 minutes by train from Moscow. That was also where the road and the railroad crossed the Protva river on the way to Maloyaroslavets. The train took 16 minutes to get from Obnino station to this good-sized town; a bus would probably take half an hour. The only morning train from Obnino to Moscow left at 0750. The possible return trains left Moscow at 1300, 1440, and 1630, giving scarcely more time there than the round trip consumed and so not "fitting well." Some ten other localities were two and a half hours by train from Moscow, but few were near rivers which might have good swimming. Of those that were, several, like Mozhaysk, were large towns in themselves; others had excellent evening train service. Obnino station thus remained the only likely place.

In August 1953 attaché photographs from the railroad looking northwest from the bridge over the Provta river showed several large buildings under construction and a completed large stack with blower house such as is usually required for a nuclear reactor. Photointerpretive measurement done by comparison of these with wartime German aerial photography showed that the stack was almost 210 feet high. Obnino was thus the location of a probable nuclear establishment containing a reactor. The Pose group moved to Sukhumi in 1952.

24   SECRET

Soviet Nuclear Start SECRET

First Western Picture of Obninsk Plant

In 1954 the Russians publicized the initial operation of the first atomic power station in the world at Obninsk (the variant name used for the town served by Obnino station).

The Special Labs

Meanwhile a 1952 report from the UK settled the destination of a high-voltage accelerator for nuclear research built by Koch and Sterzel of Dresden in the East Zone. By checking the interrogation of a bordercrosser who had taken the accelerator to Laboratory No. 3 in Moscow against reports from several returned POW's, the British had concluded that Laboratory No. 3 was in Cheremushki, a suburb of south Moscow. Evidently "Gong" had been mixed up about the numbers of Special Laboratories 2 and 3 when he identified Kikoin and his work in west Moscow on isotope separation with Laboratory No. 3. That one must be No. 2, and the laboratory of the famous nuclear physicist A. I. Alikanyan in south Moscow No. 3.

The question of Special Laboratory No. 2 was solved completely through the efforts of the Biographic Register when it undertook the monumental task of rearranging the 1951 Moscow telephone book by telephone number and by street address. For a west Moscow address given in a 1944 newspaper clipping as that of "Laboratory No. 2 of

SECRET

25

SECRET   *Soviet Nuclear Start*

the Academy of Sciences" there were three telephone numbers, and against these were listed several hundred persons, many of them renowned nuclear physicists such as I. V. Kurchatov and G. N. Flerov, known to have been involved in the uranium problem as early as 1941. I. K. Kikoin was there too. So Laboratory No. 2 of the Academy of Sciences was the same as Special Laboratory No. 2 (not 3) of the First Chief Directorate attached to the Council of Ministers, and it must conduct research on reactors as well as that on U-235 separation under Deputy Director Kikoin.

The Pow's Return

At this time Operation Dragon was girding itself for the expeditious procurement of POW's who had worked with German scientists in the USSR on many projects, including the atomic ones. By 1951 these POW's had been redeployed to "cooling-off camps" in European Russia where they worked at unclassified tasks in industrial plants. There were many hundreds of them. Some used POW camp addresses, other Moscow Post Boxes. Some idea of the complexity of keeping track of them can be gleaned from the following redeployment chart tracing the movement toward only one of the new Moscow addresses. C stands for POW camp:

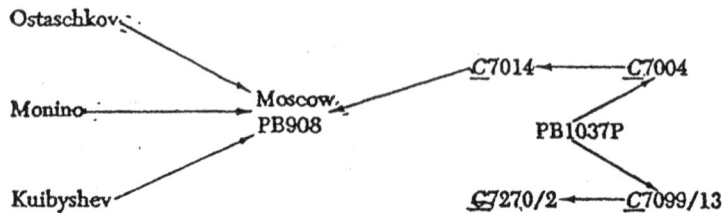

Ostaschkov
Monino — Moscow PB908
Kuibyshev

C7014 ← C7004
PB1037P
C7270/2 ← C7099/13

Most of the civilian members of Moscow Post Box 1037P, the scientists, had by 1952-3 also started their cooling-off period and were using Sukhumi Post Box 3122. For a time there was a question whether they were actually at Sukhumi, for we had only the letter postmarks to vouch for it. This question was settled neatly when a Miss Verena Weber wrote her aunt that on 30 June 1954 they had seen an eclipse of the sun reaching 97 percent totality which started at half past four and ended at half past six. A check with the Naval Observatory established that in the locale of Sukhumi the eclipse reached slightly more than 97 percent totality and that it started at approximately 1623 local time and ended at approximately 1835. This agreement, along

26   SECRET

with information in the intercepts on climate, flora, and physical surroundings, confirmed the location as in the general area of Sukhumi.

The POW's from 1037P who had cooled off since 1951 began to return in mid-1954, practically the last of those who had helped German scientists in the USSR. Though many knew little except their own particular tasks, their information tended to round out the deductions which had previously been made about the work of each of the main groups of atomic scientists. The Born group really had been located at Singul, near Kyshtym, and had worked on the biophysics of radioactive substances. The Pose group really had been at Obninsk and had worked on the design of nuclear reactors.

Of most interest at the time was the report of one Von Maydell, which established clearly that the Thiessen group was the one which had developed the nickel-wire-mesh-backed barrier of sintered nickel powder used after 1950 in the Soviet gaseous diffusion process for separating U-235. He knew technical details. The plant that put it into practice must have operated under considerably different conditions from those of its U.S. counterpart.

We were still ignorant of the location of that plant, although it had produced as early as 1951 the U-235 for the Soviet Union's third atomic test. By now our guesses were largely limited to what were known to be atomic facilities at Nizhnyaya Tura and Verkh Neyvinsk in the north Urals. Nizhnyaya Tura seemed most likely, for a large electric power plant had been built there in the postwar period. But then the function of Verkh Neyvinsk lay in question. Were the Soviets pursuing more than one kind of U-235 separation process?

Several POW's knew that German scientists from Sukhumi had visited the U-235 plant using the barrier, and we looked to them to help locate it. Imagine our consternation when it developed that they had heard the place spoken of only as "Kefirstadt," so dubbed because the favorite soft drink there was kefir, the fermented milk of the Caucasus.

Scientists Tell All

Finally, in April 1955, the German scientists returned from Sukhumi to the East Zone of Germany, the last of them except for some groups engaged in missile research. The defection plans went into action. Hertz, Von Ardenne, Vollmer, Steenbeck, Pose, and several others would not respond, but many of those working for them did. Despite the three-year cooling-off period, skillful and exhaustive interrogation

Soviet Nuclear Start

in depth revealed technical details, individual names, etc., in a richness unbelievable to one who has never witnessed this procedure.

Nikolaus Riehl defected as soon as he learned that he could not keep the proceeds from his Stalin Prize. He and others detailed the uranium processes at Elektrostal exhaustively.

Patzschke's uranium prospecting effort near Tashkent was reportedly a failure. His fate was not, and still is not, known.

Members of the Born group discussed their radiobiological research at Singul. Without knowledge of the reactor site near Kyshtym, they reported they had gotten their radioactive "soup" from Teche. Teche was listed in the file as one of the villages east of Kyshtym which had disappeared in the 1950 Deleniya, the MVD's biennial listing of administrative centers in the USSR; it was within the area of the Kyshtym reactor site as delineated by earlier POW interrogations.

Members of the Pose group discussed their abortive attempts at Obninsk to design and construct a beryllium-oxide-moderated reactor. Because graphite-moderated reactor research at Laboratory 2 and heavy-water-moderated reactor research at Laboratory 3 had both been quite successful, the decision had been taken in 1950 to build up around the German nucleus at the Obninsk site and under the direction of Academician A. I. Leipunski a third Russian center for reactor research working on power reactors and other advanced types.

The research of the Vollmer group on heavy water production turned out to be in connection with a heavy water facility built at Norilsk, where Zavenyagin's Nickel Combine was already located, in the far north of Siberia. The wartime work of the Leuna group had been used by the Karpov Institute in connection with two other heavy water production processes, according to a member of that group. Presumably he was referring to those used by the heavy water plants at Aleksin, Chirchik, Kirovakan, Dneprodzerzhinsk, Gorlovka, and Berezniki, which had been uncovered by returned POW interrogations and attaché photography.

The work at Sukhumi prior to 1952 had been mostly devoted to isotope separation, as we had supposed. The Von Ardenne group worked on the electromagnetic method and the Steenbeck group on the gas centrifugal method. Several Germans had been concerned with the thermal diffusion method. Hertz himself had worked on a variation of gaseous diffusion termed mass diffusion in the United States. None of these were actually put into practice for U-235 separation.

28   SECRET

Thiessen's group, with calculational help from the Hertz group, worked on mesh-backed gaseous diffusion barrier (as Von Maydell had reported) and on plant design. Some of the Germans had even helped set up a barrier factory at Elektrostal and knew the cutting and loss factors required to turn square footage of nickel wire mesh into completed barrier. The German mathematical theory on gaseous diffusion was strangely easy to understand; with minor exceptions the symbols and formulae somehow seemed familiar. Then someone had the bright idea of looking up several of Klaus Fuchs' wartime papers on gaseous diffusion: that was where the Germans got it.

"Kefirstadt" turned out to be Verkh Neyvinsk in the Urals, leaving the function of Nizhnyaya Tura and its associated large power plant an enigma. Presumably power was sent by transmission line to Verkh Neyvinsk, there being mention in the technical press of transmission line construction from Nizhnyaya Tura southward.[1]

In retrospect, following the trail of Gustav Hertz and his associates proved to have been a wise course of action. Despite Russian efforts at security compartmentation the Germans had valuable information which complemented that from other sources. Indeed it would not have been possible to achieve an understanding of the later U-2 photography of Soviet U-235 facilities and uranium metal plants without the information obtained from the Germans.

---

[1] For the subsequent solution of this mystery and further description of the Urals atomic complex see the author's "The Decryption of a Picture" in *Studies* XI 3, p. 41 ff.

~~SECRET~~
~~No Foreign Dissem~~

A study in perspective.

SOVIET DECEPTION IN THE CZECHOSLOVAK CRISIS

Cynthia M. Grabo

The various postmortems and retrospective analyses of the Soviet invasion of Czechoslovakia in August 1968 have revealed a considerable amount of disagreement among analysts concerning the deception measures taken by the Soviet Union during that summer. Some analysts believe that the USSR conducted a deliberate and fairly successful political and military deception campaign at least from mid-July onward (that is, from the start of major mobilization and deployment of the invasion forces), which was intended to conceal the scale and purpose of the military movements, and to deceive the Czechoslovaks and others into believing that there would not be an invasion. On the other hand, there are analysts who believe that the USSR did not engage in any significant deception effort, and that if we or the Czechoslovaks were misled at all it was a result of wishful thinking or self-deception. Aside from those relatively few specialists who have examined all the evidence in detail, most of us probably have a very inexact understanding of this question and why there should be a difference of opinion in retrospect.

This article does not purport to provide a definitive solution. It is intended rather to outline the problem and the evidence available and to draw some tentative conclusions. Perhaps more usefully, it also attempts to put the episode into perspective in relation to what we know of the USSR's doctrine and past practice with respect to deception, and to suggest what the USSR might be able to do to deceive us on another occasion. In short, there are some lessons to be learned from our experience during the summer of 1968.

Types of Deception

There are various kinds of measures which a nation bent on initiating surprise military operations can undertake in an effort to conceal its intentions. In all cases, standard security precautions would be taken. These, of course, may involve a variety of means to prevent outsiders or potential enemies from observing or otherwise detecting that military

~~SECRET~~

19

SECRET

Soviet Deception

movements or logistic buildups are in progress, or at least to conceal the full extent of the buildup, the units involved, etc. It is important to understand, however, that such measures to achieve military secrecy do not in themselves constitute an active deception effort, particularly in nations which practice rigid military security as a matter of course, and the sophisticated analyst will take care to distinguish the true deception effort from conventional security measures. Nonetheless, the line between deception and security is a narrow one; the two are often confused, and an effective security program can do much to deceive the intended victim even if no other measures are undertaken. Soviet security measures therefore will be considered in this article.

The most common and easiest to carry out of all types of deception, a political deception program may involve a variety of measures. The simplest of course is the direct falsehood. Through diplomatic channels, public statements or by other means, the nation bent on military aggression or some other venture it wishes to conceal merely states that it has no such intention and that all such charges are false. Although such tactics are by no means unheard of, particularly when the stakes are very high, many nations will seek insofar as possible to avoid the direct lie in favor of some type of indirect or slightly more subtle deception. Thus, even in the Cuban missile crisis, in which Soviet spokesmen unquestionably directly misinformed the President of the United States, an examination of public Soviet statements shows that nearly all of them were indirect rather than absolute falsehoods. The USSR as a rule did not flatly deny that it was putting IRBMs and MRBMs into Cuba. Rather it said that all weapons being sent to Cuba were "designed exclusively for defensive purposes," or that there was "no need" for the USSR to deploy its missiles to any other country, etc. This type of statement, although extremely misleading, is not totally untrue and thus permits the prevaricator to maintain some degree of credibility if or after he has been caught in the act.

Among the more subtle means of political deception is the effort to mislead by implying that the situation is not serious, that the nation does not consider its vital interests at stake or that its relations with the intended victim are really pretty good. Ordinarily such a deception effort will be maintained only over a relatively short period, usually no more than a few weeks, although in some cases it may last for several months. Generally, it will involve the downplaying of the situation in propaganda and diplomacy after political means at solution have failed and a decision has been reached to conduct a surprise attack or at least to prepare military forces for such attack. This type of situation may be

20

SECRET

marked by quite a sudden change in the tone and volume of propaganda, particularly for foreign consumption, in an effort to lull suspicions. Dictatorships, including the Soviet Union, are usually masters of this type of political deception; their complete control of the press and secrecy of the decision-making process make it relatively easy for them. For example, in the weeks and even months before the Soviet attack on Japanese forces in Manchuria in August 1945, the USSR undertook to ease political tensions with Japan and to be "almost cordial" to the Japanese Ambassador, as all the while it was building up its military forces in the Far East for the attack.

Another facet of this type of political deception is to offer to enter into negotiations in an ostensible effort to solve the matter at issue, when there is actually no intention of reaching an agreement. The Soviet Union also has been known to use this tactic. On the evening of 3 November 1956, less than 12 hours before Soviet forces struck throughout Hungary to suppress the revolt, Soviet officers began negotiations in Budapest with Hungarian defense officials on Soviet "troop withdrawal." (The growing Chinese Communist concern with Soviet intentions in late 1969 is said to have been attributable in part to Peking's fear that the USSR had proposed the border talks as a deception measure prior to attack.)

In the interests of preserving secrecy as to its real intentions, a nation bent on surprise action also may attempt to deceive (or at least not inform) its allies of its plans. There is reason to believe, for example, that the USSR informed only the top leaders of the Warsaw Pact countries, and probably belatedly at that, of its plans in Cuba in 1962. It almost certainly did not make its intentions known to the non-ruling Communist parties. As is well-known, the reluctance by the US to believe that Great Britain was preparing for attack against Egypt in 1956 was based in large part on a confidence that one of our closest allies would not undertake such action without informing us first.

We have coined the term "political-military deception" to denote a type of attempted military deception which is carried out solely by putting out false statements about the nature, scale, or purpose of a military buildup. It is in effect a political deception effort designed to camouflage or conceal the real intention behind the military buildup by attributing it to something else. This type of deception, to be distinguished from true military deception described below, proceeds from the premise that since the enemy is likely to detect the military movements, it is therefore desirable to offer him some seemingly plausible explanation, other than planned aggression, for the activity.

The most usual explanation is that the troops are "on maneuvers." It may also be possible, on occasion, to find some other pretext for troop movements, such as alleged internal disturbances in a border area. US intelligence has long recognized that the Soviet Union would probably seek to mask preparations for aggression under the guise of maneuvers. Similarly, the USSR and its Warsaw Pact allies are extremely suspicious of major NATO exercises as potential covers for attack.

True military deception, as opposed to the various means described above, is the most difficult and complex of all types of deception to orchestrate, at least on a large scale. It is most commonly used when hostilities are already in progress, when it may be used with other deception measures to disguise the scale of a buildup, the date or place of attack, and/or to lead the enemy to believe that an attack is planned in one area when in fact it is not. It involves such techniques as permitting seemingly valid, but actually false, military orders to fall into the hands of the intended victim; the sending of invalid military messages in the clear or in easily read ciphers, or the maintenance of completely spurious radio nets; assignments of false designations to military units; setting up of dummy aircraft or other equipment to suggest that units have not left home stations; sending out false "defectors" with erroneous but plausible reports, etc. Measures of this type call for very sophisticated and highly coordinated planning, since the chance that an obvious slip would be detected is great, and detection might betray the whole plan. Such measures can, however, be highly effective in tactical situations in leading the enemy to misdeploy his forces or to misjudge the timing or area of the main thrust. Obviously, such tactics have a more limited use when one is trying to conceal that an attack is planned at all.

The planting of false reports, through established intelligence channels or the diplomatic service, may be used as a part of the political or military deception methods described above. A military attaché is a useful channel for putting out a seemingly plausible explanation or disclaimer concerning a troop buildup, as is a diplomat to provide a false political story. These channels, along with the professional clandestine services, also may be used simply to flood the market with a mass of conflicting stories and reports. Particularly when reports are sensational but otherwise appear to have some authenticity, they can be a tremendous distraction. If the volume of such planted disinformation is large enough, the analytical system can be so overwhelmed by it that the truly reliable or useful intelligence may become lost in the mill. It is difficult to overestimate the damage that this type of deception can do to the process of assessing and evaluating information in a crisis situation.

Soviet Deception   SECRET

Actual Soviet Security and Deception Measures in the Summer of 1968

With this brief background, we shall attempt to analyze what the USSR did and did not seek to do in the way of deception prior to the invasion of Czechoslovakia. This requires that we also attempt to determine whom it may have wished to deceive—the Czechoslovaks, the US and NATO, or others, including other Communist parties.

The USSR's objective in Czechoslovakia was to reverse the course toward liberalization and to restore orthodox Communist Party control there. Insofar as possible, the USSR wished to achieve these aims through the Communist apparatus in Czechoslovakia rather than by overt military intervention. The objective was not to carry out a surprise military operation, which was only the final means to the end. The USSR and its Warsaw Pact allies decided on massive military invasion only after a series of lesser political and military steps had not been successful. It is thus obvious that the amount of deception which the USSR could usefully employ against Czechoslovakia was limited. In order to induce the Dubcek regime to comply with its wishes, the USSR clearly had to insure that its political pressures were such that Czechoslovakia would have no doubts concerning the seriousness of Soviet intent. To lend added weight to the political effort, it was also desirable that Czechoslovakia recognize the possibility of Soviet military action—and indeed the first device used by the USSR to attempt to put troops into Czechoslovakia was simply to request that Soviet units be stationed there.

So far as the West was concerned, it was not in the USSR's interests to attempt to mislead us unduly concerning its military movements lest these be misinterpreted as a threat to NATO. And the future support of other Communist parties was of importance to the USSR; it wished these parties to understand its concern with and actions toward Czechoslovakia. To deceive them unnecessarily would be counterproductive.

Military Security Measures

As everyone knows, Soviet military security is extremely tight. As a matter of normal practice, the USSR never identifies an active military unit by its true designator in the open press, and never reports a buildup of its military forces anywhere (except temporarily for exercises). Moscow has occasionally reported a reduction of forces, although not necessarily accurately, when it has seemed politically expedient to do so. It usually identifies by position only a small group of top-ranking commanders, and

SECRET   23

the names and locations of its military districts, groups of forces, and other major commands such as the fleets. It may or may not report the whereabouts of top military officials, including the Minister of Defense, as it chooses. It nearly always denies travel in the USSR to US and other Western military attachés (and sometimes to all diplomats and tourists as well) to any area in which significant military movements are under way; it is most unusual for any Westerner to see a unit redeployment. The same security restriction is carried out in East Germany by imposing restricted areas, some permanent and some temporary, on the three Allied Military Liaison Missions.

A review of the military security measures taken by the USSR from early May (when the first deployments to the Czechoslovak border were made) up to the date of the invasion on 20-21 August leads to the conclusion that the steps taken were about normal for the USSR. Security was not relaxed (at least not intentionally—there were a few slips), but neither was it drastically tightened. There was no announcement of the early May deployments in the Carpathian Military District, Poland, and East Germany, and no announcement that a partial mobilization had been carried out to bring these units up to strength where needed (we learned this after the invasion from a defector). Throughout the summer, the USSR denied most travel by military observers to areas of the Soviet Union where the buildup had occurred, and in East Germany a "temporary" restricted area was continuously reimposed throughout the summer in the southern area near the Czechoslovak border. At least one unusual security measure was taken in East Germany: in early August an unprecedented ban on travel by virtually all foreigners was imposed in the area of the military buildup along the Czechoslovak border.

In Poland, however, which was to be the major line of communication for support of the invasion, there was only the most minor effort on perhaps two occasions during the summer to restrict movements of attachés, diplomats, tourists and newsmen. Only the actual encampments of Soviet forces were ever placed off limits. There were any number of observations by Western sources of the Soviet troops along the Czechoslovak border, and the start of the massive movement into Poland in late July of troops from the Baltic and Belorussian Military Districts was fortuitously witnessed and promptly reported to the US Embassy by several US tourists and other travelers. Why this contrast with the security measures in the USSR and East Germany? Did the Soviets want us to learn about movements in Poland but not elsewhere? A more likely explanation is that Poland traditionally does not impose major restrictions on travelers, and that it either was not prepared to or did not

wish to do so in the summer of 1968, particularly at the height of the
tourist season. Presumably the Soviets made no major issue over this
policy (although we do not know this for certain), but it would appear
unlikely that they really wanted us to learn about their troop movements.
We would judge that they would have preferred secrecy (there was a
report that the Poles had a public announcement ready in late July that
Soviet troops were entering the country, but never issued it), but that
secrecy was not considered of overriding importance.

In Hungary, the other area of pre-invasion deployments, partial but
not complete restrictions were imposed on attaché movements. Western
attachés did observe the major deployments of Soviet units from their
garrisons toward the Czechoslovak border in late July.

Political Deception Measures

The USSR, from at least the time of the Dresden conference in late
March, repeatedly and progressively made it evident that it was most
gravely concerned with the course of events in Czechoslovakia. All
indications are that it used virtually every political device at its
command to bring pressure on the Dubcek regime to reverse the trend
toward liberalization. Thus it is evident that there was no political
deception in the strategic sense, no attempt by the Soviets to play down
the importance of the issues. And this message also came through loud
and clear to us.

More difficult and controversial is the question whether the USSR was
engaged in a political deception effort at the Cierna and Bratislava
conferences and in the succeeding days prior to the invasion. The theory
that the conferences were deception, convened at Soviet insistence to
mislead the Czechoslovaks and to gain time for the continuing military
buildup, rests largely on a presumption that the Soviet leadership took a
final decision in mid-July that any further political effort was useless and
that the only recourse was military invasion, that all developments from
that time forward were in preparation for that invasion, and that the
timing was determined solely by when the military forces were ready.
This hypothesis assumes that the Soviet leaders went through the motions
at Cierna and Bratislava only for political effect; they had already
decided to invade as soon as all military preparations were complete; and
that they concealed such an intention from the Dubcek regime.

A review of the military evidence alone yields much to support this
hypothesis, and a quite plausible case can be made that the date for the
invasion (or at least the date when the forces would be ready) was set well
in advance. The chain of military preparations from about 20 July

onward appears almost unbroken, and a final review and inspection of
the deployed forces was apparently completed by the Soviet high
command on about 16 August (their visits to the forward area between
13-16 August were announced by the Communist press). It may be
conjectured that Marshal Grechko then returned to Moscow, informed
the political leadership that all was ready, whereupon the final military
orders were issued and the invasion proceeded on schedule.

The political evidence, however, is not so readily explained. From
what we know of the Cierna conference, it appears that the USSR was
compelled to expend a tremendous effort to get the Czechoslovak
leadership to hold the talks at all (finally agreeing to the border town as
the site after other proposed sites had been rejected), that a great deal of
hard bargaining went on at the talks, and that an agreement of sorts was
reached whereby Czechoslovakia undertook to carry out certain
measures to strengthen Party control and its relations with the Warsaw
Pact. A case therefore can be made, also with considerable plausibility,
that the talks were a genuine, albeit desperate, effort by the USSR to
reach some sort of political accommodation so that the invasion would
not be necessary. The reduction in Soviet polemics which followed the
talks was then part of the agreement, not just a deception to lull
Czechoslovak suspicions.

If this is correct, one cannot view the Cierna and Bratislava talks as
pure political deception. This, however, does not resolve the question of
what the Soviets actually told the Czechoslovaks and whether or not they
misled them—by omission, direct statements, half truths or
innuendoes—concerning their military buildup and intentions.
Unfortunately, on this crucial question, our evidence is far from
adequate. The contention, which appears logical to us—that the USSR
should have given Dubcek some unequivocal warning that Warsaw Pact
forces were prepared to invade unless he complied with the terms of the
agreements—may or may not be valid. It was reported in Budapest
following the invasion that the purpose of Kadar's meeting with Dubcek
on 16 August was to warn him that the USSR would invade unless its
demands were fulfilled, and it has been implied that others also warned
Dubcek of this. Charges have been made that Dubcek withheld from his
colleagues some of the communications which he received from the
Soviet Union, including a letter from Brezhnev on 16 August and a letter
from the Politburo of the CPSU to the Czechoslovak Party on 17 August,
which in the view of Dubcek's opponents allegedly provided some
warning of impending Soviet action. Dubcek, on the other hand, is
reported to have denied to the Czechoslovak Central Committee plenum

26   SECRET

in September 1969 that Kadar had mentioned possible imminent intervention, or that the letters from Brezhnev and the CPSU contained warnings of impending armed action. Although Dubcek was of course attempting to justify his actions and his statements therefore are suspect, there is some evidence to support his denials. We do not know the content of the Brezhnev letter, but we do have the reported text of the CPSU letter of 17 August. While it called for immediate action to implement the Cierna agreements and said that delays in this matter "are extremely dangerous," there was no threat of *military* action in the letter. Also, it must be noted that Soviet public commentaries were notably devoid of saber-rattling and statements or even direct hints that massive Soviet forces were capable of overrunning Czechoslovakia at any time.

In short, we lack sufficient evidence to make a firm judgment whether or not the Soviets directly threatened Dubcek and his colleagues with invasion and if so how convincing this was to the Czechoslovaks. Similarly, we do not really know whether most of the Czechoslovak leadership was as surprised by the final military action on the night of 20 August as it has appeared. It is probable that those who really had understood the Soviet position did expect invasion sooner or later. They may have been tactically, but not necessarily strategically, surprised. On the other hand, those who did not understand the USSR's attitude and tactics—foremost of whom was probably Dubcek himself—may have been impervious to any kind of warning and hence genuinely surprised. It is not unlikely that many Czechoslovaks, like ourselves, were the victims of a good bit of wishful thinking—they just could not believe that the Soviets would invade.

There is another type of Soviet political deception against the Dubcek regime, which was quite likely considerable although we know little about it. This would have involved an attempt to subvert the regime from within using pro-Soviet elements in the Czechoslovak Party, the security services and the armed forces. According to General Sejna, the Czechoslovak party and governmental machinery was so well controlled by the Soviets during the Novotny era that virtually nothing went on without Moscow's knowledge and usually prior consent. Although there is little direct evidence, there is some reason to suspect that the USSR hoped in the spring to carry out some type of coup within the Party whereby the conservative element would take over from Dubcek, but that it was unable to effect this. We may be almost certain that the USSR subsequently tried any number of devices, without success, to undermine Dubcek's position and to promote the conservatives. On the night of the invasion the USSR clearly had expected an overthrow of Dubcek and the

Soviet Deception

installation of a new conservative leadership, but again the plan failed. It has been suggested that one reason for this failure was that most of the conservatives were not apprised of the timing of the invasion and therefore were not ready to act. If this is so, the argument that the USSR did not directly forewarn the Czechoslovaks—other than those agents actually involved in the operation—gains considerable weight.

In sum, the evidence which we have concerning Soviet political deception of the Dubcek regime is certainly incomplete and in some important respects inconclusive. These uncertainties, however, apply more to the USSR's techniques than to any attempt to conceal its objectives. On the fundamental issue, the USSR's intent to restore orthodox Party control, there is no good reason to suspect that the USSR ever sought to deceive the Czechoslovaks.

With regard to the West, and particularly the US, there is little indication that the USSR conducted any long-term or elaborate political deception effort—certainly nothing remotely comparable to what it undertook in the Cuban missile buildup. But, since its objectives in Czechoslovakia could hardly be kept secret from us as well, there was comparatively little room for any deception. There may be some basis, however, for believing that in the few days prior to the invasion the USSR sought to lull US suspicions by reaching an agreement to open talks soon on strategic arms limitation. Exactly what happened will have to be revealed by a policy-level official of President Johnson's administration. According to an article in the *Washington Post* on 23 August 1968, a meeting between President Johnson and Premier Kosygin to discuss strategic arms limitation was to have been announced by the White House on the morning of 21 August. The article also noted that on the evening of 20 August, while Ambassador Dobrynin was at the White House informing President Johnson of the invasion of Czechoslovakia, Secretary of State Rusk was telling the Democratic Platform Committee in Washington that "we anticipate early and important talks with the Soviet Union on the limitation and reduction of offensive and defensive strategic missiles."

A final note is in order on the CPSU's conversations with and communications to non-ruling Communist parties. A substantial body of evidence is available that the USSR did not attempt to deceive these parties but in fact took steps to inform them between about 15 and 20 July that it might have to take drastic action, including invasion, to control the situation. While we have little information on any subsequent communications, the evidence is that these parties were forewarned about a month before the invasion to prepare their membership for this

28

Soviet Deception   SECRET

contingency and that few if any of them were surprised. Many were dismayed by the final action, but not surprised.

Political-Military Deception Measures

We shall now examine the nature and possible intent of the various public statements made by the USSR relating to the buildup of its forces against Czechoslovakia. As we have noted, consistent with its security doctrine the USSR never announced that it was deploying any units to the Czechoslovak border. Following the initial deployments in early May, however, it prevailed upon Czechoslovakia, after considerable pressure, to announce that Warsaw Pact exercises would be held in June in Czechoslovakia and Poland. This "agreement" provided the pretext for the subsequent introduction of Soviet forces into Czechoslovakia under the guise of conducting Pact exercise "Sumava," which was held, according to announcements, during the last ten days of June. The announcement may also have been intended to provide a pretext for the presence in Poland of the troops from the Carpathian Military District which were introduced in early May, and whose movement had been reported in the Western press. Although "Sumava" was concluded on 30 June, TASS immediately retracted its announcement of the termination, and a series of subsequent statements from Prague made it evident both that the USSR had introduced much larger forces than originally announced and was seeking to keep them there. This was the first of the USSR's efforts, and a transparently evident deception, to bring military pressure on Czechoslovakia under the guise of "exercises."

On 23 July, the USSR announced that rear services exercises would be held in the western USSR until 10 August, would cover an area from Latvia to the Ukraine and would involve the recall of reservists, requisitioning of transport from the civilian economy and demothballing of military equipment. Subsequent announcements outlined a scenario of the "exercises," repeatedly described them as very large-scale, and stated on 30 July that the exercises were being extended into Poland and East Germany. The USSR also announced that a large antiaircraft defense exercise was conducted in the USSR from 25-31 July. On 10 August, a Soviet announcement implied that the rear services exercises had terminated, but no announcement was made that any of the recalled reservists or requisitioned transport were being released. Concurrent with the start of the announced rear services "exercise," the USSR began the major buildup of additional forces along the Czechoslovak border. By 31 July it was evident that substantial forces in East Germany had deployed to the Czechoslovak border, that the bulk of Soviet troops in Hungary

SECRET   29

had moved into positions near the Czechoslovak border, and that large numbers of additional Soviet troops, both combat and rear services, were moving into Poland from the Baltic and Belorussian Military Districts. It was indisputably clear that a major deployment of forces was in progress. It was less clear at the time whether exercises were also under way, although there was no discernible indication that any of the deployed forces were engaged in exercises.

What was the purpose of the announcements? Were they intended to provide some ostensibly plausible reason for the forward deployments of forces and supply columns? To lead us to believe that the only mobilization was in the rear services? To deceive us and the Czechoslovaks as to the real purpose, or primarily to put more pressure on the Dubcek regime?

Much of the disagreement concerning Soviet deception is over this issue. It has been argued, and with considerable reason, that the Czechoslovaks (who would be familiar with Soviet deception tactics and who already would have known the Pact training schedule for the year) could not have been so naive as to believe that an exercise was under way. Therefore, it is maintained, the primary purpose of the announcements was to put more pressure on Czechoslovakia, to warn but not to deceive. Perhaps so. We do not know how the Czechoslovaks interpreted the announcements.

But what about the West? Were the announcements intended to deceive us and NATO, or at least to confuse? To most observers, it would seem that they were, and that in fact many were deceived. To judge from current intelligence coverage at the time, it would appear that a majority of analysts were reluctant to say that these were not exercises, or to draw the conclusion that the *only* thing which was in progress was a mobilization and deployment. Only a minority probably firmly believed the latter at the time. And it may be noted that, even in retrospect, some analyses have persisted in referring to the "exercises."

At the same time, however, the Soviet announcements provided us the clearest indication which we had that a mobilization was actually in progress. If they left unclear the extent of it, and whether combat as well as rear services units were involved, they did serve to warn us, even before the military movements became evident, that an extraordinary Soviet military effort was under way. Thus the Soviet statements, if intended to deceive, also were an asset both to analysts and collectors.

Active Military Deception Measures

There is reason to believe that the USSR engaged in some active military deception against Czechoslovakia at least as early as June when

Soviet Deception   SECRET

it began moving forces into that country ostensibly for exercise "Sumava." Numerous Czechoslovak statements both then and later suggest that the Soviets brought in much larger forces than the Czechoslovaks had agreed to, and possibly attempted to conceal the identity and size of these forces as well. Because there was so little Western observation of these movements, it has been suspected that the USSR moved forces covertly at night, or in small contingents over secondary roads to conceal the extent of this peaceful invasion during June. This may be partially true, particularly of the first elements which were introduced. A Soviet defector from a regiment which entered Czechoslovakia from the Carpathian Military District at the start of the exercise has stated, however, that his unit moved on main roads with no unusual attempt at concealment, although it did travel at night.

We are not sure whether the USSR finally agreed to withdraw its forces from Czechoslovakia during July (the withdrawal was not finally completed until 3 August) as part of a deception plan in connection with the buildup of the invasion forces, or because it really saw no practicable alternative at the time. Similarly, we know relatively little about any deception measures which may have been taken before the invasion to mislead the Czechoslovaks as to its timing. The USSR did employ some active deception against the Czechoslovaks during the invasion, perhaps more than we know. The best-known example was the flight into Prague shortly before the invasion of ostensibly civil aircraft carrying the military personnel who seized the Prague control tower to vector in the military transports. It is likely that other measures also were employed. For the most part, however, the USSR appears to have relied on security and speed of movement to insure tactical surprise.

So far as the West and NATO are concerned, there is virtually no indication that the USSR attempted any active military deception measures designed to mislead us as to the scale, location or purpose of the military buildup or the possible timing of the invasion. The Soviet military leadership had ample time to plan and complete its military buildup, and presumably could have undertaken a more elaborate and sophisticated deception effort than it in fact did. Such a plan would logically have been put into effect as soon as the major military deployments were begun in late July. The argument has been advanced that, if Soviet leaders did not decide to invade until mid-August, they had little time to devise and carry out any active deception measures. This argument appears both unconvincing and unrealistic. It presumes that the Soviet political leadership had not taken any fundamental decisions on possible military action until a few days before the invasion.

SECRET   31

A far more realistic assessment is that the Soviet leadership in mid-July initiated the massive military buildup because it then believed that a solution by political means was unlikely and that the probabilities were that military invasion would be required to bring the situation under control. Or, to put it another way, the Soviet leadership reached the basic decision in mid-July to carry out an invasion unless a political solution could be reached, but deferred a final decision on whether military action would inevitably be required and hence also a decision on its timing.

Apart from this, however, it is in large part irrelevant to the military deception program just when the political leadership reached the final decision to invade, since the military leaders clearly were directed in mid-July to make all necessary preparations as if invasion were to be carried out, and they did so. Active deception measures would have been an integral part of the military preparations, not something reserved for the last few days.

The apparent lack of major military deception measures may indicate that the USSR saw no need for them against the Czechoslovak forces or did not wish to reveal its more sophisticated war plans and capabilities. It would be optimistic to suppose that more elaborate deception efforts would not be employed in event of attack against the West.

Confusion and Disinformation Measures

Possibly the most conspicuous missing element in the picture was the almost total absence of deliberately planted false reports by the Soviet intelligence services, whose disinformation capabilities are well recognized. There was almost no apparent effort to distract and confuse us with this type of material. Again the USSR may have seen no need for this type of effort in the circumstances. It may have preferred not to release a flood of misleading reports which might cause alarm in the West and raise suspicions that the Soviet buildup might be directed at some nation other than Czechoslovakia. Indeed, one of the most notable features of the entire Soviet military and political effort in the summer of 1968 is that it was so clearly directed at Czechoslovakia that there was no cause for any undue alarm in the West, despite the scale of the military buildup. It appears likely that this was a consequence of a deliberate decision by the USSR to keep the temperature in Europe as low as possible.

SECRET

Soviet Deception SECRET

Implications of the Soviet Effort

The predilection of Soviet leaders for secrecy, security, and surprise makes it almost impossible to conceive that they could have carried out an operation such as the invasion of Czechoslovakia without employing some of their traditional deception tactics. So deeply ingrained is the concept of deception that there is reason to suspect that the USSR has sometimes employed such tactics when there was no evident political or military necessity to do so. In the case of the invasion of Czechoslovakia, it was probably also very important to the Soviets that the actual timing of the invasion and the details of the military plans be concealed in order to achieve tactical surprise and reduce the likelihood of any Czechoslovak resistance and loss of life on both sides.

The scope of actual deception measures employed by the USSR was probably far less than might be expected under other circumstances. The security measures were less than we would normally expect to see during a major redeployment, and the buildup was quite evident to us, and presumably to the Czechoslovaks as well. The amount of political deception, although somewhat debatable as regards Czechoslovakia, does not appear to have been very extensive or elaborate. There seems to have been very little active military deception, except possibly during the actual invasion phase. We were spared a disinformation effort by the KGB. About the only significant Soviet effort at deception, at least as far as the West was concerned, appears to have been the attempt to portray the logistic buildup and troop deployments as "exercises," and even here some observers suspect that the USSR never expected us to be deceived. This effort certainly would have been more effective had it been accompanied by drastic security measures to deny US observation of the troop movements and logistic preparations in Eastern Europe. In short, the situation was unusual and should not be regarded as a typical Soviet performance or as an illustration of what the USSR could do in circumstances calling for maximum security and surprise—particularly in an attack against the West.

Even the limited Soviet deception effort, however, serves as a useful reminder that we should always be watchful for the possibility of deception, and that we must continually look behind what the enemy says to what he is actually doing. This becomes even more essential when it is evident that a crisis situation exists in which the use of deception should be anticipated. The fact that any US analysts were taken in by the Soviet announcements on "exercises" is cause for considerable concern that intelligence analysts also might fail to recognize a deception effort

SECRET

33

when it might be vital to US security to detect it. Our experience in the invasion of Czechoslovakia has reinforced the opinion long held by warning analysts that the US, at both its intelligence and policy levels, is extremely vulnerable to deception. The intelligence community has profited greatly in other respects from the Soviet invasion, which provided us with valuable data on Soviet mobilization, logistics, and operational concepts. It is to be hoped that the lessons learned with regard to deception will also be the subject of further study. Perhaps there should be more provision in the intelligence schools and in publications such as this journal for study and analysis of this kind of problem.

New photointerpretation illuminates
a grim chapter of history.

THE HOLOCAUST REVISITED:
A RETROSPECTIVE ANALYSIS OF THE
AUSCHWITZ-BIRKENAU EXTERMINATION COMPLEX

Dino A. Brugioni and Robert G. Poirier

The authors have been strong advocates of the application of aerial photography to historical research and analysis.* Our convictions about the utility of this medium to the professional historian have been strengthened as we became increasingly aware of the many historical problems to which the exploitation of aerial photography can contribute an added dimension. In this paper, we attempt to demonstrate the application of aerial photography to a historiographical problem.

Our interest in the subject of Nazi concentration camps was rekindled by the television presentation "Holocaust." In the more than thirty years since VE Day, 8 May 1945, much has happened to these camps. Some, like Treblinka, have been completely obliterated; others, such as Dachau and Auschwitz, have been partially preserved as memorials.

Aerial reconnaissance was an important intelligence tool and played a significant role in World War II. We wondered whether any aerial photography of these camps had been acquired and preserved in government records. If imagery was available, we thought it likely that the many sophisticated advances in optical viewing, and the equipment and techniques of photographic interpretation developed at the National Photographic Interpretation Center (NPIC) in recent years would enable us to extract more information than could have been derived during World War II.

We had a number of advantages not available to the World War II photographic interpreters. Instead of .7X tube magnifiers, we had micro-stereoscopes. Our modern laboratory photo-enlargers were vastly superior to those available to earlier interpreters. While the World War II photointerpreter performed his analysis by examining paper prints, we would use duplicate film positives allowing detailed examination of any activity recorded on the film. The present day imagery analyst also has the advantage of years of training and experience, while the World War II photointerpreter was extremely limited in both. Most importantly, for this project, we have the advantage of hindsight and abundant eyewitness accounts and investigative reports on these camps.[1] We therefore had the opportunity to study the subject from a unique perspective.

We faced two immediate problems as we began our investigation. We knew that the cameras carried by World War II reconnaissance aircraft were limited to about 150 exposures of Super-XX Aerocon film per camera and that this film resolved about 35 lines per millimeter. The film was exposed at "point" rather than "area" targets

---

*"Rome East of the Jordan: Archaeological Use of Satellite Photography," *Studies* XXI/1. p. 13; "Satellite View of a Historic Battlefield," *Studies* XXII/1, p. 39.

[1] The "intelligence collateral" for this paper was drawn mainly from O. Kraus and E. Kulka, *The Death Factory*, New York, 1966; N. Levin, *The Holocaust*, New York, 1973; and the official Polish government investigations, *German Crimes in Poland*, 2 Vols., Warsaw, 1946-47, which draw on primary sources.

11

which were selected for their strategic or tactical importance. Thus, when the reconnaissance aircraft approached the target, the pilot or aerial photographer would switch on the cameras shortly before reaching the target and then turn them off again as soon as the target was imaged. There was nothing like the broad area coverage which modern photoreconnaissance makes available to the photo researcher. To find photos of a concentration camp, therefore, we would have to identify one which was located close to a target of strategic interest.

Since the Nazi concentration camp system was so widespread, we also had the immediate chore of narrowing the scope of the investigation to manageable proportions. Our research revealed that the Auschwitz-Birkenau extermination complex was only 8 kilometers from a large I. G. Farben synthethic oil and rubber manufacturing facility. We knew that oil and rubber production plants were high on the Allied bombing list. Auschwitz, then, in addition to providing us with a high degree of name recognition, offered a strong probability of having been filmed as a by-product of tactical reconnaissance. Our research soon produced positive results.

The Defense Intelligence Agency, which is the custodian of World War II aerial reconnaissance records, was given the coordinates for Oswiecim (Auschwitz), Poland, through NPIC's film distribution and control center. DIA ran a computer search against the coordinates within the time frame we had selected and produced a print-out of all the unclassified photographic references to film stored in the National Archives' records center at Suitland, Maryland. From this list we were able to order the photography we desired sent to NPIC for photographic analysis. On off-duty hours, we examined all the available unclassified aerial imagery for evidence of the Holocaust at Auschwitz.

The Auschwitz-Birkenau Extermination Complex

The Auschwitz-Birkenau complex had its origins in spring 1940. A concentration camp was organized in a former military camp in the suburbs of Oswiecim (Auschwitz), Poland. When the first trainload of German criminal prisoners arrived in June 1940, it marked the beginning of a system which would eventually total some 39 subsidiary camps and make the name of Auschwitz synonymous with terror and death.[2]

In the fall of 1941, the Auschwitz concentration camp entered the most sinister phase of its expansion with the construction of a camp on the moors of Brzezinka (Birkenau). Under cover of a prisoner of war camp, it would become a center for *Sonderbehandlung,* i.e., "Special Treatment," the Nazi codeword for extermination. During the following three and one-half years, an estimated two to three and one-half million people would meet their deaths on this remote Polish moor.

Details of the horrors perpetrated at Auschwitz have been reported many times and at length. It is not our purpose to reiterate that type of detail but rather to see if any of that activity had been recorded by the World War II aerial reconnaissance cameras.

Auschwitz is located in a remote area southwest of Warsaw on the Krakow-to-Vienna rail line. We found no evidence of any Allied reconnaissance effort in the Auschwitz area prior to April 1944. On 4 April 1944, an American reconnaissance aircraft approached the huge I. G. Farben facility for the first time.

The format employed in the balance of this paper will present the background information for a particular topic and then a photographic analysis of the pertinent

---

[2] Kraus and Kulka, *The Death Factory,* p. 8.

12

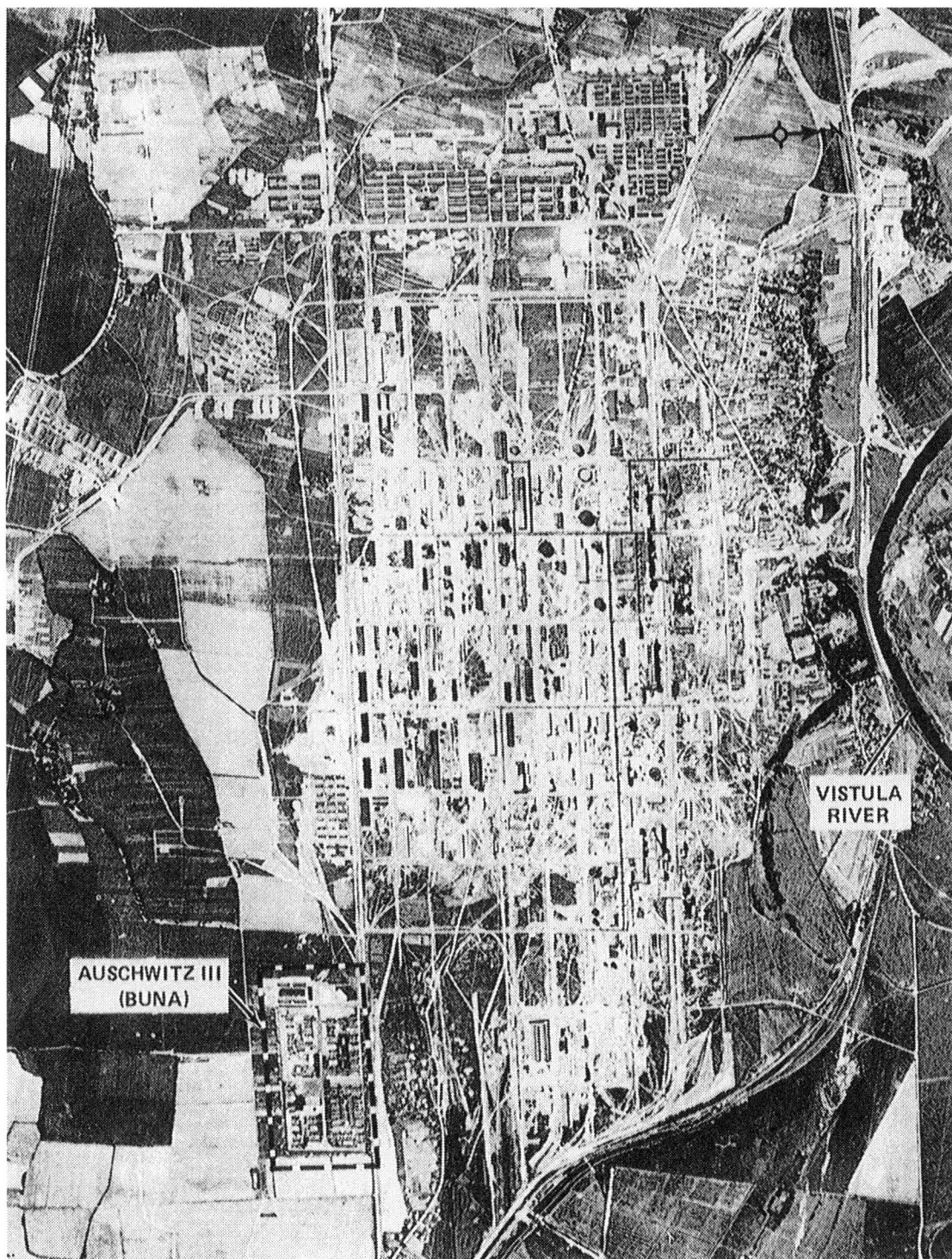

I.G. FARBEN COMPLEX

13

The Holocaust Revisited

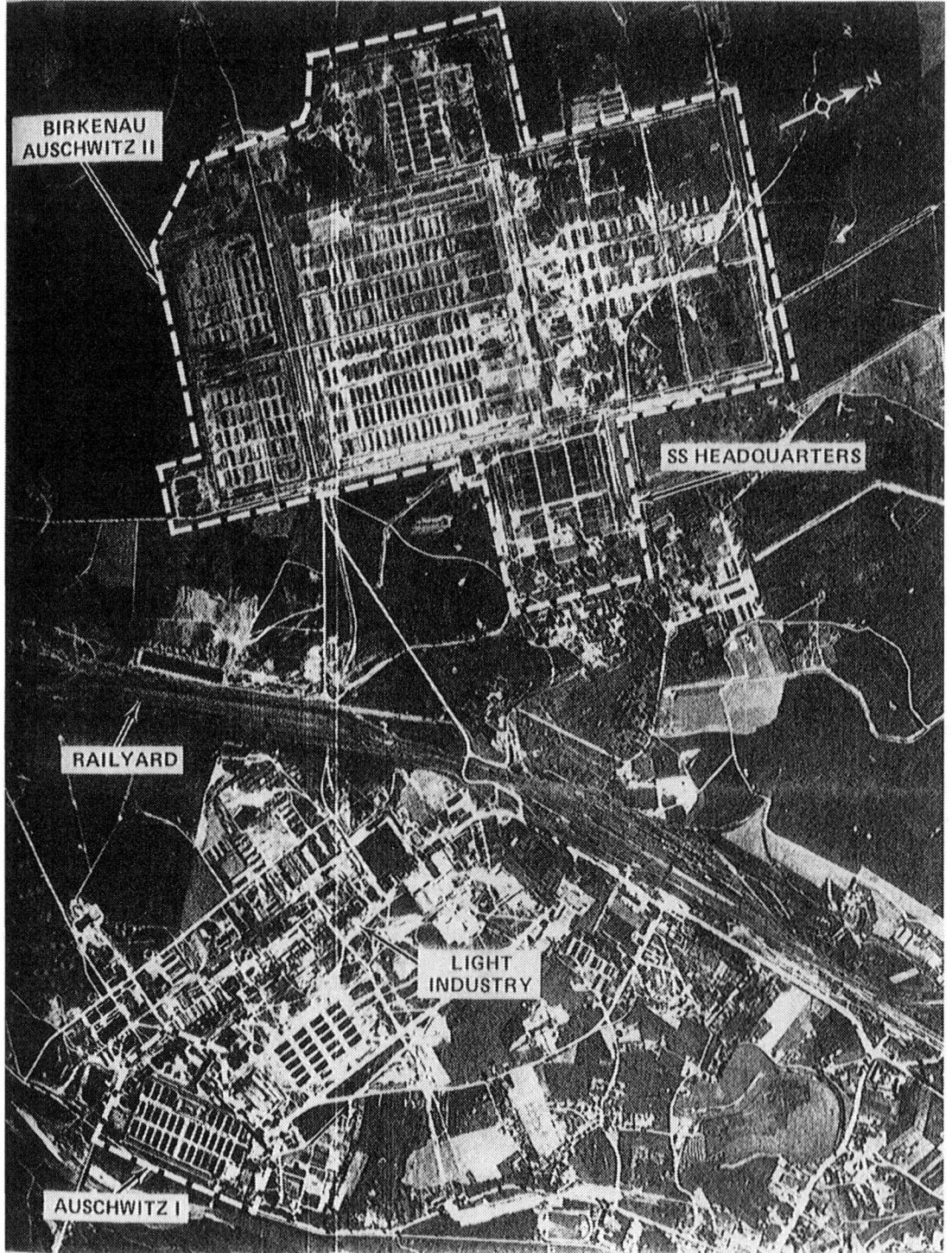

FIGURE 1. THE AUSCHWITZ-BIRKENAU COMPLEX, 26 JUNE 1944

The Holocaust Revisited

imagery. All available imagery on Auschwitz acquired between 4 April 1944 and 21 January 1945 was examined.

Background: Construction of the various Auschwitz camps began in spring 1940. Auschwitz I, the so-called Main Camp, was operational by fall of that year. The development of Birkenau (Auschwitz II), began in fall 1941 with Russian prisoners of war as construction crews. The I. G. Farben industrial facility, referred to as "Buna" (Auschwitz III), was begun at Monowice in April 1941. Expansion of these facilities was virtually continuous until the evacuation of the area by the Nazis in January 1945. The operation of these vast petrochemical facilities was a joint SS and I. G. Farben venture. Farben had full access to a source of slave labor—prisoners from Auschwitz and local British prisoners of war—and the SS received the salaries paid their prisoners.

Crippling the German petrochemical production system was a high Allied priority, so the targeting of the Farben complex was inevitable. The late date of the reconnaissance effort is probably attributable to the plant's production status; it produced no significant amounts of fuel until 1944. Another factor was probably the distance from Allied air bases—about 750 miles from England and 700 miles from Italy.

Photo Evidence: The mission of 4 April 1944 produced very little photographic coverage of the I. G. Farben complex. It was not until the 26 June 1944 mission (Photos 1 & 1A) that an overall view of the complex, both as to extent and purpose, could be interpreted. For our study, however, even the partially successful mission of 4 April provided positive evidence.

Auschwitz I

Background: Details of the origin of the camp have been outlined earlier, but some additional comments are appropriate. It was at this facility that experiments in mass extermination by using *Zyklon-B* gas were first carried out. Rudolf Höess, the notorious camp commandant, initially tested the use of that gas on Russian prisoners of war in 1941. The first gas chamber and crematorium, number I by the Nazi numbering system, was later constructed at this camp. The Main Camp penal barracks for problem prisoners (Barracks Block 11), and the medical experimentation barrack located here would both become infamous.

Photo Evidence: Analysis of the facilities at Auschwitz I (Photo 2) combined with the collateral information, corroborate eyewitness accounts of its description. We can identify Gas Chamber and Crematorium I, the Commandant's quarters, the camp headquarters and administration buildings, the prisoner registration building, the individual barrack blocks and the infamous "execution wall" between barrack blocks 10 and 11. This latter facility was used for the exemplary execution of "problem" prisoners. Death was inflicted either by hanging or shooting against the execution wall. In addition to the above, the camp kitchen, guard towers, and the security fencing can all be identified.

On the photography of 4 April 1944, a small vehicle was identified in a specially secured annex adjacent to the Main Camp gas chamber. Eyewitness accounts describe how prisoners arriving in Auschwitz-Birkenau, not knowing they were destined for extermination, were comforted by the presence of a "Red Cross ambulance." In reality, the SS used that vehicle to transport the deadly *Zyklon-B* crystals. Could this be that notorious vehicle? While conclusive proof is lacking, the vehicle was not present on imagery of 25 August and 13 September 1944 after the extermination facility had been converted to an air raid shelter.[3]

---

[3] *Ibid.*

15

The Holocaust Revisited

The preferred method of shipping prisoners to Auschwitz was by rail. Large transports arrived in the railyards of Auschwitz from all sections of Europe. To the west of the camp, as shown in Photo 2, a number of transports are present in the railyard and an additional train is arriving. A new rail spur from the main line into Birkenau is under construction. Eyewitness accounts indicate that work on this spur continued round the clock in anticipation of special shipments of Hungarian Jews in May–July 1944.[4] Some equipment, probably construction gear, appears to be at work on the new spur. It was complete and operational when seen on imagery of 26 June 1944.

Birkenau

Background: Birkenau, the "Birch Wood," underwent continuous expansion from autumn 1941 until the suspension of the extermination effort in November 1944. As a "Special Treatment" facility, it had a planned capacity of 200,000 prisoners. Had Nazi Germany won the war, evidence presented at the War Crimes Trials revealed that it was destined to be the extermination center for the Czech and Polish nations.[5] The camp contained more than 250 barrack blocks subdivided into sections and some 95 support buildings. Four large gas chambers and crematoria were contructed here in 1943.

Photo Evidence: A 7X enlargement of the 26 June 1944 imagery reveals the camp layout in considerable detail (Photo 3). The rail spur and debarkation point near Gas Chambers I and II are complete. A rail transport is present within Birkenau. The site of the four gas chambers and crematoria can be identified. The locations of the various Birkenau sub-camps, e.g., the "Gypsy Camp," the "Women's Camp," could also be traced. Expansion of the facility into Section III is under way. The SS Headquarters and Barracks complex is seen east of the camp. The security arrangements can be traced in considerable detail.

Several indications of extermination activities can be identified in the camp. Smoke can be seen near the camp's main filtration facility. While this is to be expected near the camp crematoria, where bodies had to be burned in open pits during the hectic days of the Hungarian Jewish influx, it is a surprise to see it here. There are a number of ground traces near Gas Chambers and Crematoria IV and V which could also be connected with extermination activities. Ground scarring appears to the rear of Gas Chamber and Crematoria IV and is very noticeable to the immediate north and west of Gas Chamber and Crematorium V. These features correlate with eyewitness accounts of pits dug near these facilities; they were no longer present on coverage of 26 July and 13 September 1944. The small scale of the imagery, however, prevents more detailed and conclusive interpretation.[6]

In portions of the imagery not shown in Photo 3, activity in the rail yards, the layout of the surrounding countryside, to include several of the Polish villages forcibly evacuated when the Nazis established Auschwitz, and the marshes south of the camp used for human ash disposal can be identified.

Imagery acquired on 26 July 1944 added little new information to the study. The first evidence of Allied bombing at the I. G. Farben complex and a very large transport of prisoners in Birkenau could be identified. While an overall view of the complex was obtained, the exceptionally small scale of the imagery precluded detailed interpretation.

---

[4] Kraus and Kulka, *The Death Factory*, p. 132.; *German Crimes in Poland*, Vol. I pp. 88-89.

[5] Kraus and Kulka, *The Death Factory*, p. 17.

[6] *German Crimes in Poland*, Vol. I, pp. 88-89.

16

The Holocaust Revisited

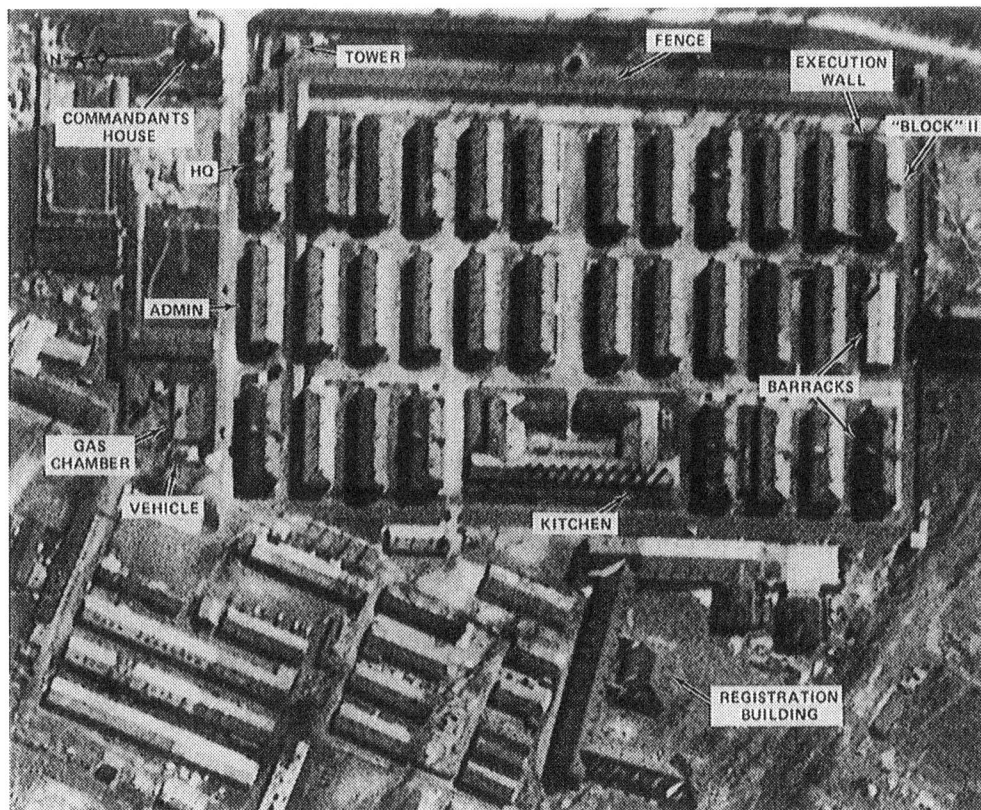

Photo 2: Auschwitz I, 4 April 1944

The Extermination Process

Background: Extermination operations in progress at Birkenau were recorded on aerial photography of 25 August 1944. By that time, rail transports of prisoners were being channeled into Auschwitz from locations throughout occupied Europe in a desperate attempt to achieve the "Final Solution" prior to the collapse of the Nazi war machine. After a trip lasting from a few hours to days, those who survived the journey faced a selection process. SS "doctors" screened the prisoners to determine those fit to be used as slave laborers and those to be exterminated. Those selected as laborers were sent "to the right" while those to be exterminated were sent "to the left," according to numerous eyewitness accounts of these last tragic moments.[7]

Photo Evidence: A 10X enlargement of imagery acquired on 25 August covers only the southern third of Birkenau and is of very high quality for its day (Photo 4). The imagery illustrates eyewitness accounts of the death process at Birkenau. A rail transport of 33 cars is at the Birkenau railhead and debarkation point. Prisoners can be seen beside the train. The selection process is either under way or completed. One group of prisoners is apparently being marched to Gas Chamber and Crematorium II.

---

[7] Kraus and Kulka, *The Death Factory*, pp. 130-141.

17

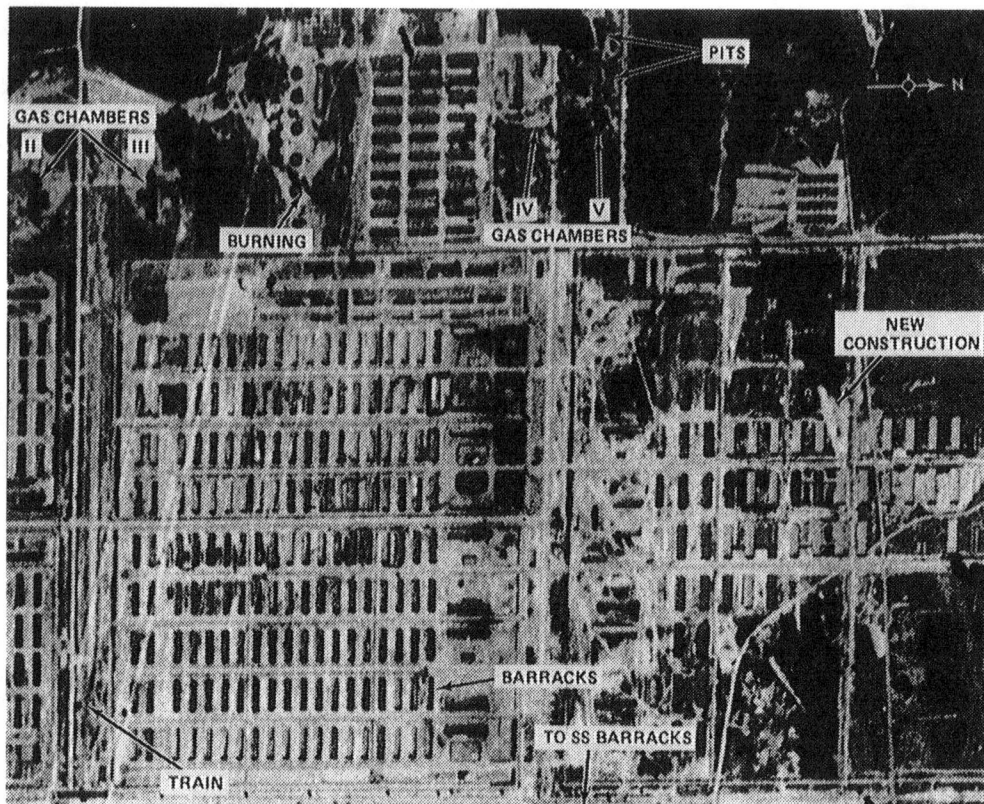

Photo 3: Birkenau Extermination Camp, 26 June 1944

The gate of that facility is open and appears to be the destination of that ill-fated group.[8]

Groups of prisoners can be seen marching about the compound, standing formation, undergoing disinfection and performing tasks which cannot be identified solely from imagery. A detailed view of the Women's Camp and individual barrack blocks was obtained. (Many of the so-called "barracks" provided as living quarters were originally prefabricated stables intended for use in Africa with the *Afrika Korps*.) We can also identify details of the camp security system—the electrified fences, guard towers, the camp main gate and guardhouse, as well as the special security arrangements around the gas chambers and crematoria.

High quality imagery of the entire Birkenau complex was obtained for the first time on 13 September 1944. A huge transport of some 85 boxcars is present at the Birkenau railhead. Details of the compound, including the expansion into Section III

---

[8] Collateral information indicates that this transport is very likely from the Lodz ghetto. This was the last Jewish ghetto in Poland to be liquidated. This action took place between 2–30 August 1944. A less likely possibility is that the victims were members of the French underground, who are known to have been sent to Birkenau during this period.

18

The Holocaust Revisited

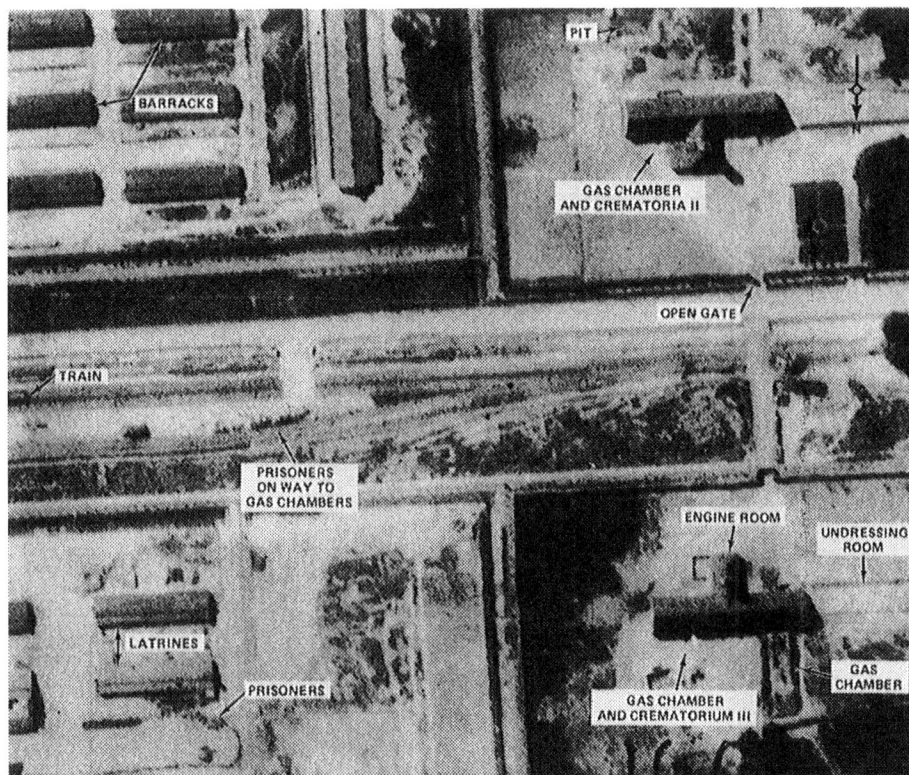

Photo 4: Extermination Process at Birkenau, 25 August 1944

necessitated by the large influx of Hungarian Jews, were observed.[9] A large column of prisoners, estimated at some 1,500 in number, is marching on the camp's main north-south road. There is activity at Gas Chamber and Crematorium IV, and its gate is open; this may be the final destination of the newly arrived prisoners.

Registration

Background: Prisoners selected as slave laborers were processed through a registration system which culminated in numbers being tattooed on their arms prior to their being quarantined and assigned to work details.

Photo Evidence: In Auschwitz I, we have the other part of the drama, those sent "to the right," being enacted at Birkenau (Photo 5). In front of the Main Camp Registration Building, a long line of prisoners is visible. This was undoubtedly the group spared death in the gas chambers but condemned to a living death in an SS work detail. They stand frozen in time, awaiting their tattoos and work assignments.

---

[9] It was not possible to specify the nationalities of the groups in the photographs from the collateral information. They might have come from either the remnants of the Lodz ghetto or from Czechoslovakia.

19

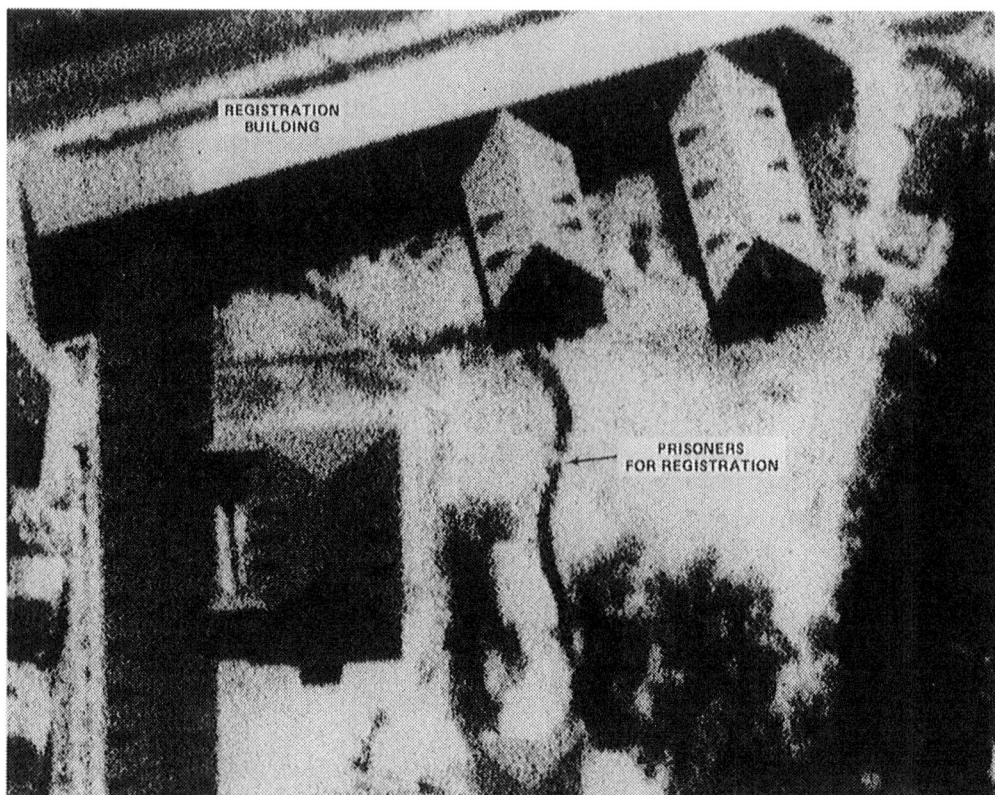

Photo 5: Registration, Auschwitz I, 25 August 1944

The Gas Chambers and Crematoria

Background: The gas chambers and crematoria at Birkenau were designed to process some 12,000 people a day. The prisoners sent "to the left" were deceived into thinking they were going to be showered and disinfected. After undressing in an anteroom, they were herded into the shower/gas chamber and put to death by means of *Zyklon-B* gas crystals introduced into the chamber through exterior vents. The bodies were then moved to the crematoria or external burning pits for disposal.

Photo Evidence: The photography of the gas chambers and crematoria in the southern section of Birkenau appear to be historically unique (Photo 6). As far as we have been able to determine, no other photography of these facilities exists. The Birkenau gas chambers were special access facilities, even for most Nazis, and all photography was forbidden. The extermination facilities at the camp were destroyed by the Nazis prior to the camp's being liberated by the Red Army in January 1945.[10]

We can identify the undressing rooms, gas chambers and crematoria sections as well as the chimneys. On the roof of the sub-surface gas chambers, we can see the

---

[10] Kraus and Kulka, *The Death Factory*, pp. 134-140.

20

The Holocaust Revisited

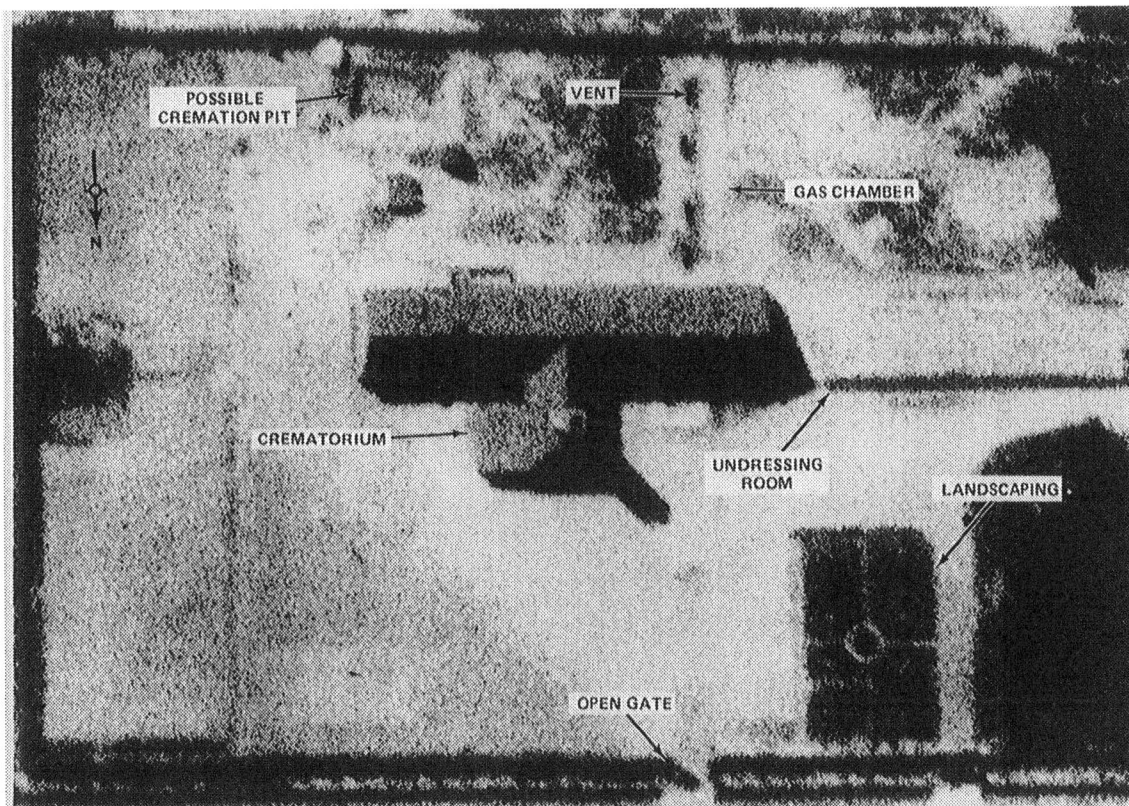

Photo 6: Gas Chamber and Crematorium II, 25 August 1944

vents used to insert the *Zyklon-B* gas crystals.[11] A large pit can be seen behind both Gas Chambers and Crematoria I and II; it is probable that these were the pits used in summer 1944 for the open cremation of bodies which could not be handled in the crematoria. Measurement of Gas Chambers I and II by NPIC photogrammetrists provided construction data on the crematoria not available from the architectural plans.

Numerous sources speak of the well-kept lands and landscaping around the crematoria; some described the buildings as "lodge-like," "industrial looking," or having a "bakery-like" appearance. These descriptions are borne out by the imagery of 25 August 1944 in which a park-like rectangle is visible. In the imagery of 13 September 1944 landscaping is visible around all four extermination facilities. Although survivors recalled that smoke and flame emanated continually from the crematoria chimneys and was visible for miles, the photography we examined gave no positive proof of this.[12]

---

[11] *Ibid.*

[12] The imagery examined from records of the extermination period include 4 April, 26 June, 26 July, 25 August, and 13 September 1944.

21

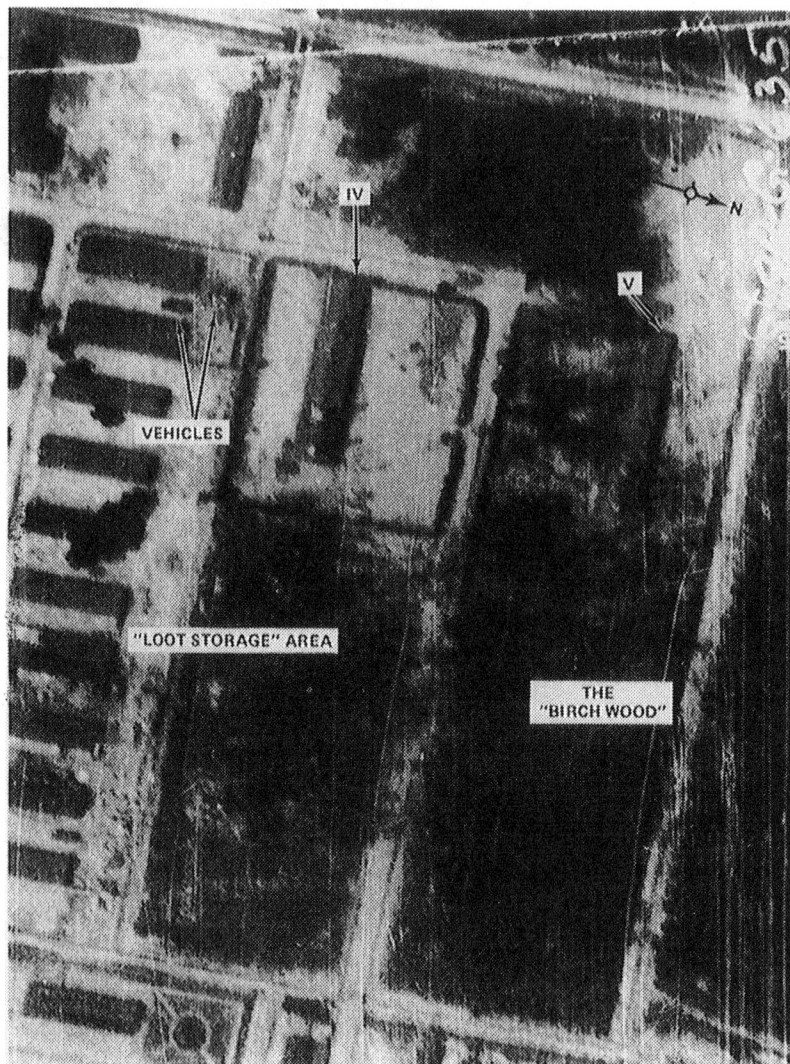

Photo 7: Gas Chambers and Crematoria IV and V, 13 September 1944

The imagery acquired on 13 September 1944 provides a unique view of Gas Chambers and Crematoria IV and V (Photo 7). Located among the trees of the "Birch Wood," these facilities could not be seen by surviving prisoners in the camp. They were of a different design than Gas Chambers and Crematoria I and II; they had two rather than one chimney each, and were built totally above ground rather than having underground sections. An additional piece of information, not included in Photo 6, is the view of two large buildings some 500 meters west of the disinfection block. It is probable that these are two of the 1942–43 era extermination facilities used prior to the construction of the four main gas chambers in 1943.

22

Deactivation and Dismantling of the Complex

Background: When imagery of Birkenau was next acquired, the operational status of the camp had changed radically. By 29 November 1944, the Nazi war effort on all fronts was on the verge of collapse. A dramatic though futile revolt of the *Sonderkommando* had occurred on 7 October 1944 at Gas Chamber and Crematorium IV.[13] Extermination at Birkenau was officially terminated on 3 November 1944. The first stages of evacuation of the prisoners and the technical equipment began shortly thereafter.

Photo Evidence: Photography of 29 November and 21 December 1944 enables us to monitor the progress of the Nazi evacuation efforts (Photo 8). For the first time since Allied photography had been acquired, no train is located in the Birkenau railhead. The exterior of all extermination facilities, with the exception of Gas Chamber and Crematorium IV destroyed on 7 October 1944, appear to be intact. The dismantling of Section III of Birkenau has begun.

On imagery acquired on 21 December 1944, the progress of the evacuation effort is clearly discernible. The electrified fence around Section III and the guard towers there have been dismantled. The former location of the various barrack blocks and support buildings can be identified. The light snow cover provides an aid to our interpretation efforts by highlighting soil marks and depressions, making it easier to identify man-made disturbances. There is a clear view of Gas Chamber and Crematorium IV's former location.[14] Additionally, Barracks Block B II/C 11 has been destroyed, probably by fire. We were able to find no reference to this event in the collateral material.

Photo 9 details Nazi efforts to dismantle the technical equipment at Gas Chambers and Crematoria II and III. We can trace the dismantling of the special security fencing around these installations, the removal of the roofs and the underground dressing rooms, the dismantling of the chimneys, and the filling of the pit to the rear of Gas Chamber and Crematorium III. As far as we know, this is a unique photo of that activity.

Evacuation

Background: The final period of Auschwitz is that immediately prior to the evacuation of January 18-21, 1945. By that time, the Nazis faced defeat on every front and were trying desperately to erase all traces of the extermination program. When prisoners could not be evacuated, their destruction was the alternative. Many of the Auschwitz facilities had, in fact, been dismantled and shipped to Germany for use in other concentration camps.

Photo Evidence: The heavy bomb damage inflicted upon the I. G. Farben complex is visible in Photo 10. This 14 January 1945 imagery revealed more than 940 bomb craters and 44 damaged buildings at that facility.

The camp at Buna (Photo 11), is still operational as evidenced by the melting snow on the barrack block roofs. Cleared footpaths and streets are further evidence of movement in and around the compound.

Auschwitz I is also occupied on 14 January 1945 (Photo 12). It was the last camp to be evacuated. Snow melt on the roofs indicates that the barracks remain occupied,

---

[13] The *Sonderkommando* was a special unit of prisoners forced by the Nazis to assist in the extermination activities, especially in the disposal of bodies. Themselves marked for extermination, one group attempted to rebel. Although they succeeded in destroying Gas Chamber and Crematorium IV, they were all killed.

[14] See *The Death Factory*, pp. 261-263 and *German Crimes in Poland*, Vol. I, pp. 90-92.

23

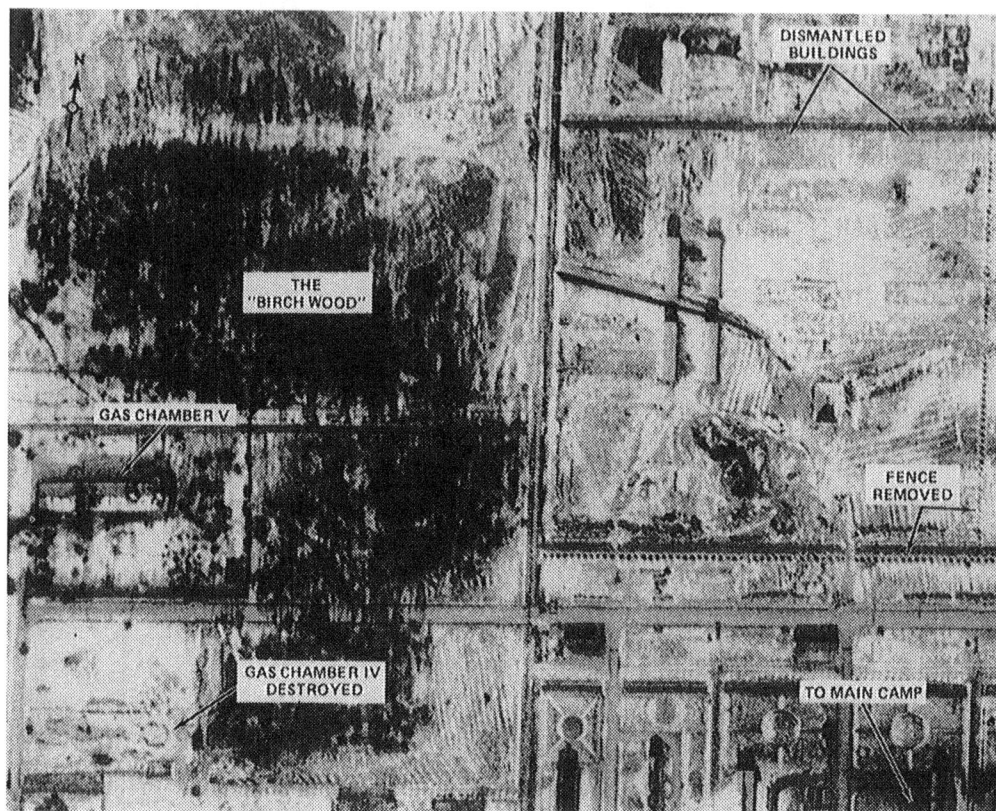

Photo 8: Evacuation Process at Birkenau, 21 December 1944

with one important exception. The lack of heat and presence of snow on the roof of Barracks Block 10, site of the infamous medical experiments, indicate that it is empty.[15]

Imagery of Birkenau (Photo 13) also presents an informative and surprising record. Section III of Birkenau has been completely dismantled and evacuated, including the guard towers. The snow cover on the roofs of the Women's Camp indicates that it had been evacuated. Within Camp II, it is easy to detect which of the barracks are probably still occupied as evidenced by the melting snow on the barrack block roofs. The camp had been partially evacuated. Several buildings had been dismantled in the Women's Camp since the 21 December 1944 coverage.

The most revealing photographic evidence to emerge from analysis of the 21 December 1944 and 14 January 1945 imagery centers on Gas Chambers and Crematoria II and III. The official Polish investigation stated that these facilities had been dismantled and blown up in November 1944, but this is clearly contradicted by the presence of the installations on imagery of 29 November and 21 December 1944,

---

[15] The SS conducted hundreds of "medical experiments" on prisoners during the existence of Auschwitz. These included pseudo-scientific investigations into infections, attempts to "create" twins, starvation experiments, etc. carried out by SS doctors.

24

The Holocaust Revisited

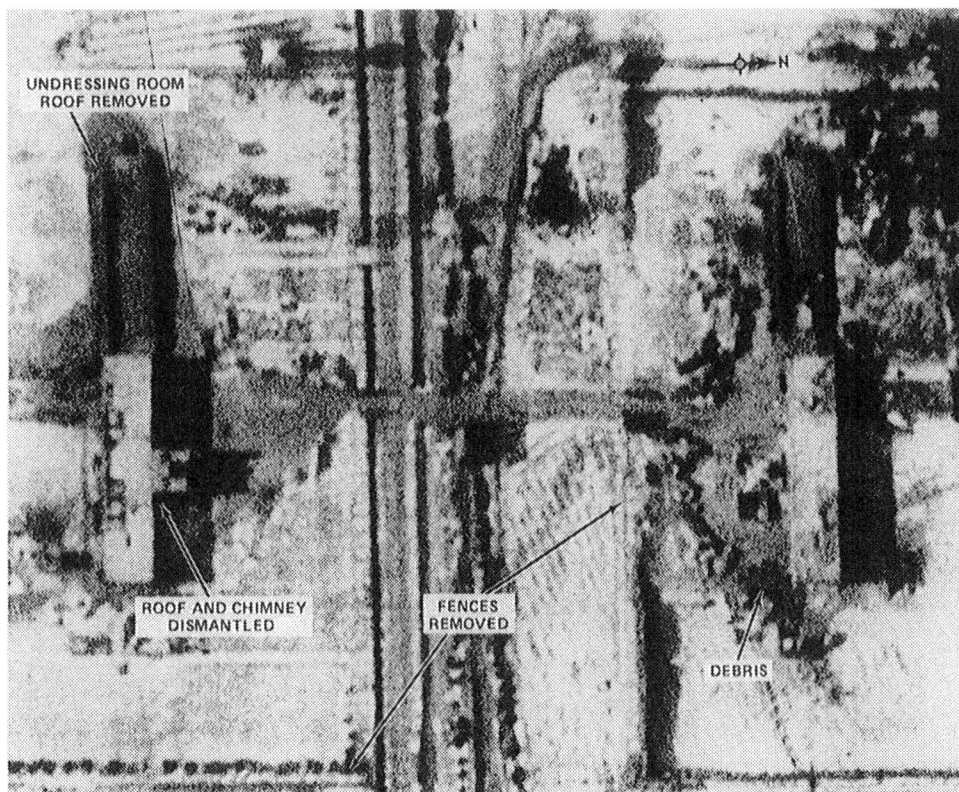

Photo 9: Dismantling of Gas Chambers II and III, 21 December 1944

and that of 14 January 1945.[16] Examination of those facilities shows them to be only partially dismantled. On the 14 January 1945 imagery, however, evidence of final preparations for destruction may be under way. Snow patterns indicate activity by vehicles and personnel at these sites. In any case, they had been destroyed prior to the camp being liberated by the Red Army.[17] Here in a small way, photographic intelligence contributes evidence clarifying the official history of Auschwitz.

Conclusion

Our review of the imagery acquired over the Auschwitz-Birkenau extermination complex was interesting and, we think, historically valuable. The photographs illustrate a major historical phenomenon from a new perspective and in some cases provide data unavailable from other sources. Our experience strengthens our belief that aerial photography, interpreted with modern intelligence techniques and equipment, is a research source which could be profitably mined by the professional historian.

---

[16] *German Crimes in Poland*, Vol. I, p. 91.
[17] *Ibid.*

25

The Holocaust Revisited

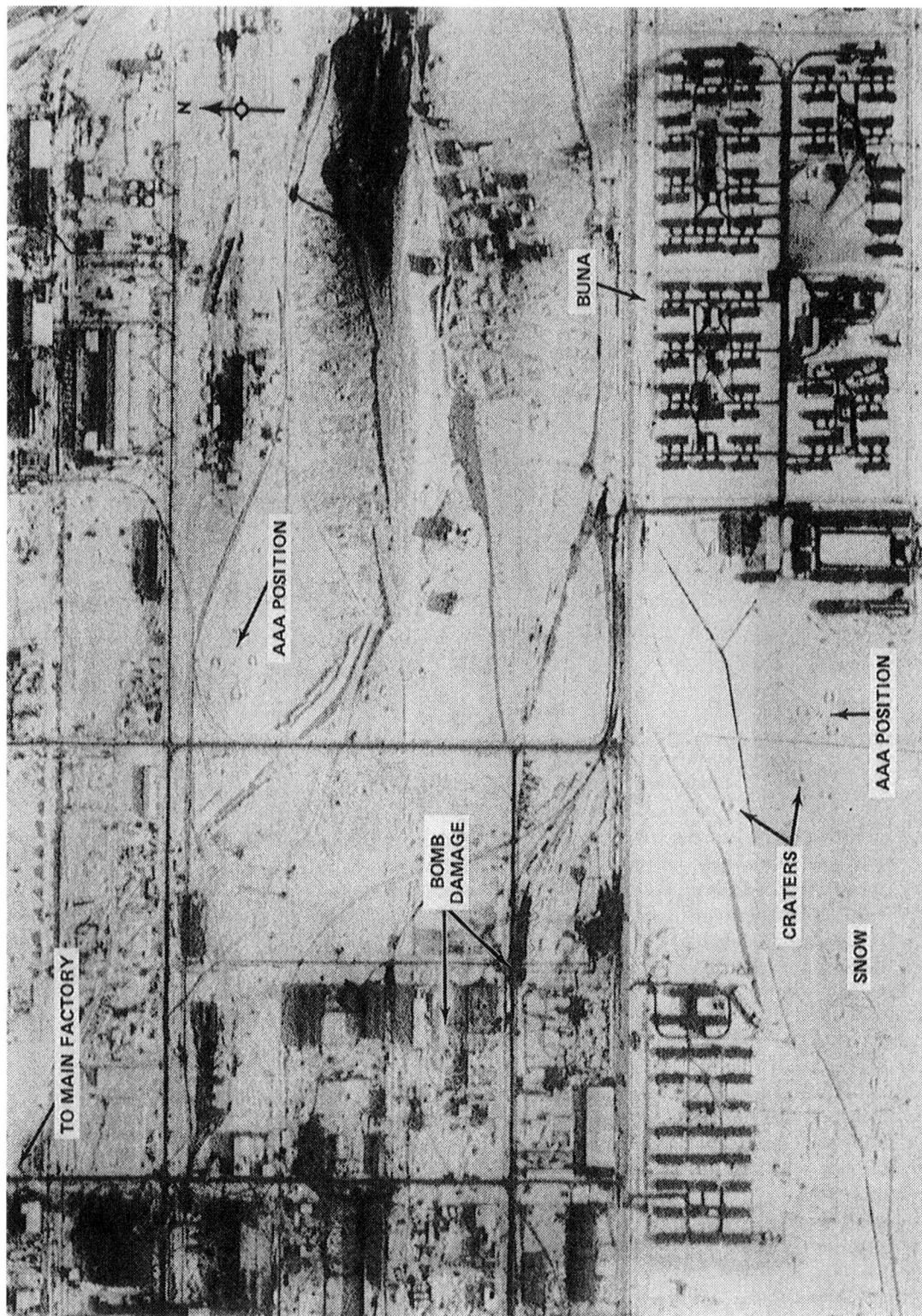

Photo 10: I. G. Farben Complex and "Buna," 14 January 1945

BUNA

AAA POSITION

AAA POSITION

CRATERS

SNOW

BOMB DAMAGE

TO MAIN FACTORY

N

26

The Holocaust Revisited

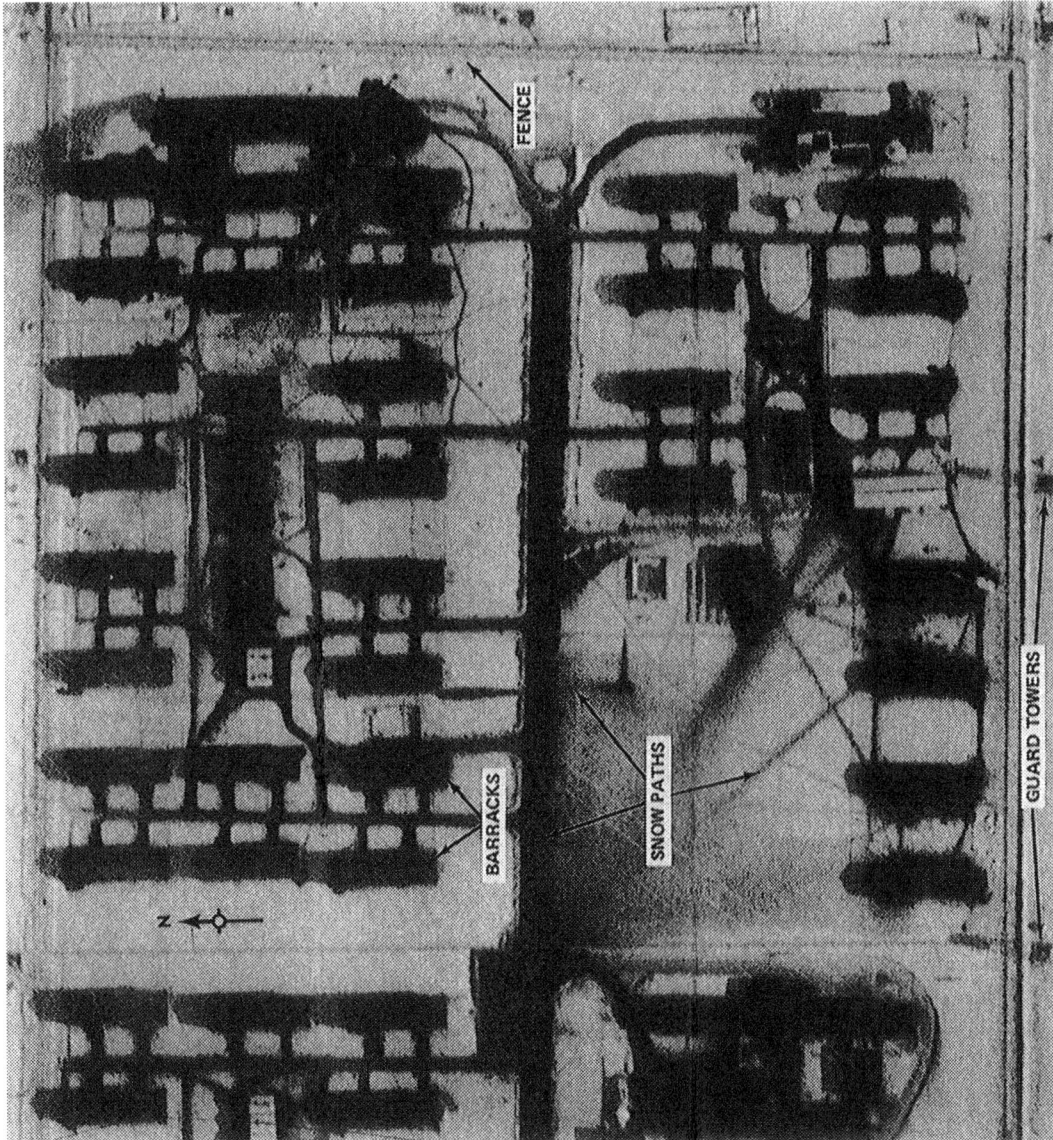

Photo 11: Section of "Buna," Auschwitz III, 14 January 1945

27

Photo 12: Auschwitz I, 14 January 1945

28

The Holocaust Revisited

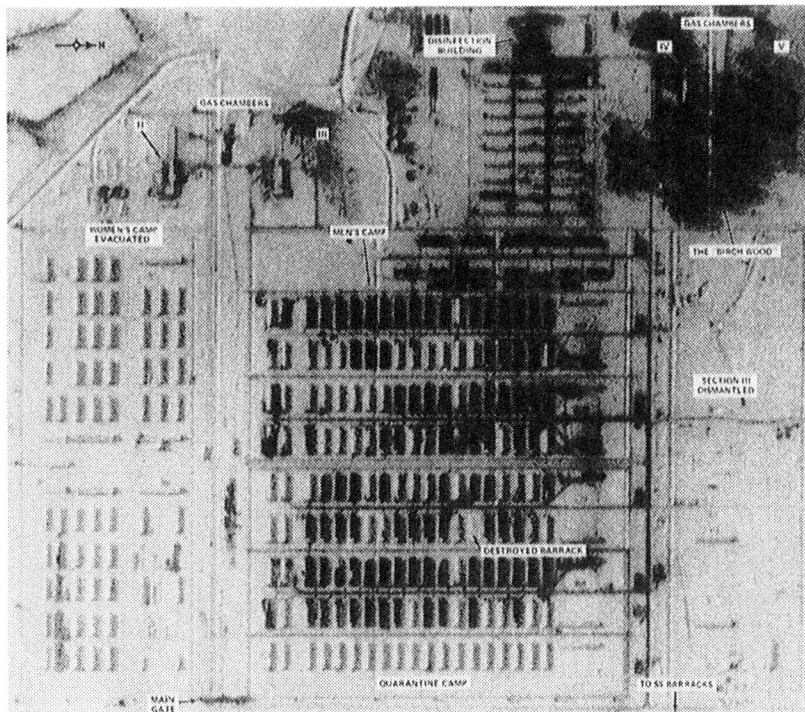

Photo 13: Birkenau Extermination Camp, 14 January 1945

The reconnaissance pilots who risked their lives to photograph the I. G. Farben complex had no idea that their efforts would one day be remembered not for that particular target but for the grim evidence subsequently revealed on the fringes of their photographs. The World War II photointerpreter probably could identify nothing more than the Farben plant and some labor/prisoner of war camps. He could neither see nor imagine the scope of the human drama hidden beneath his eyes, which modern imagery analysis and retrospective historical analysis would eventually reveal.

29

AN INTERVIEW WITH RICHARD HELMS*

As you look back over your long career in the CIA what would you say was the high point, the greatest moment, and what was the lowest or the saddest?

Well, it is a little difficult to say what was the greatest moment because there was some success that was not manifest, perhaps, to the public. I think that one of the high points was the time that we predicted beforehand how long the Six Day War would last almost within a matter of hours. In other words, before the war began we told President Johnson that it wouldn't last more than seven days no matter what combination of forces was brought to bear by the Arabs.

When you come as close as that in the intelligence business, it has to be regarded pretty much a triumph.

I think the lowest point came after I had left when in 1975, during the investigations, I saw what was happening to the Agency and heard the charges being brought against it and saw the amount of material pushed into the public domain at the time. I think that was probably the lowest point. It was not while I was in the Agency itself.

If you'd known at the outset what you know now, how many things would you have done differently in your life?

That is impossible to answer, as you knew when you asked it. But if you mean would I spend a good part of my life as I did working on intelligence, I would be glad to repeat the experience, because I think that it was not only useful to try and get intelligence established in this country, I think it was a help to the country. I was interested in it. I enjoyed working at it and I would like to do it over again if I had to retrace my steps.

With minor modifications?

Certainly with some minor modifications, but that is true of everyone. But in the last analysis the association with the people and the work in intelligence has been a privilege and anybody who is fortunate enough to work there is a fortunate man indeed.

If you were drawing up a balance sheet to answer the question, "Okay, what have we got out of having the CIA since 1947? What are its triumphs? What has it achieved?" What would be your sort of condensed balance sheet?

It would be that we had brought into being and had, up to a point, settled into American society an intelligence organization which not only was designed to prevent

---

* Adapted from an interview with Mr. Helms taped by David Frost in Washington, 22-23 May 1978.

1

RICHARD HELMS
DIRECTOR OF
CENTRAL INTELLIGENCE
1966-1973

another Pearl Harbor, that is an intelligence organization which could review and analyze independently and objectively all of the material coming into the United States Government, but we also made some significant contributions in the technical field. The CIA has been in the vanguard of that quantum jump in the use of intelligence derived from photographics, satellites, electronics, overflights—a whole series of technological achievements. Some were developed in consort with the Department of Defense but the ideas for many of them originated in the Agency itself.

Then last, but by no means least, we did develop a worldwide network of intelligence collection which has made a significant contribution.

What about the complaints of liberal critics of the CIA that we always end up in the name of freedom on the side of the suppressors of freedom? Where has the CIA advanced human rights?

That is simply an unfair charge. The whole history of the CIA, if you care to examine it, was to support the non-communist left, not only in Europe but in Latin America and elsewhere, and I think the record will show that this is what was done. Obviously, we have dealt with dictatorships of the right in various places where it seemed required in the anti-communist context which certainly governed this Government's policies overseas during the 50s and the 60s. But if you examine the record, I think that a great deal was done to support the non-communist left against takeover by the Soviets. Take the youth movement of the 50s and 60s when the Agency was supporting the young people at international conferences. The Soviets put on about two of these meetings after we began to do so and then never put them on again because young people from the free world were able to dominate the conferences and prevent the Soviets and their satellites from controlling youth movements the world over.

So do you think in a sense there is a double standard in the media that applies to right wing dictators as opposed to left wing dictators?

There is no question that there is a double standard; left wing dictators seem to be treated very well by the media, whereas right wing dictators are beyond the pale. We suffer, it seems to me, from a bit of provincialism in thinking that the kind of democracy that developed in the United Kingdom and in the United States is exportable everywhere. That simply isn't true.

But there are certain irreducible human values that are universal, wouldn't you say?

I would and I believe that firmly. But I don't find that those values are adhered to any more in left wing or communist dictatorships than in any other.

Is it practical that the public be informed of what Intelligence is doing in its name?

I don't quite see how, particularly in the secret intelligence field. It may be possible to tell them about oil imports and wheat estimates and things of that kind, although I happen not to agree even with that. I don't think that the Agency ought to make documents public, even if theoretically they are sanitized. Anybody reading them knows that a lot of the information came from secret sources and even if it's fuzzed up, the fact remains that there is put in the public domain more evidence, more material, for the opposition to examine and to study and to deduce how the data have been gathered.

2

What would happen if we were to disband the clandestine services?

We would run a real risk, particularly with a country as powerful and having as good an intelligence service as the USSR. They would simply run us off the map in the rest of the world—if they are not doing so already.

Presumably the public must accept the fact that for clandestine activities to work, some of it has to be dirty work by definition?

It is by definition. I believe that the American public is mature enough to understand. Except for certain very shrill voices, you don't find very much ill-will when you travel around and talk to people in this country. They think it is quite sensible that we should protect ourselves. We have a right to survive, to protect our way of life. The allegation that the Agency and the FBI have eroded our civil liberties is nonsense.

This country has never been more democratic than it is today. Civil rights have never been so vigorously defended. How anyone can say that their personal liberties have been impinged upon by these various things, except in the abstract or theoretically, I don't know.

Should the American public trust CIA employees or anyone with engaging in "dirty work" in their behalf?

A professional intelligence service is essential to our survival.

Who are these CIA people, after all? They are the men and women living next door, down the street or across town—these are normal Americans who have gone through an extraordinary experience to get into the Agency in the first place.

They are interviewed, then they take a difficult intelligence test and if they get through that they take a probing psychological test to establish their stability and their personality and so forth. They are then the subject of a detailed security investigation during which their entire past, from the time they were born, is combed out. Last but not least, they are asked to submit voluntarily to a lie detector test in which they are asked very intimate questions.

These are people serving this country very well and very loyally and very patriotically, in some cases under very difficult circumstances. But too often they are reviled and cast as second-class citizens.

If this is the way the public wants to deal with its intelligence professionals, then we ought to disband the Agency and go back to the way we were before World War II. Otherwise, it is up to the citizens of this country, the Congress and the President, to support these people and to support them adequately or else there is no reason to expect them to do these kinds of dirty jobs. It isn't fair, it isn't right, and it won't work.

We went from a hot war, World War II, into a Cold War, and then into something called Detente. Are we back in a Cold War situation today?

I happen to agree with George Will who says we have never left the Cold War. The underlying antipathy between the East and the West is as real today as it was when Winston Churchill warned in 1945 about the Iron Curtain descending over Central Europe. Detente was a term used to describe limited efforts by the U.S. and USSR to get on a better footing and a better relationship, and there was nothing wrong with attempting to do so. But the basic hostility between us and the goals which the Soviet Union has espoused from Lenin through Stalin, Khrushchev and Brezhnev, have not changed.

3

Do you think that the weakened position of the intelligence community has made our ability to warn of another Pearl Harbor questionable?

I am not so concerned about that aspect. We have a first-rate indications and warning capability. The Central Intelligence Agency still has a top-notch analytical and estimative capability. There is nothing secret about that function of the CIA. Pearl Harbor might have been avoided or its impact lessened had information available been brought together and properly analyzed and presented to the leaders of the United States.

The clandestine service established by Executive Order can contribute only a small amount of information compared to the hoard acquired by other means. Nevertheless, sometimes that tiny bit can be terribly important—particularly if it tells you what the other fellow's intentions are.

There are two memorable quotes in your speech of 1971. The first, as you may have guessed, is, "I cannot, then, give an easy answer to the objections raised by those who consider intelligence work incompatible with democratic principles." And, "The Nation must, to a degree, take it on faith that we too are honorable men devoted to our service." Do you stand by both, and if you would want to amplify them now?

I stand by them. I think they sound fine.

You still couldn't give an easy answer to those who are worried?

I could not. In fact, I think that it has even become more difficult, because the problems have multiplied as a result of the charges, the allegations, and the efforts to write charter legislation in the Congress, and so forth. In a democratic society there are endless ambiguities; it is inevitable by the very nature of the society in which we live. These things cannot be made black and white; there have to be gray areas.

We have to do the best we can, take some chances and hope for the best. And this is why I advocate that authority over a Clandestine Service should be in the Office of the President where it is now, that it should have Congressional oversight, certainly, but that the responsibility should not be shared. The President is the Commander-in-Chief of the Armed Forces, he is the formulator of American foreign policy; intelligence is a tool available to him.

How would you compare Presidents Kennedy, Johnson and Nixon in their approach to the CIA? In what way were they different to deal with?

The CIA got off to a very weak, rocky start with President Kennedy because the Bay of Pigs came along not long after he was inaugurated and after that we had to pick up the pieces. One dealt with him on a personal and very straight forward basis. He held a lot of meetings, calling to the White House experts at lower levels in the government in an effort to find out to his satisfaction what the facts in any given case were. He wouldn't even have the Secretary of State or the Secretary of Defense there. Gradually, I think by the time 1963 had rolled around, we had rather reestablished ourselves, and he could see the Agency's good points, as well as the warts, if you like.

As for President Johnson, it was not very clear to him, I believe, what role intelligence could play until the Six Day War in 1967 when suddenly he realized that intelligence could be premonitory and could keep him informed in a way that was helpful to him. After that, I was invited to the so-called Tuesday lunches which he held almost weekly. I did not play a policy role, however. I don't want to be misunderstood on that score. But I was at the table. If I may put it this way, having me

4

there kept the game honest. The other people present had to be a little careful about the way they pushed their individual causes on policies, because they knew very well that I probably had the facts fairly straight and wouldn't hesitate to speak up.

I think it is fairly clear that President Nixon was very distrustful of the CIA—largely because of the missile gap which was alleged to have existed at the time of his 1959 campaign against Mr. Kennedy. He felt that he lost that election because of the so-called missile gap and held the CIA at fault. He had it in for the Agency in the sense that he was very distrustful of what we advocated and felt that our estimates had been wrong at times. There was not very much opportunity to talk to him personally. He liked to deal through Kissinger and Haig, and so we had an arrangement whereby written reports were sent to him and he read them. When necessary, one could talk to him, obviously, but it was a more stylized and formalized arrangement. He took it in faster through the eye, and preferred to do so. So did President Johnson, for that matter. He liked to read reports; he didn't want to be talked to.

*In his book, **The Ends of Power**, H. R. Haldeman claims Nixon also resented the fact Kennedy had been briefed by Allen Dulles on the possibility of a Bay of Pigs operation so Kennedy was able to advocate aggressive action against Castro while Nixon, since he knew it was really going to happen, had to seem to oppose it in order not to tip the administration's hand.*

I have seen that, but I know nothing about the merits of the allegation.

In the same book, Haldeman refers to an unspoken feud between CIA Director Richard Helms and Nixon.

There was none on my part. He was my President. I worked for him, and I had no sense of a feud at all. I was doing the best I could to satisfy his requirements and the requirements of the office. Haldeman must have got the notion of a feud from President Nixon—not from me.

Is the story in the Haldeman book that Nixon wanted certain documents on the Bay of Pigs and that you resisted handing them over true?

It isn't only in the Haldeman book but in President Nixon's book, as well, that I was asked for certain documents by Ehrlichman. I collected the documents, ones that I felt would be satisfactory for the purpose. I then insisted on seeing President Nixon, because I wanted to be sure that he wanted them himself and that he, as my boss, asked me for them.

The appointment was arranged and I did go down to see him in October of '71. I turned over the documents that he had requested and, as far as I knew, they were satisfactory. He never told me later that he hadn't received what he wanted. So, I don't understand the complaint in the Haldeman book—or in Nixon's—that they asked for more material than I provided.

After all, under the law the Director of Central Intelligence reports to the National Security Council, which, in effect, is the President. He was my boss. We have one President at a time and if he wanted a document from the CIA, what right did I have to decline to give it to him?

Haldeman says in his book that when Ehrlichman read the materials you had delivered, he found that several reports, including the one on the Bay of Pigs, incomplete. But they never said that to you?

They didn't. They just said it among themselves apparently. As I recall, I took three documents with me. One was about the Bay of Pigs, the second about Trujillo

5

and his demise, and the third—written by John McCone—made it clear that the Agency had had nothing to do with President Diem's being killed in Vietnam.

You wanted to hear directly from the President that he wanted these documents. What were your misgivings?

The documents dealt with episodes that had occurred on other Presidents' watches and I wanted to be very sure that Mr. Nixon, himself, wanted them and that they were not going to fall into the wrong hands or be used for purposes other than what I thought might be proper.

It turned out that that was not the design, but I didn't know this. I just simply wanted to be sure that this wasn't an Assistant to the President asking for information which might be used politically. It seemed only proper to me that the President himself should ask for them.

Given that the motive of the President himself seems now to have been political, was that abuse of the Agency?

It might have been. He assured me at the time that he would protect the Agency, that he did not intend to use the documents for political purposes. I had no choice other than to accept his word. But I don't think in the end that actually they were used for any nefarious purposes.

Do you think there was abuse of the CIA by the Nixon administration?

I think that the effort to involve the CIA on 23 June 1972, vis-à-vis the FBI, was an abuse. So, too, was the effort by Mr. Dean to get us to put up bail money and so forth for the break-in men. I don't recall anything else. The materials for Howard Hunt and certain related things I didn't like, and it may just be that we should have stood up more firmly against the requests even though we didn't know what they were for. I mean all of those second guesses by the Monday morning quarterbacks do come at issue, but the things I have mentioned were real abuses. Had we gotten involved in those, I think the consequences for the Agency would have been very serious.

The Epstein book, Legend: The Secret World of Lee Harvey Oswald, which tries to pull together a lot of fragmented information, contains two great mystery quotes of Nixon. Presumably when he said, "We protected Helms from a lot of things," when he actually probably meant the CIA, and when he said, "Bring out the whole Bay of Pigs thing," he meant the assassination plots against Castro?

Well, Mr. Nixon makes clear in his book and also has made clear in an affidavit in a law case, that the only thing he meant when he said, "We have done a lot of things for Helms," was that he helped me get a lawyer appointed in the Department of Justice to seek to enjoin Marchetti from publishing a book about the Agency. That is the only case mentioned in his book, and the only case mentioned in a legal affidavit, and I assume that is the only case he had in mind. I know of no favors he did me, other than the perfectly official interchange of business.

As for the Bay of Pigs, I don't know what Haldeman was talking about. All I knew was that that was a failure that the Agency had had, but I didn't see any reason to drag it into conversations that we were having at the time. The efforts to upset Castro are well-known and I didn't have a moment's thought about this.

So if this is Haldeman's interpretation, it is his and his alone.

When I talked to Richard Nixon in Monarch Bay in the Spring of '77 his criticism of the CIA was that it had not done a good job on Cambodia, that it failed

6

to warn of the Yom-Kippur War, and that it thought that Allende was likely to win the Chilean election, albeit not with the plurality.

Do you think he was right on those three things?

We did miscalculate the flow of arms, weapons and supplies provided to the Viet Cong or North Vietnamese forces through the port of Sihanoukville in Cambodia. The economists built a model to try to do so, and we underestimated, I think rather considerably underestimated, what was going through Sihanoukville. Later, when we had access to things in Cambodia, and found the bills of lading for the ships that had called at Sihanoukville, they totalled up to a larger volume than we had estimated.

As for the Yom-Kippur War, I was in Tehran as ambassador and I don't know the merits of that case.

I don't see how he could assert that we were mistaken on Chile, because we said relatively early on there was a very real question whether Allende could be defeated. And all of that hugger-mugger that took place in Chile was a result of that estimate. I can't imagine that President Nixon should have been surprised when Allende was the winner.

Did the Nixonian idea that there must be a sort of "bamboo pentagon" somewhere in Cambodia, a sort of "Dr. No's Palace," to be found by the April 30 incursion, emanate from the CIA?

They were looking for but never found something called "COSVN" which was the North Vietnamese Command of the forces in South Vietnam. The CIA had no illusions of a "bamboo pentagon." We knew that there was kind of a command structure which may have been no more than a General and two or three aides and maybe a table that moved from place to place, but you can't run armies without communications and without a headquarters.

If President Nixon had kept the American troops in the area longer and really had cleaned it out, as the operation was designed to do, I think we would have found a lot more. But the operation started and then stopped suddenly and the troops withdrew because of domestic pressures in the United States. It is hard to say today that there was no headquarters in there just because we didn't find it.

There are people who told us that the idea of an incursion into Cambodia was one of Nixon's greatest passions, and that in fact there was a good deal of information, that such an incursion would not be successful, that you had some of that material but you thought that it was hopeless to show it to Nixon because he was intent on doing it come what may. Did you have evidence that the thing wouldn't be a success that you didn't give to Nixon?

I don't really know, in this context, how you define success. We did our very best to provide Mr. Nixon information on what we thought was there. There was a very real concern about what would happen if Cambodia were invaded. We had no illusions about domestic dissent in the United States, either, but that wasn't our job to assess.

It has always seemed to me, quite frankly, that President Nixon early-on paid a very high price for that invasion and therefore should have seen it through to the bitter end. It didn't help him any to pull out before it was finished. And we will never know whether it could have been more productive.

7

Did you have evidence that it wouldn't be successful unless he stayed there for a long time?

That is too minute a detail for me to remember.

Do you think that overall, the CIA was responsible for overly optimistic assessments by both Presidents Johnson and Nixon of how we were going to do in Vietnam, or do you think that was political optimism overlapped on not overly optimistic CIA estimates?

I don't think that the CIA was in the vanguard of optimism about the Vietnamese war at any time. As a matter of fact, one of the most difficult problems for the DCI during that period with both President Johnson and President Nixon was the charge of negativism, that after all you are Americans, you are on the team, why is it you see these things so negatively? Why is it these things are never going to work? What is the matter with you fellows?

The OPEC oil embargo came about in October '73 but the Nixon people seemed to have resented the lack of any contingency plans for an embargo going back months or years. Is that a fair point?

I would not have thought so. I would have thought that the United States Government should have had a contingency plan for an embargo of that kind because it affected the entire country.

Were there ever CIA people in any other government department without the knowledge of the head of that department?

Never. But there might have been instances in which a responsible person in the department knew, whereas the head may not have been personally aware, if you want to make that qualification. However, the CIA did not go about planting agents or spies or the like in any agency of the Government or—most importantly—in the White House. I would like to put this myth to rest forever.

There were as many as 90 or 100 employees of the CIA in various parts of the White House at different times—in communications, handling telegrams in the Secretariat, in the Situation Room. There were Agency secretaries working in parts of the White House. We loaned telephone operators. It was our effort to help the White House staff itself in the way that it thought was required. There was nothing secretive about it. For a long time, the White House was staffed largely by people seconded from other agencies—the Department of State and Defense, the CIA and from any place that they could borrow people. That was one of the ways the President kept the White House budget down.

To revert to H. R. Haldeman, was Alexander Butterfield a CIA plant?

He was not.

Let's come on to that 15 September 1972 meeting after Allende had already won the popular election on 4 September though not with a plurality. You said later that if ever you left the Oval Office with the marshal's baton in your knapsack, it was on that day.

Well, that was one of those zingy phrases which one should refrain from ever using.

8

But it is basically true, that Nixon was extremely exercised?

He was very interested in preventing Allende's accession to the presidency. There wasn't a one of us who thought we had any chance whatever of achieving that objective and I had tried to make that point but it was like talking into a gale. We were to go out and do the best we could and that was all there was to it.

The possibilities of succeeding in the short time span were so remote that we had a most difficult time putting together anything that was even a semblance of an effort.

One of the things not generally realized by people who are not familiar with the process, that advanced planning is critical for any covert operation. You have to have assets in place—real estate, individuals, money and sometimes automobiles, newspapers, printing plants and even loud speakers. You have to have everything organized and ready to use.

We had nothing in place in Chile. We really had to extemporize from the very beginning and it was an almost impossible situation.

Why do you think Nixon was so worked up about Chile?

I think that he makes the point clearly in his book that with Castro in Cuba, right off the coast of the United States, that another communist-led country with frontiers contiguous with Argentina and Bolivia and Peru would make things in Latin America difficult for the United States.

One of the reports critical of the operation asked "Did the threat to vital U.S. national security interests posed by the Presidency of Salvador Allende justify the several major covert attempts to prevent his accession to power?"

Answering that question today would you say yes or no?

With benefit of hindsight, I think that the Chilean business would be handled differently. I can't imagine wanting to go through such a nightmare a second time. When President Kennedy launched the Agency into the 1964 Chilean election, the work was started many months ahead of time so that there was some chance it would be effective. Against Allende it was started much too late to be very effective. The thing went from bad to worse.

Any judgment as to whether Mr. Nixon was justified in trying to defeat Allende or whether President Kennedy was right earlier in wanting to defeat him, rests within the foreign policy establishment. The President has the right, under our Constitution, to formulate foreign policy—whether everybody agrees with it at the time or their perceptions change through the years.

The Agency is often criticized, "Well, you did what the President wanted." What is the Agency for? It is part of the President's bag of tools, if you like, and if he and proper authorities have decided that something has to be done, then the Agency is bound to try to do it. We would have a very strange government, indeed, in this country if everybody with an independent view of foreign policy decided he was free to take or not take the President's instruction according to his own likes and beliefs.

But when you left that meeting on September the 15th you knew that the brief was impossible?

Let's say, most difficult.

Were you tempted to resign or did you think "This is part of my job"?

No, I thought it part of my job.

9

Chile was central to what I think Harold McMillan once described as "local difficulties" that you experienced. Looking back on those Senate hearings at which you said "No sir," to the question about CIA activities in Chile and so on, if you had your time over again, would you handle it differently?

I don't know how I could handle it differently because the dilemma posed at that time has never been resolved. If I was to live up to my oath and fulfill my statutory responsibility to protect intelligence sources and methods from unauthorized disclosure, I could not reveal covert operations to people unauthorized to learn about them and that was the predicament I was in before Senator Church's committee. If I had to do it again tomorrow, I don't see that I would have had any choice. It should be made clear what Congressional committees a Director of Central Intelligence must confide in or to which he must provide operational details. The chairmen of at least eight committees, four in the Senate and four in the House, can summon the Director of Central Intelligence and swear him, ask him any questions they want, and force from him any information they want.*

There have been suggestions that, when you were called to Camp David and then sent as Ambassador to Iran, you held a pistol of some kind to Nixon's head. Did you, and, if so, what was in it?

I certainly did not. Of all the accusations made about me and about my leadership of the Agency and about the Agency itself, I have resented none more than the charge I blackmailed President Nixon. It is nonsense. I did not blackmail him; I threatened him with nothing. When he said that he wanted me to leave, I said fine. It never occurred to me to argue. I was never one of those presidential appointees who thought he had an entitlement to his job. You serve at the pleasure of the President of the United States; when he wants you to leave, this is time for you to leave.

And, last but not least, why should I want to blackmail my boss, the President of the United States? I worked for him. The Agency worked for him. What point would there have been to do this?

When he asked you to leave, did he also offer you your new appointment? Did you feel you were being fired and then given another appointment or promoted or what?

He told me that he wanted me to leave and that he wanted to appoint a new man. There was some conversation about timing and then he asked "Well, would you like to be an ambassador?" We discussed this and I said "I wanted to think it over, because I didn't know." So the two were not put together, no.

Was Iran mentioned at that meeting?

Yes, it was, because by the time I said that I wanted to think about the idea, he asked "If you would like to be an ambassador, where would you like to go?" I thought for a minute and I said "I thought Iran would be a good post." I never regretted it.

Presumably, one of the reasons that you thought the appointment appropriate was that the CIA has enjoyed good relations with Iran ever since it helped restore the Shah to power in 1953.

That is the conventional wisdom, and while it may be true that the Shah appreciated the help that both the British and the American governments gave him in 1952, his later feeling about the Agency had a great deal more to do with the quality

* The Intelligence Oversight Act of 1980 subsequently established the sole authority of the Senate and House Select Committees on Intelligence to oversee the Agency and the Intelligence Community.

10

of its personnel who had served in Iran and whom he came to know over the years than with the earlier events. He thought them a first-class group of officers, who knew their business.

You have testified that you didn't know about the Watergate break-in in advance.

Given that in an organization as large as the CIA, there are things that the Director doesn't get to hear about, like the Lee Pennington Affair, until later, I could quite believe the theory that since Martinez was reporting to his case officer and had reported his contacts with Hunt as early as November '71 and that Hunt was working for the White House in March of '72, I could quite believe that although word never reached you, somebody in the CIA knew that a break-in was going to happen.

The FBI, Special Prosecutors, grand juries, Senate committees, House committees, Lord knows who all, have been trying to find who it might have been. As far as I know, he doesn't exist. Martinez did not share his information with his case officer.

Nobody has ever been found, in the Central Intelligence Agency, who knew about the Watergate break-in beforehand, period. And let's put a period to it right now.

But everybody has such a vast respect for the intelligence gathering capacity of the CIA that it seems almost incredible that they didn't know that something like this was going on.

Do you think they ought to have known?

No, because we don't have a charter to do any investigative work in the United States. Why would we have people around the Democratic National Committee or around the White House or around the CRP, the organization to re-elect the President?

The CIA had nothing to do with any of them. We were very conscious that we ought to stay out of anything having to do with the political process in the United States and to the best of my knowledge we did. So why would a tip-off to the break-in come to our attention.

Only under the guise of self-protection, I suppose. But once you had found out that Hunt was a potential troublemaker in August of '71, shouldn't some one of your underlings have kept track of him in self-protection?

That would have been the worst thing we could have done. Then we would have been tied into the thing and never could have extricated ourselves. I think it would have been a disaster if we had tried to keep an eye on Howard Hunt. He was working for the White House. He was their man. And he was doing their bidding. And he paid a horrendous price for it, but that was the way it was.

When you first learned that Hunt had come to the Agency for help in August of '71 and you and Cushman switched him off because he was getting to be a bore or potential danger or whatever and when Osborne called to say that various people with CIA connections, including Hunt, had been detained in connection with the Watergate break-in, and—without knowing any of the details—didn't your mind go, click, click, click, what the Whole Bloody Hell, and your heart sink?

Well, I didn't like the notion of any people that formerly worked for the Agency being involved, but the interesting thing about Hunt was that, when I got the call from

11

Osborne, I believe it was a Saturday evening, but then the papers the next morning made no mention of Hunt's name at all. So on Monday when we had our staff meeting, I turned to somebody and said "Osborne tells me that Hunt is involved in this. I haven't seen his name in any of the papers. How come he is making that allegation?"

Then I called Osborne and he said that Hunt was involved in it and in what way.

So during the 24 hours in between, I was more concerned about the names in the paper than I was about Hunt.

To go back just a moment, I don't know why Gray didn't believe me when I told him early-on back at the time of the Watergate break-in, that those fellows were involved with Ehrlichman. I did tell him that. I am certain he will tell you I told him. But for some reason his people seemed to feel that the Agency was involved. But I didn't hold back from the head of the FBI. As a matter of fact, I told him in a telephone call I made at the time of the break-in. I think he was in Los Angeles. I said, "You'd better watch out because these fellows may have some connection with Ehrlichman." I knew Ehrlichman was the one who had arranged for the hiring of Howard Hunt.

We were notified when the White House hired Hunt. We were never asked about it beforehand. We never asked about his background or anything. Not that it might have changed the course of history, but it interested me that the White House hired him without ever going to his employer of many years standing for a recommendation or a reference.

There have been allegations since, whether in books by prosecutors or commitee reports, that while the CIA wasn't involved and didn't know about Watergate in advance, it could have been more cooperative sooner. Do you regret that the CIA didn't blow the whistle a bit quicker and perhaps shorten the agony of Watergate?

I don't think that it would have shortened the Watergate agony. That should have ended in 1974 with President Nixon's resignation, but it seems to have been continuing. Something in our psyche likes to keep working this one over. My problem as Director was to distance the Agency from anything which looked like involvement. That problem began the minute the announcements about the break-in were made. Who were those fellows? They were Cubans that had worked for the CIA. There was McCord and there was Howard Hunt.

I knew that we were not in any way culpable with respect to Watergate, and it seemed to me that the thing I had to do and what I was paid to do, was to adhere to truth, to distance the Agency from the whole problem.

I recognize that I have been accused of not having turned out my pockets and made everything available to the prosecutors, but the fact remains that their office and the FBI and so forth were leaking information to the press in a way that looked very dangerous to me.

If I had said to them, "talk to this man, here is a fellow who did such and such," the next thing you know we would never be able to unsnarl the Agency from the Watergate thing.

If I was wrong, I was wrong. Monday morning quarterbacks always have a better way to play the game.

12

To clarify the record, Haldeman says, in his book: "Interestingly the CIA never allowed the Ervin Committee investigators to see reports of Martinez's case officer. . . ." When they asked to interview the case officer they were told he was on safari in Africa.

There were no reports from Martinez's case officer for them to see?

I don't recall ever having gotten into it and they may not have been able to get them, but certainly the FBI could have, if they had wanted to, or a Special Prosecutor or a grand jury. You know there is nothing that you can deny to a grand jury if they want to subpoena it.

*Again Haldeman, in November of '73, "Andrew St. George said in **Harpers Magazine** that he had visited CIA Headquarters and discussed the break-in with his former associates. What he discovered was that Martinez had indeed reported to the CIA hierarchy on the planning of the Watergate break-in."*

Who said this?

*Andrew St. George said it in **Harpers Magazine**.*

That fellow is a discredited individual. The Senate Armed Services Committee went into his background and so forth, and if you take Andrew St. George as a witness, you can believe anything.

When did you realize that what you had been invited to take part in was a cover-up?

"Cover-up" became a word of art much later in 1973. At this particular point the things that concerned me were Dean's requests to give money for bail and things of that kind.

Now, this is not the first time that the Agency had been asked to use its un-vouchered funds for things that were not strictly our business. I don't want to go into the history of this; there is no sense in dredging it up. But, this was not the first time by any means and we were used to turning these things off—or pointing out that we had an understanding with the Chairmen of the Appropriations Committees of the Senate and the House, that any monies expended this way would be reported to them.

This we religiously abided by. So when Dean's request was denied and then the pressure dropped off and so forth, we resumed our own normal business.

Now this whole area of cover up and so forth developed much later.

In fact, it was May '73 before Walters informed the Department of Justice of these White House efforts to have the CIA stop the FBI investigation—11 months after they happened.

It was 11 May before General Cushman provided testimony that it was Ehrlichman who had telephoned him to assist Hunt, rather than that he couldn't recall.

It was the same month, May '73, before the first James McCord letter, which Osborne had shown you in August '72 came to light. It was January '73 before the casting photographs of the Fielding break-in came to light. Those four things together might have held up the investigation considerably.

In retrospect, perhaps it was a mistake that those things were not brought to light sooner?

13

Possibly, and I don't have any reason to argue with your recital of the events. I left the Agency in February of 1973 and I don't remember any more the exact dates on which these things came out.

But I don't recall either any people from the Department of Justice or any place else up until the 1972 election asking for any of this material.

The real investigation began in March 1973 and that was when the thing really started to move. The Ervin Committee was organized, etc. There were just small pieces of it being nibbled around the edges in February of 1973 when I was being confirmed as Ambassador to Iran. The first questions were being asked about it. Prior to that, I don't recall anybody asking about these things. If they did I have forgotten about it. I am not ducking here, I just don't recall it.

Your priority was that you felt the whole future of the Agency might be at stake here, in fact?

I did indeed.

And you told Gray right at the time of the break-in that there was a link between Hunt and Ehrlichman?

I did indeed.

It was a major lead?

I would have thought so.

Given that the CIA got quite a lot of "stick" for the fact that for 11 months General Cushman didn't name Ehrlichman as the man who called him about Hunt, as I mentioned, why didn't the CIA ever get credit for your call to L. Patrick Gray right after the break-in, when you said that it was Ehrlichman who had called Hunt?

I don't know to this day because at the time we were attempting to deal with all of these various factors. I didn't see Gray. I had asked to see him on one occasion, but he cancelled the appointment. I learned later he cancelled on instructions from the White House.

I think that he was in a most unfortunate position. He had taken over the Bureau at a most difficult time. I think he had a very tough time of it. And I have no interest in picking on Pat Gray. He doesn't deserve it.

Who was "Deep Throat," do you think?

I haven't the faintest idea.

Someone I talked with yesterday is convinced it was you. Was it?

No. I never even met Bob Woodward or Carl Bernstein. I think it is most unlikely that they would even have thought of me in this connection.

Wouldn't it be very good for your image if you had been?

I would prefer not to have that image. There would be no reason for a person in my position to sneak around in garages and so forth to keep a couple of reporters straight. If I had all of this information I should have walked out and said something about it, publicly, or before a properly authorized body.

Moving away to broader issues of Watergate, taking a broader philosophical view, in retrospect, is there any period when you wish that you had resigned because the demands made upon you were improper?

14

The only time that there was a real question in my mind as to what was going on was at the 23 June 1972 meeting because neither Walters nor I, especially, could figure out what this was all about. Everyone must realize that at that time we knew nothing about money being laundered in Mexico, we knew nothing about money at all.

We couldn't figure out what the preoccupation with Mexico was. We didn't want to bring Walters into that aspect of it too much because he had only been with the Agency for six weeks, but after all he is a clever man and he obviously was wondering, too, about why they were interested in Mexico and what was going on down there that might cause a problem for the CIA.

When I left that office that day, therefore, I was in a quandary trying to figure out what we could be involved with here.

But you must remember, as I had said earlier, the President was the boss, and if he had information about something that I apparently didn't have, I wanted to find out what it was and see what it portended for the Agency or for any of us.

So when I got back to the Agency and we finally got to working on these things, I realized that there was nothing in Mexico that was going to affect our operations. Gray eventually was told this when we had been able to ascertain it.

Then gradually those several names came to light. They didn't mean anything to us at the time. It was only later that I understood that they had to do with something in this line of laundering the money.

So, during that period, that weekend Walters and I talked frequently and later on Dean called Walters down on Monday, Tuesday, and Wednesday.

If you had to choose an adjective to characterize your personal relationship with J. Edgar Hoover, what word would you choose?

I can't choose any adjective except "correct." I used to see Mr. Hoover at an occasional reception and we held very pleasant conversations on those occasions. In some respects, I came to know him relatively well—in contradistinction to most because he never saw very many outsiders.

When I say I came to know him relatively well, that is only by contrast; other people didn't know him at all. We always greeted each other with proper respect and cordiality. It has been said often that we didn't meet very frequently in a formal way. The reason I didn't call on him more frequently, rather than handle the business between the agencies through liaison officers or memoranda, was that when I went to his office I was lectured the entire time and then left when it was time to leave. I could barely get a word in edgewise. I used to succeed a little bit when I had something important to talk about, but Mr. Hoover liked to dominate the conversation, and he was quite a figure around this town for 40 years. A lot of people are throwing arrows at him and saying unkind things about him now. I didn't see very many people including Presidents, who said unkind things about him when he was in office.

One of the reasons that is given for the feeling that you may have felt no more than correct toward him is that throughout the Nixon administration Hoover was adding legal attaches to embassies around the world everytime he saw Nixon and that he was encroaching on your territory. Broadly speaking, is that so?

Broadly speaking, it is accurate, but it really had nothing to do with this, so-called, breakdown of relations because, after all, we were grown-up people. I

15

recognized that Hoover was encroaching on my territory, and I did my best to keep this encroachment down to a minimum. President Nixon wanted it, and since he did, we would accommodate to it.

There is no sense in being immature about these things. I felt that the breakdown over the Colorado affair was quite unnecessary, but this was, obviously, in a fit of petulance on Mr. Hoover's part, and, like most things that come as a fit of pique or petulance, it was short-lived. It wasn't very many days before we were back to the status quo ante, but the papers had been going back and forth, and people were talking informally, and the work of the two agencies was not impeded.

A lot has been made out of it. It is one of those episodes that are easy to dramatize, but the working level in both agencies kept things on an even keel.

After all, you must recognize that if these two organizations don't work together, the United States is ill-served, and I think most of us had that sense.

You knew that Hoover was trying to encroach on your territory. How did you limit that encroachment?

I think the word "encroach" is too strong. There have been so-called "legal attaches" in embassies abroad since World War II. Those legal attaches were Hoover's men. Hoover wanted to expand those legal attache officers in certain places. This would not "encroach" on the CIA's efforts. We have a great deal of work to do. There is a certain specialized kind of work the FBI did overseas and it did not get in our way. What was involved here, more than encroachment, was the fact that the embassies had to absorb additional people—which the State Department and the Foreign Service obviously didn't like very much.

I didn't like it much either, but I was in no position to remonstrate about it, since it was quite clearly delineated that the legal attaches were not going to duplicate any of the work that our people did.

Do you think Hoover, knowing Nixon didn't like the CIA, sold the plan to him partly by intimating that he could also keep an eye on the CIA?

I never suspected that because, frankly, what was there to keep an eye on? We had a highly disciplined organization overseas with first quality people doing the best job they knew how to do and if somebody wanted to mind their business for them, let them mind it. But I doubt very much that the FBI fellows wanted that kind of job or would have done it anyway.

In the last resort, who do you think was responsible for exposing CIA to the public? Was it Ehrlichman? Nixon? Daniel Schorr? Was it William Colby?

I don't think there is any place to lay it except at the feet of Director Colby who, after all, was the one who made available all of this material. To this day, I am not sure why he handled matters the way he did. He explains his reasons in his book and obviously I am required to accept his explanation.

But the thing that had bothered me, quite frankly, is Mr. Colby's belief that he had a constitutional obligation to do all this. I am no lawyer, but it has always been my understanding that any question of constitutionality has to be decided by the courts, with the Supreme Court the final arbiter.

But the legality or the requirement for the release of these hordes of documents to the House and Senate Committees never was tested before the fact in the courts. Finally, President Ford stood aside and watched it happen, when if it was going to be

16

stopped, he had to dig in his heels and say "Don't send down those documents. We are going to find out here whether it is required that secrecy be breached in order to conduct this investigation in public."

That would have forced the issue into the courts. If the Congress then insisted on subpoenaing the documents, the courts would have had to decide.

I would have felt a lot more comfortable if they had done so, if there had been an order from the courts to Director Colby, to turn over those documents—but this never happened. In the end, it was decided by Mr. Colby's interpretation of the Constitution.

Could Colby have stopped the hemorrhaging? What should he have done?

Once one starts to bleed it becomes a question of quantity. The time to try to head this off was at the beginning. That was the time for the President of the United States to take a firm stand in favor of the security of the CIA's files. President Ford could have forced the issue into the courts and maybe to the Supreme Court. I would have felt a lot more comfortable if the Supreme Court had directed the Executive to turn over those secret documents to the Legislative Committee. But they didn't have a chance to rule. We must not forget that the Office of Strategic Services, the forerunner of the CIA, a secret service or a clandestine service, was founded just before our involvement in World War II and the concept never has been tested in the courts.

One review of Colby's book said that he could have scarcely done more damage to the cause of U.S. intelligence or counterintelligence if he had been a KGB agent. Would you go along with that?

I think Colby did considerable damage, but he explains in his book why he took the actions he did. He has gone to great pains to explain himself and I think only History can judge the merits of the case.

I don't believe that Colby was a KGB agent. I don't believe that we had any KGB agent in the inner circle of the Central Intelligence Agency. The nightmare of every Director is that one day he will be told that somebody inside his immediate organization has been spying for a foreign power.

So I was very conscious always of the charges and countercharges that some individual might be off base or something of this kind. It was my conviction that none of the people with whom I was closely associated was in any way working for any foreign intelligence organization. I certainly do not believe it about Colby and I don't think such allegations serve the cause of the United States at all.

So much paper and so much information were released that it is almost impossible to tell what has been compromised. Moreover, the legal requirement to satisfy inquiries under the Freedom of Information Act are further eroding security. The Agency is trying to be careful about what it releases, but blotting out something with black ink on a piece of paper doesn't mean it can't be recreated by somebody who knows the facts. I find that this is a very difficult on-going kind of "leaking" and I put the "leaking" in quotations because it is done under the guise of legality and by law. I have pleaded with the Senate Select Committee to exempt the intelligence and security agencies from the Freedom of Information Act.

FOIA is good legislation if it results in someone learning from the Department of Transportation or the Department of Interior or elsewhere information the American public has the right to know. But it is used as a device to ferret out information about intelligence and security operations and I think that is bad and ought to be changed. I

17

realize that I am opening myself up to criticism about the public's right to know, but the public's right to know is the Russian's right to know. It is everybody else's right to know. The Russians read our newspapers and our magazines and our technical journals very carefully indeed.

Colby says in his book that he felt that he had to go to the Attorney General's office and that it was an unpleasant thing for him to do and so on. How do you feel about it?

Obviously I have always wondered why he did it, but I haven't anything further to say. If he felt he had to do it, then he did and it has been done. I would have preferred, however, that he had gone first to the President, his boss, and said "Mr. President, I am going to turn over this material on one of my predecessors and I just want you to know it is being turned over to the Attorney General."

Have you seen Mr. Colby on a personal basis since he decided that he had to advise the Attorney General's office that you might have committed perjury in the Chile hearings?

We have seen each other in public since that time, but we haven't had any detailed conversation. But I don't mark it from that time. I just haven't had any detailed conversation with him since sometime in 1975 when I went to his office for lunch and talked about a particular situation. That was the last time I had any conversation with him.

In retrospect, do you agree with the findings of the Rockefeller Commission that some domestic activities, such as Operation Chaos, exceeded the CIA's statutory authority?

Yes, I think there were two or three cases in the Operation Chaos context where we went too far. I would like to explain though, if I may, that the word "chaos," which has such an unhappy connotation, was not chosen because it was descriptive of the operation. You will remember that Winston Churchill always said that you should have happy optimistic cryptonyms when engaged in any big undertaking in the world. This was not all that big an undertaking. We didn't think anything about it at the time. But, I have noticed since that the word "chaos," although only a cryptonym, has been seized on as an indication of some terrible thing that the Agency was involved in, whereas in point of fact, the operation was an attempt to collect information on foreign involvement with American dissidents and domestic bombings and things of that kind.

What about the mail opening, HTLINGUAL or SRPOINTER from '52 - '73? The Rockefeller Commission said that was unlawful. Do you think it shouldn't have happened?

Mail opening is a very important counterintelligence technique, particularly if it can be done as we did it, under conditions of secrecy. Whether it should have continued as long as it did is debatable, but it was useful at the outset. The Korean War was just winding down and then American soldiers were being killed in Viet Nam. We were looking for evidence of the involvement of Americans with the Soviets and so forth. After all, the Soviets were backing the North Vietnamese, just as they had backed the North Koreans.

I can't imagine that Allen Dulles embarked on the program without President Eisenhower's knowledge. President Kennedy was briefed. There is some controversy over whether I informed President Johnson, but I am relatively certain that I did on 10

18

May 1967 when we went over certain things that the Agency was doing. There is no record of it, however.

I did not testify to this effect before the Church Committee because there was no document to support such testimony. It was solely my word; President Johnson can't speak for himself. So, I didn't want to get this into any controversy. I don't feel, however, that it is was the wrong thing to do in terms of our efforts to see what the Soviets were doing to us.

Let me say that this issue is important for the future. We still have a problem with counterintelligence in this country. Not only has it fallen into disrepute, but there isn't very much being done.

Now is the moment for the Executive and Legislature to decide how they are going to protect this country against spies, saboteurs, and terrorists at home.

It is an important question. Our young people seem to be rather cavalier about such questions because of a lingering distaste for the Vietnamese war and other things, but they are the ones who are going to be affected. I think they ought to decide whether the right of survival of the country takes precedence over human rights in certain cases.

But, the Agency did end up with files or a cross index or whatever on over 300,000 Americans, files on protest organizations and 7,000 details of those figures?

These were names—most provided to us by the FBI. To hold names you need lists. Sometimes you open a file, but that doesn't mean you are targeting anyone. As a matter of fact, most of the files in the CIA aren't targeting anybody. They simply hold material, like the filing case in your office, the kind of correspondence you conduct.

For example, someone in the CIA today receives a letter from the FBI mentioning David Frost. Now, do you file the letter or throw it away? Usually you file it because you don't destroy material in the government except under a certain process. So, it would be filed and henceforth there would be a file on David Frost, who might be innocent as a lamb. Maybe it just said you went across the street and had a beer.

So that this question of the files on Americans has been blown out of all proportion and I am delighted to have the opportunity to set the record straight.

Including photographing individuals attending anti-war demonstrations?

There were two cases of this. There were two fellows for whom we were trying to build overseas cover so that when they went abroad they would have the proper credentials to penetrate foreign dissidents working against the United States.

We overstepped the line by encouraging these two to become a part of the demonstration, to get their credentials by meeting the leaders, so they could say when they went overseas that I was with Joe in that May Day demonstration and so forth.

In one of these cases all that material was put aside and never used or passed to anybody. But, when the boss of the section left, a new man arrived, found this material and distributed it all over the place.

When finally it was taken down to the Senate, it looked as though we had been spying on everybody in the United States. I want to wipe out that impression. We were not spying on people in the United States. We were not spying on anybody; we were trying to get this fellow prepared to go overseas. In retrospect we overstepped the line and I am sorry.

19

Nobody was damaged that I know of and nobody was disadvantaged.

Do you agree with the Rockefeller Commission's view that you exercised poor judgment in January of '73 by destroying documents that might have contained evidence?

Tapes—not documents—were destroyed. No, I don't agree.

One recorder was attached to my telephone and the other could be used to record conversations in my office. Neither, may I say, was activated by sound; both required the pushing of a button.

These tapes contained material having to do with foreign policy and US intelligence; they would have been damaging to our foreign policy, if they had gotten into the public domain. I thought that then, I think so now. I would do the same thing today. A great deal has been made of the fact that Senator Mansfield wrote various government agencies not to destroy material having to do with Watergate. I did not destroy material having to do with Watergate. Nobody can examine those tapes, so there is no way to verify my assertion—but I promise you it is true.

In the case of Operation Mud Hen, do you think you overstepped the line there with the surveillance of Jack Anderson?

When I was testifying before the Senate Select Committee in May 1978, I said this is a totally unclear area and needs to be looked at.

I was criticized in the Rockefeller Commission Report for undertaking this surveillance of Anderson, saying I had no authority to do so under the Director's charge by statute to protect intelligence sources and methods from unauthorized disclosure.

Now if you are going to give the Director this responsibility in the future, then I think you have either got to define it, give him the wherewithal to achieve his purpose, or don't give him the responsibility.

This is an unclear area to this day, and I think it ought to be cleared up one way or the other.

The drug testing is a mystery to me. How did the CIA feel that LSD and such things fitted in with national security?

All of this started back in the very early fifties, when you will recall we were just coming out of the Korean War and there was deep concern over the issue of brain-washing.

As a matter of fact, a man named Hunter had written a book entitled *"Brainwashing in Red China,"* and "brainwashing" was a literal translation of the Chinese words, and we wondered what it was all about. Did they use sodium pentothal or drugs of one kind or another?

We had learned that something called LSD had been discovered in Switzerland by a scientist named Hoffman. It was tasteless, odorless, and colorless and taken even in small quantities created a kind of schizophrenia.

Coincidentally, I think it was in 1952, Ambassador Kennan came out of Moscow and made a speech in Berlin that the Soviets regarded as so egregious that they declared him *persona non grata*. We wondered whether he'd been administerd some

20

drug that caused him to act in such an aberrant fashion. There were a number of things going on that puzzled us.*

We felt that it was our responsibility not to lag behind the Russians or the Chinese in this field, and the only way to find out what the risks were was to test things such as LSD and other drugs that could be used to control human behavior.

These experiments went on for many years. There is the inevitable question of whether they should have been ended sooner.

Allen Dulles, who was the Director back in those days, authorized this thing to be undertaken, but we all felt that we would have been derelict not to investigate this area.

Who else in government was going to investigate it? It was our field. Maybe our people abroad would be administered drugs. In other words, in a defensive way we felt we would have failed in our responsibilities if we hadn't investigated what was there, if anything.

The commission said it is clearly illegal to test potentially dangerous drugs on unsuspecting US citizens.

There was one instance in which that was the case, and in retrospect I agree we should not have done it.

There is virtually no drug-related MK-ULTRA material in the files, we gather? In terms of destruction of those files, the seven boxes of progress reports that I think you had recalled from the Archives and destroyed on 31 January, was a booklet called "LSD 25, Some Unpsychedelic Implications." Why did you decide to do that?

It was a conscious decision that there were a whole series of things that involved Americans who had helped us with the various aspects of this testing, with whom we had had a fiduciary relationship and whose participation we had agreed to keep secret. Since this was a time when both I and the fellow who had been in charge of the program were going to retire there was no reason to have the stuff around anymore. We kept faith with the people who had helped us and I see nothing wrong with that.

In principle, do you think there is ever an occasion when somebody has a right to lie in the national interest?

I don't recall specific episodes, but it seems to me that if one goes through history there are examples of it and that it has been upheld by public opinion at the time. I don't encourage lying. I have never been confronted with this problem. I testified many years before various Congressional committees cleared to hear my testimony.

---

*The remarks in question were delivered at a plane side press conference at Templehof in Berlin on 19 February 1952. Ambassador Kennan, en route to a Chiefs of Mission meeting in London had learned shortly before his departure from Moscow that his study in Spaso House had been bugged and had seen Soviet militia keeping Soviet children away from his two year old son at play in the Embassy garden. In his own words, he was both depressed and irate. He thought that his remarks to the press in Berlin were off the record, but later admitted that they and particularly a young reporter for the *Herald Tribune* may not have sensed his intent. In any event when asked by the reporter for the *Tribune* whether diplomats in Moscow enjoyed social contacts with the Russian people, Kennan snappishly compared life in the Embassy in Moscow with that he had known in an internment camp where he was imprisoned by the Germans in 1941-42.

On 26 September he was attacked by *Pravda* in an editorial which said he'd "lied ecstatically" and made "slanderous attacks" on the Soviet Union. He was declared *persona non grata* on 3 October.

For a full account of the incident see *Memoirs 1950-1963*, Volume 2, George F. Kennan, Little, Brown and Company, Boston, 1972, pp 145-167.

21

This is the first time I was questioned about operational matters before a committee that I had understood the Congress did not want me to testify before on such matters. The consensus in the Congress, it always seemed to me, was quite clear. There were two attempts, one in 1955 and another in 1965, to broaden the committees that had oversight of the CIA. Both were defeated in the Senate. That should have settled the matter it would seem to me. But apparently it didn't.

So that there can be situations in which a Director of the CIA would have a right to lie in the national interest?

I don't think there is any question about that—just as other officials of the United States government would. I would suggest that if you unearth the transcript of the hearings of the Senate Foreign Relations Committee after the U-2 was shot down over Russia, you will find that there were very high members of the United States Government who were not telling the truth, the whole truth, and nothing but the truth. They were trying to protect the President. He later admitted that he knew about the U-2 flight and revealed it. I am sure there are other examples of testimony before the Senate and House where the whole truth was not disgorged by members of the Executive Branch.

In fact you were not charged with lying, but rather with withholding information. I suppose that critics of the Intelligence Community would say that the sorry state that the intelligence business finds itself in now is not so much that things were made public but that the CIA and other agencies had done things which made news, that if there hadn't been assassination plots, if there hadn't been Operation Chaos, if there hadn't been drug testing and so on, then public disclosure would not have been harmful?

If the CIA had done nothing, then there would have been nothing to expose. When Vice President Humphrey came out to speak at the 20th anniversary of the founding of the Agency, he made the point to the audience very strongly that, "You are criticized and you will be criticized, but if you are an activist and get out and do the work that you are supposed to be doing in the world, you ought to be able to bear the criticism, but the only people that aren't criticized are those who do nothing, and I would hate to see this Agency get in that state." I grant you that the point you make is a valid one except that I would like to submit in evidence that the way that these matters were brought to public attention in the most flamboyant manner possible and sometimes almost in an atmosphere of hysteria, was most unfortunate.

Have you ever had any doubts about the Warren Commission's conclusions that J.F.K. was killed by a lone gunman acting alone?

No, I have never had any doubts about it. I didn't have any doubts when the Warren Commission made its report, and I don't have any today. I have never seen any persuasive evidence that anyone other than Lee Harvey Oswald shot President Kennedy.

How close did either of the Kennedy brothers get to ordering attempts on the life of Fidel Castro?

I can't answer the question directly. If you read the transcripts of the Church Committee, and there are many pages in the public domain, you can see what the problem is all about.

All I would like to ask is what did these so-called assassination plots against Castro amount to? The business about the suit that was supposed to have powder put on it

22

and some big sea shell and so forth are just pipe dreams. There were fellows trying to figure out if some device could do this, but the idea was never seriously considered, and the gadgets never left the laboratory.

As for the Mafia, that is one of the great regrets of my life. We were under great pressure to make contacts in Cuba. I let the pressure to do something—because we didn't have very many contacts—overwhelm my judgment. We never should have gone forward the second time with that Roselli thing.

When I found out about it, I should have corked it off then and there. I am genuinely sorry that I didn't. It was a case of poor judgment.

I was told Roselli was attempting to find out if there were Mafia elements or organized crime elements still in Havana. That was all I authorized, but I shouldn't even have authorized that, and I am sorry.

On the other hand, let's not exaggerate what was involved. There isn't the slightest creditable evidence that any poison pellets ever reached Havana. We have only the word of a gangster that they did, and I don't believe him. I think he and his case officer grossly exaggerated what they were trying to accomplish.

What about the testimony of Nosenko the Soviet defector who is referred to in the Epstein book? You told Earl Warren there were two opinions about Nosenko. Do you believe his claim that the KGB had no contact with Lee Harvey Oswald while he was in the Soviet Union?

I went to Chief Justice Warren because I didn't know what to believe then; and I don't know what to believe now. I don't know what the facts are today. But it did strike me at the time that it would be a great mistake for the Warren Commission to shape its findings on the basis of a statement made by a man whose bona fides we could not establish.

I told Justice Warren that I did not know what the truth was but that we could not vouch for Nosenko, and the Commission should take this into very serious consideration in their conclusions. I think that was the right thing to do.

When Nosenko was given a new identity, after three years of hostile interrogation, had you decided on his bona fides?

By this time, the issue was what to do with him. Obviously, I recognized we couldn't keep him in durance vile, as we had, against the laws of the United States. Lord knows what would happen if we had a comparable situation today, because the laws haven't been changed, and I don't know what you do with people like Nosenko.

We sought guidance from the Justice Department at the time. It was clear we were holding him in violation of the law, but what were we to do with him? Were we going to release him and then a year later have it said "Well, you fellows should have had more sense than to do that. He was the whole key to who killed President Kennedy."

The controversy has been bad enough without our having done that, but everything would have come down on our heads, I am sure, if we had released him before we did, and we would have been bitterly criticized. So, we did the best we could, but eventually it became necessary to give him a chance to go on about his life. There were those who felt he was bona fide, and others who felt that he was not. As far as I know, that controversy endures. May I say one of the most difficult things about counterintelligence is that it tends to be very untidy. There is no answer to the Lee

23

Harvey Oswald and Nosenko cases and there won't be unless the KGB in Moscow or the Soviet leadership is going to tell the United States exactly what the facts were. I think that unlikely to happen and, therefore, these cases are going to remain untidy. They don't end up like novels; they end up with long Irish pendants.

What about the assertion that during his residence in the U.S.S.R. Oswald provided information on the U-2 to the Soviets?

I was totally unaware of that until I read Mr. Epstein's book, and I know nothing about the merits of the assertion. In other words, I have no way of verifying it. I don't call up the Agency about matters of this kind. After all, when I was DCI, I wasn't interested in having former Directors guide my hand.

In retrospect, do you think the Warren Commission should have known about AMLASH and those contacts?

This is a very confused area, as far as I am concerned. Allen Dulles, who had been Director of the Agency for many years, was on the Warren Commission. I don't know what he did or did not tell the Warren Commission about what the CIA was doing.

When one is running secret operations, there is a great reluctance to spread knowledge of them. In retrospect, I can't question the fact that it might have made for some clarity if these things had been laid on the table for the Warren Commission.

On the other hand, that is a hindsight judgment. I just don't know why Allen Dulles didn't make these things clear to them or John McCone go down and talk to the Warren Commission about these, or the Attorney General go down, or somebody go down.

But suppose they had known it, what different conclusion would they have come to? This is a question I simply raise. I am not making judgment; I am simply raising it, as if to say, what does it signify?

One of the Senate reports makes the point that you were on the horns of a dilemma because you were in contact with the Warren Commission and you knew about AMLASH.

It wouldn't have occurred to me to go to the Warren Commission with information about on-going, covert operations without the clearance of the Director and maybe the clearance of the executive committee that passed on those things at the time. In those days I think it was known as the Special Group.

But the thing that seems to be quite forgotten, with respect to the Kennedy Administration and Castro, was the Missile Crisis. Nobody talks about that anymore. The Russians came along at Castro's invitation in 1962 and were about to score one of the great strategic coups of the century by placing medium range ballistic missiles in Cuba—missiles which could shoot right into the American heartland and hold us hostage in a way which their intercontinental ballistic missiles could not. We seem to have forgotten that Castro was a co-conspirator of Khrushchev's; he was making it possible. But that never seems to be mentioned anymore. We become snarled up in the question of whether CIA was running this or that operation against Cuba, as though that had everything to do with what later happened to President Kennedy; whereas the antipathy between Mr. Kennedy and Castro was manifest at the time of the Missile Crisis and for good and serious reasons.

The Missile Crisis happened in October 1962. In December 1962 when the Brigade that had landed at the Bay of Pigs, Brigade 2506, was repatriated as a result of

24

the arrangements made by Attorney General Robert Kennedy in exchange for drugs and medical supplies and so forth. President Kennedy went to the Orange Bowl in Miami and greeted them with words to the effect that "I can assure you that this flag will be returned to this Brigade in a Free Havana."

President Kennedy himself was keeping the pressure on the Castro government. This wasn't anything hidden or anything of that kind. I mean, if provocations were needed, both Castro and Kennedy had provided fine provocations for each other. But what does it say in the end?

If History renders the verdict that President John F. Kennedy did not rule out the assassination of Castro, and even said in so many words that he would quite welcome it, would History be unfair?

I don't know how to answer that and I think one is simply going to have to wait for History.

You were asked if Robert Kennedy told you to kill Castro and you said "Not in those words, no." Can you remember what the words were?

No, I don't recall any more. Let's leave this judgment to History. We are not going to contribute anything by trying to make a judgment today.

If the Kennedy family, for reasons of national security and so on, had endorsed or not turned off assassination plans, if the CIA didn't want the details of something like AMLASH to be made public, then there was a vested interest between the CIA and the Kennedys that these facts not be put before the Warren Commission, just as you didn't mention them to Rusk in '66 or LBJ in '67.

I know of no conspiracy about these matters. If there were oversights and things that should have happened didn't, I assure you there was no conspiracy involved.

Turning to the subject of assassinations in general, you made your point that you think assassination is unacceptable as a policy tool, both because of the public aversion to it and also for practical reasons. Is the most practical reason the danger of reciprocity?

No, that is not the most practical reason. But I think this is a good place to note that the CIA never has assassinated anyone.

There were many of us who never liked any idea of assassination. Plotting such an act is one thing and committing it is another. Plotting is a buzz word—all you have to do is say somebody is plotting and it reeks of crime and all kinds of horrible things.

But the fact remains that none of this happened.

Let's leave aside the notion of theology and the morality of all good men for just a moment.

Leaving that aside, one comes smack up against the fact that if you hire someone to kill somebody else, you are immediately subject to blackmail and that includes individuals as well as governments.

In short, these things inevitably come out. That is the most compelling reason for not getting involved.

But then there is an ancillary consideration. If you become involved in the business of eliminating foreign leaders, and it is considered by governments more frequently than one likes to admit, there is always the question of who comes next. If

25

you eliminate one leader, have you really improved your position? That is a very critical point.

And if you kill someone else's leaders, why shouldn't they kill yours and so forth.

On the other hand, may I say that there isn't a chief of state or chief of government in the world today who does not feel vulnerable to some terrorist or would-be assassin, and they all take great precautions. There isn't one so naive as to think he isn't a possible target by someone, some disgruntled individual.

Do you feel the world would be a safer place if those assassination attempts on Castro had succeeded?

It is an awfully hard thing to bring a case against a specific individual. But I think the world would have been a nicer place if somebody had gotten to Hitler before he had a chance to eliminate six million Jews and cause God knows how much destruction.

Discussing assassinations is a very difficult thing, for an American, particularly for one of any religious persuasion, because we are against killing. But we are peculiarly ambivalent; we are glad to have certain people eliminated if we don't have to do the eliminating.

I cited the case of Hitler. But there are others. What about the thousands of people killed in Cambodia in 1977-78? There would be a revulsion in this country if it was thought anybody in our government was trying to kill Pol Pot. The same was true with Idi Amin, and, yet, the death of a tyrant might save hundreds of innocent people. A human life is a human life. Nevertheless, assassination is not a way for the American government. It is not a way for the CIA.

Nonetheless, I can only say I agreed with Clark Clifford, when he testified that it should not be barred by law. That would make us look silly.

It makes us look silly, or there might be a Hitler-type situation where it should happen?

If there were, maybe you would have to break the law, but I don't think anybody would notice particularly. We don't notice if laws are broken in the best causes. It is when somebody questions the causes that we get uptight, but the fact remains that if you say we are going to bar assassination and to bar this and to bar that, there are a lot of other things you are going to permit—by implication.

When you say that the subject of eliminating foreign leaders is discussed more than anyone would like, does that mean that you, on your initiative or that of others actually said "No," or turned off such discussion or had suggested to you other assassinations plans?

I don't want to go into any details but obviously I have heard such suggestions and turned them off. But the idea does come up, because it looks like a quick and relatively cheap way of achieving something in the foreign policy or national security area.

Right. You said "No" for the reason that you have just given, I suppose?

Yes. I have never believed in assassination.

There are two accounts, one of them very fresh, to put it in perspective, in the case of Lumumba, where lethal biological substances were supposed to have been

26

transmitted to the Congo and two Europeans with criminal backgrounds were allegedly involved.

I have read that you told CIA officer Michael Moroney that you thought that the Lumumba plan was ill-founded.

Now Leonard Mosely in his book, **Dulles: A Biography of Eleanor, Allen and John Foster Dulles and their Family Network,** *says that in fact you planned one operation with lethal toothpaste but that Lumumba did not use toothpaste and that the joke was that he preferred halitosis to no breath at all. Which is the truth?*

Leonard Mosley has a fascinating imagination. I don't know the gentleman. I have never met or talked to him. I don't believe that story. I have no recollection of any such plot. I had nothing to do with the Lumumba business. Moroney, as you call him, which is obviously not his name, asserts that he came to discuss this business with me and I intimated that I didn't think that this was a very good idea. But I was not the boss and it was the boss who was talking about this at the time.

But I don't think we should leave on the record any suggestion that anything came of this, even though certain things may have been transported to the Congo. The final decision was to do nothing and that is the important thing. What happens in the end is important. This is what we are all judged on.

But given there were so many plots.

There weren't so many plots.

There were plots against five leaders.

What five?

Well, there was Castro, obviously.

We have discussed Castro.

To quote the Senate report, which you said is your Constitutional right to say was wrong, the CIA encouraged or was privy to coup plots which resulted in the deaths of Trujillo, Diem and Schneider. That was the final result. But there were also plans against Lumumba and Castro?

A "coup plot" is very different from an assassination—maybe. Let us take an example. President Daoud of Afghanistan was killed in a coup. Was he intentionally assassinated or was he simply killed in the course of the coup? I don't konw—but he is dead.

The Agency had nothing whatever to do with the demise of Diem and didn't plot it. If there was any plotting, it was someone else in the United States Government.

As far as Trujillo was concerned, he was killed but there has never been any real evidence that those guns that were allegedly sent to the Dominican Republic were used to shoot him. We did not pull the trigger.

I think that it has been abundantly pointed out that Schneider was killed accidentally, that he was not killed intentionally by anybody—let alone the CIA. I think that what this line of questioning tends to lay out is that no matter which of these leaders dies, if the Agency was anywhere around they were the ones who are assumed to have plotted. Whereas if you had an objective rendition of history, I think you would find that a lot of people at all levels of the United States Government were involved in these things.

27

But I suppose the point on Schneider is that if the CIA gave ammunition, albeit to other kidnap groups, as they did, the Agency must have been aware that ammunition might be used in a kidnap. Isn't that fair?

It is perhaps a fair question, but who can prove that any ammunition was given. One of the difficulties with the Senate report about this business in Chile was that it is all based on second-hand stuff—from CIA case officers' documents, allegations and so forth. But nobody has ever demonstrated exactly what went on down there, and in 1975 it was very popular to pick on the CIA and give the worst cast to all of these things. Someday, with the aid of the Chileans who took part, maybe the proper history of this will be written, and then maybe we will have a correct rendition.

My own feeling about the Schneider affair is the irony of it, that given President Nixon's instructions, the United States was a party to removing a democrat in order to install somebody else, who would support overthrowing the democratic process in Chile?

Who was the democrat in this?

Schneider was the man who believed in constitutionalism in Chile.

That is a better term, constitutionalist, rather than democrat.

Should we really not have been on the side of a constitutionalist, rather than trying to have him removed?

We could discuss for hours the backings and forthings of what went on during this period of time in Chile, but I agree that it is ironical. Let's leave it there. I have no other insights to contribute, to help unwind the tangled skein of who did what to whom in connection with Schneider's kidnapping and death. I don't know the facts to this day and I don't believe they have ever been put down any place accurately.

It will only be with the aid of the Chileans that were involved?

I would think so.

How many Chileans were involved?

I don't remember any more.

It has often been reported that Israel, with the help of persons in the United States, achieved the wherewithal for the atomic bomb. What was the reaction in the Intelligence Community to the news that the Israelis had almost certainly joined the nuclear club?

Intelligence officers are so used to the Quixotic developments of life that what they are really interested in is trying to make a correct assessment and getting something right. In the study of the proliferation of nuclear weapons, there were certain countries referred to as "threshold countries." These were countries thought to have the capability to make an atomic bomb if they chose, but most have not done so.

If you don't test such a bomb, it is not difficult to make one secretly. You can put the bomb together and the only way that anybody is going to know that you have it is either to spy it out and take a photograph or have you explode it. Anyone who wants to assume that the Israelis have nuclear weapons is free to do so. There has been enough evidence in the newspapers and so forth to argue both ways.

For the record, during the Johnson administration, did you hear that the Israelis probably had a nuclear capability and did President Johnson tell you that that must remain a secret?

28

I have no recollection of President Johnson ever enjoining me in this fashion. I don't think it happened, but I obviously can't swear to it.

One of the most interesting incidents in your life must have been when you had the opportunity to interview Hitler.

It was unforgettable, particularly since I was only 23 years old and didn't expect it. It was only on Saturday afternoon (the day before) that I had been invited to have lunch with the Fuehrer. He talked with us for almost an hour, so that I had a chance, being as close to him as I am to you, to hear his views and see his gestures, the expressions on his face, how he treated various questions and so on.

One of the problems of dealing with history is that everybody wants to run it together—run it on real time, rather than historical time. But this happened in 1936 when one couldn't help being impressed then with how astute he was in the geopolitical sense, what a good politician he was, German-style. He understood his people very well, what they wanted, what their aspirations were, how to appeal to them.

The luncheon took place in connection with the Party Congress which was run annually in Nuremberg and in the course of the conversation somebody asked him "Why have this party congress?" He said, "Well, this is the way I reward the faithful party workers. . . . Besides, they come for two days and then they go back home, and it is exactly the kind of an operation that the German railways would be involved in if we had a mobilization, so it is very good practice." The statement gives you pause in the light of what happened later.

Whereas former secret agents in Britain tend to defect to the Russians, in America former secret agents tend to defect to their publishers. When you look at somebody like Phillip Agee would you describe what he does as treason or what?

I find the terminology a little bit difficult to come by. I am not a lawyer and I realize that certain words have legal implications which other words do not have, but I don't have any difficulty agreeing that what he did and the way he did it was treasonable.

What about people like Frank Snepp that have a moral crusade about the fall of Saigon or Stockwell talking about Angola?

Well, I would think of them in a different category entirely. I am not in favor of turning off dissent or suppressing disagreement. The thing that I think somewhat unfortunate about Snepp and Stockwell is that they published without abiding by earlier agreements both made to clear their writings with the Agency. It doesn't seem to me that is such a bad agreement. I can't conceive that the points that these gentlemen wanted to make about mistakes and misfeasance and so forth would have been censored by anybody at the CIA. They certainly were not classified or anything. I don't know why they didn't go the normal course and submit their books for review.

It is very different, it seems to me, to want to correct abuses by making points in a book rather than by going out and comprising the names of agents in a way designed to do harm literally to human beings. And that is what I criticize about Agee.

29

aka Rudolf Ivanovich Abel

A STONE FOR WILLY FISHER

████████████

On 11 July 1903 in Newcastle-upon-Tyne, England, a son was born to Henry M. Fischer and his wife, Lyubov. The child was named William August; the family name was anglicized to Fisher.

Genrikh Matveyevich Fischer and his bride, Lyubov Vasilevna Karneyeva, a midwife, had emigrated to England from Baltic Russia in 1900, joining the more than 30,000 Russian emigres already in London. Henry (as he called himself) settled in Newcastle and began to work intensely on behalf of Lenin and the Bolsheviks by smuggling copies of the revolutionary newspaper *Iskra* into Russia aboard Russian ships that called at Newcastle as well as nearby Blyth and Sunderland. The Fishers quickly integrated into local life and their son Willy grew up in Newcastle as a typical local schoolboy except for his involvement with the senior Fisher's underground party work. At school, Willy excelled in mathematics and was enthusiastic about sports, but his greatest delight was helping his father in the distribution of anti-war leaflets to factory and dockworkers. The leaflets carried a message urging workers to refuse to bear arms and turn against the imperialist, colonialist powers fighting for foreign territory. Willy was 12 years old when World War I broke out. The Fisher family was perceived by the British government and neighbors to be Germans and they suffered a good deal of the animosity directed against Germans and other "enemy aliens" during the war years. (Both of Henry Fisher's parents were descended from German settlers in the Baltic as were some of Lyubov's family; however, the family considered itself to be Russian). After the Bolsheviks seized power in November 1917 and were faced with Allied disapproval and a threat of military intervention, a "Hands Off Russia" movement was established. Willy was soon helping his father distribute leaflets and organize street corner meetings for this new movement.

In 1921, Henry Fisher yielded to persuasion from Moscow and decided to return to Russia. In Moscow, the Fishers were given temporary quarters in the Kremlin until permanent arrangements could be made. The important position Henry Fisher hoped for in the new government failed to materialize. Henry Fisher reluctantly accepted the fact that he was destined to remain on the fringe of the new Soviet government, but his idealistic enthusiasm for communism never flagged.

Young Willy was sent to a special school for English-speakers which followed a regular Soviet curriculum but included a daily period of Russian language instruction. He experienced great difficulty with Russian and never attained native fluency and, although he ultimately learned to speak, read, and write Russian quite well, he always retained his noticeable foreign accent.

19

Willy was moved into a student dormitory. Together with some other students, he acquired an enthusiasm for the new marvel of radio communications. This enthusiasm led him to become a radio amateur and his new hobby would alter the course of his life. In a 1966 magazine article, he recalled:

> In our free time many of us diverted ourselves as radio amateurs. That was the time of detector receivers, spark transmitters—we only heard of radiotelephony as something that was in its infancy. It would be hard for today's youth to conceive of the inventiveness of amateurs of that time. We obtained the wire for coils by removing it from old apartment doorbells that did not work. We found the crystals used for detectors in rocks or in geological collections. The condensers for tuning were of all sizes and shapes. I remember how I managed in 1923 to obtain an R-5 lamp that took an incredible amount of energy to heat up. I remember how we had to improvise to make the wet cells feed this lamp, which shone while in use no worse than any good burner.

In 1922, Willy Fisher was accepted for membership in Komsomol, the Communist Party youth organization. At the same time, he decided to become a radio engineer. When he had completed his technical schooling and passed the qualifying examination he was able to obtain employment in a radio components factory. He also enrolled in an evening study course concentrating on science, physics, and mathematics.

In 1924 he was called up for military service and was assigned to a Soviet Army independent radiotelegraph battalion. He was demobilized during the winter of 1926 and had to decide what his future employment would be. According to his recollection, "I had two offers—a scientific research institute and the OGPU's Foreign Department. I was attracted by radio technology as well as by the romance of espionage. Comrades argued that my knowledge of foreign languages must be used in the service of the motherland. Finally the decision was made, and I became a Chekist on May 2, 1927." [1]

Training

The reasons why the organs of state security would have an interest in young Willy Fisher are clear:

— His background indicated political reliability;

— He was native-fluent in English; adequate in French and German;

— He was a radio communications expert;

— He had a genuine British passport.

William August Fisher, like all other new recruits, went through an intensive training course. His instructors gave him high evaluations and noted, in

---

[1] There is reason to believe that Willy's decision was more difficult for him than it was later made to appear. He was under pressure by recruiters from the OGPU, his friends and, most importantly, his father, to accept the offer from state security. Major General V. Drozdov of the KGB observed, "It must be said that Abel himself reacted to this without any enthusiasm, as he was interested above all in radio technology and dreamed of a scientific career. But, like a disciplined Komsomol member, he did not refuse the new appointment."

20

Fisher/Abel

particular, his unusual manual dexterity; he could do anything with his hands. While at the KGB training school, Fisher became friendly with another student, an open and forthright young man named Rudolf Ivanovich Abel. They would remain close friends and colleagues for life.

Upon completion of training, Fisher was assigned to KGB headquarters in Moscow for work in the Illegals Administration. In Moscow, he met an attractive young music conservatory student, Yelena Stepanovna Lebedeva, and they were married during the next year. Not long after the wedding, he received orders for his first foreign assignment as an "illegal." Willy Fisher was assigned to work in Great Britain and was supervised by Alexander Orlov, who operated from the rezidentura in Paris. (Although Fisher entered Britain under his own name with his British passport and his presence there was technically "legal," the KGB considered him to be an illegal.) He worked in Britain until 1931, then returned to the Soviet Union. Willy and Yelena's only child, a daughter named Evalina, was born the following year. Shortly after Evalina's birth, Willy was alerted for his next assignment: Copenhagen. When he arrived in Denmark, Fisher learned that all intelligence networks in Nazi Germany that had survived the Gestapo had been removed. Only individual agents, able to continue to work alone, were left in place.[2]

Fisher's superiors told him that the nets had been relocated to nearby countries such as Belgium, Denmark, the Netherlands, and Switzerland, but that he was not to become involved in German operations. In the event of war, Moscow expected that most of the small countries of Europe would fall under Nazi occupation. Willy Fisher's mission was to organize stay-behind networks; to train Danes, Norwegians, and Swedes as radio operators for the nets that would be activated when a German occupation took place. For the next several years, he was kept busy traveling throughout Scandanavia in this work.

In 1937, Fisher was ordered to return to Moscow immediately. The Soviet Union was in the middle of the "Great Purge." Fisher had reasons to be nervous. His status as the son of an "Old Bolskevik" no longer offered him any protection; many "Old Bolsheviks" had already dissappeared. His foreign birth and former assignment to work under Alexander Orlov (who had recently defected) were additional black marks against him. Soon after his return, he was called into the head office and dismissed from the service without explanation. Yelena was furious and wanted to initiate an intensive campaign for reinstatement. Willy was more sanguine; he calmed Yelena down and explained that such an effort was bound to have negative effects. He told an old friend in conversation, "The organs of state security may leave you, but you do not leave the organs." He and Yelena agonized because dismissal was usually followed by arrest. Fisher, however, was allowed to remain at liberty and he obtained employment as a radio engineer.

After Hitler's invasion of Russia in June 1941, Fisher expected recall into active military service. Instead he found himself recalled to the KGB and assigned to the Fourth Administration to conduct partisan warfare against the

---

[2] Stalin ordered removal of the nets in Germany because he feared Hitler would use evidence of their existence as an excuse for an attack on the Soviet Union.

21

Germans. Fisher and his old friend Abel worked together training radio operators who were infiltrated behind German lines to work with partisan groups.³ They also trained "stay-behind" agents and ran a "funkspiel" operation in which German agents were doubled back to German intelligence.

After World War II ended, Soviet-American relations deteriorated and in 1948 the leadership in Moscow became more concerned about the possibility of war with the United States. Soviet-trained and equipped military forces in North Korea were planning for the invasion of South Korea and a Soviet nuclear weapon was in the final stage of development prior to detonation. Against this background, the Soviet intelligence services began planning for new contingencies.

In the event of a war with the United States, the KGB's legal residencies would be closed and espionage activities would have to employ the "illegal" residencies and some possible limited help from "friendly" embassies in Washington. The KGB's Illegals Administration assumed a more important role in planning future espionage activities targeted against the United States. Willy Fisher's extensive capabilities and experience made him an obvious candidate for his next assignment. He was a trained engineer with studies in nuclear physics and had a broad base of practical experience in organizing and planning stay-behind operations and clandestine communications. The Illegals Administration was planning for activities which could make use of all of his skills.

On 14 November 1948 the ship Scythia, which had sailed from Hamburg, arrived in Quebec and a man with identification as Andrew Kayotis, a naturalized US citizen, debarked and entered the United States several days later. The real Andrew Kayotis had been a Latvian immigrant who lived and worked in Detroit for many years. After World War II, Kayotis returned to Latvia to seek out and visit relatives still living there. In Latvia, he fell ill and died in a local hospital. Kayotis' passport was used by Fisher for his entry into the United States. Before settling in New York City, he traveled around the country for almost a year. In New York, he normally used the name Emil R. Goldfus and, occasionally, the name Martin Collins. (The real Emil Goldfus was born on 2 August 1902 and died several months later; the birth certificate for Goldfdus used by Fisher was genuine. There was no Martin Collins; the Collins birth certificate carried by Fisher was a forgery.)

Fisher worked diligently to meet the agents for whom he was responsible and apparently worked to develop some new agents.⁴ After settling in New York City where he assumed a cover as an artist and photographer, Fisher was informed that Moscow was sending an officer to assist him in his work.

Assistant

The Moscow Center selected an individual of Finnish background and equipped him with a cover establishing that he was born of Finnish immigrant parents in Enaville, Idaho on 30 May 1919 and named Eugene Nicoli Maki. (The

---

³ One of the young radio operators trained by Fisher was Konon Molody, later to become well known as a spy using the name of Gordon Lonsdale.

⁴ Among Fisher's agents were the Rosenbergs and the Krogers (Morris and Lona Cohen, later to become famous in the Portland Naval Base spy case in Britain).

22

Fisher/Abel

Maki family returned to Finland in 1927 and their eventual fate is unknown.)
Upon arrival in New York on 20 October 1950, the assistant (whose real name
was Reino Hayhanen) made his initial contact with Mikhail N. Svirin, first
secretary of the Soviet UN delegation. (This contact by an "illegal" with a "legal"
resident violated longstanding operational procedures. It is believed that the
instructions were based upon the rationale that Hayhanen, a novice, would need
money and communications and these could be provided through the "legal"
rezidentura.) Hayhanen located himself in Brooklyn and performed his assigned
duties as a contact officer or courier and also serviced dead drops for Svirin. He
spent most of his time, however, drinking in Brooklyn bars in Finnish neigh-
borhoods and his KGB masters began to be disenchanted with him. Toward the
end of 1953, Hayhanen's behavior began to attract the attention of local authorities and in April 1954, he found it necessary to leave the United States. Upon
his return, he had his first operational meeting with Fisher sometime in July or
August 1954 in the men's room of a Flushing movie theater.

During 1954 and 1955, Hayhanen tried to satisfy the demanding Fisher,
but without success. Fisher was completely dismayed by the inept and alcoholic
Hayhanen. The more pressure Fisher put on Hayhanen, the more Hayhanen
drank. In June 1955, while on a visit to Moscow, Fisher complained to Moscow
Center about his assistant. Moscow agreed that Hayhanen should be relieved but
instructed Fisher to exercise care. Fisher returned to New York in December
and learned that during his absence Hayhanen had embezzled $5,000 that was
supposed to have been delivered to an agent. Hayhanen also had shrouded the
windows of the photographic shop he was supposed to be operating as a cover,
thus drawing attention to the place. Hayhanen and his wife drank such quantities of whiskey that the garbage collectors threatened to stop picking up the
empty bottles.

Fisher met Hayhanen in July 1956 and told his assistant that because he had
been working under a strain and since his store had not been opened, he ought
to take a vacation. Several months later, Hayhanen received a message from
Moscow notifying him that home leave had been approved and that he had been
promoted to lieutenant colonel. Hayhanen, while incompetent, was not stupid.
He concluded that his trip to Moscow was probably not going to be a vacation
and he was unenthusiastic about the promotion. He had heard about individuals
who were promoted just prior to a trip home and who were never heard from
again. He stalled and made excuses about his departure but Fisher was persistent
and Hayhanen finally sailed for France on 24 April 1957. In Paris, Hayhanen
met a KGB officer and received additional funds and instructions to travel to
Moscow via Frankfurt on the following day. The next day, instead, he went to
the American embassy and defected. The embassy made arrangements to turn
Hayhanen over to the FBI.

Hayhanen gave the FBI a physical description of Fisher and information
concerning his activities. While he did not know the precise location of the studio
loft that Fisher had rented for his cover as an artist-photographer, he provided
enough details for the FBI to find the building and establish surveillance. Fisher
had taken a short trip to Daytona Beach, Florida and on his return 11 May, the
FBI surveillance picked him up. (The FBI was able to spot Fisher because, as

23

Hayhanen had told them, the bald Fisher habitually wore a unique dark snap-brim fedora with a distinctive white band.) Apparently Moscow had alerted Fisher to Hayhanen's disappearance, and Fisher made plans to depart for the USSR by way of Mexico.

Arrest

On 20 June Fisher was sleeping in a New York hotel when FBI agents knocked on the door. Three agents burst into the room and told him that they believed he was involved in espionage and if he refused to cooperate he would be placed under arrest. The agents referred to him only as "Colonel" and Fisher concluded that Hayhanen must have defected because, aside from his rank, Hayhanen knew him only as "Mark." Fisher told his interrogators there was nothing for him to cooperate about. At the time of his arrest, the FBI agents searched his apartment and studio and found a radio communications receiver, instructions for a clandestine meeting in Mexico City, $6,500 in small bills, a bankbook showing a balance of $1,386.22, and a sandpaper block which had been hollowed out and which contained a transmission schedule for Moscow Central as well as hollowed pencils containing microfilms. They also found the key to a safe-deposit box which was later found to contain $15,000 in cash, birth certificates for Emil Goldfus and a smallpox vaccination certificate for Goldfus, and a forged birth certificate for Martin Collins.

After several days Fisher was transported to the Alien Detention Facility in McAllen, Texas where his interrogation continued. Fisher revealed nothing for about a week and then, suddenly, said that his name was Rudolf Ivanovich Abel and that he was a Russian citizen. Fisher's admission surprised the FBI. If he was, in fact, an illegal resident it was expected that he would deny any connection with the Soviet Union. The FBI reasoned that Fisher decided that while he could continue to insist he was Emil R. Goldfus, he knew that the US government could prove beyond question that the real Emil R. Goldfus was long deceased. The authorities could also prove that there was no Martin Collins and it would also be easy to produce people from the Detroit area who had known the real Andrew Kayotis. If he remained silent, the Department of Justice could prosecute an alien known as Mark with the aliases of Goldfus, Collins and Kayotis. FBI investigators concluded that by claiming the identity of Rudolf Ivanovich Abel, Fisher communicated to Moscow that he had not and would not cooperate with the FBI; at the same time, the US government had no way to

24

refute his claim that he was Abel. Informed that there would be a hearing in his case, Fisher selected a local lawyer. Fisher apparently hoped that since the FBI had transported him to Texas, close to the Mexican border, and because he had admitted to be an illegal alien, the US might simply deport him as it had many other illegal entrants. At his hearing, he provided many details (all false) concerning his background. The only correct information he gave was his mother's name and birthplace and that he had departed Moscow in May 1948. In response to the hearing examiner's question, "To what country do you desire to be deported?" he replied, "to the USSR."

On 7 August, Fisher was served with a criminal warrant for his arrest and, after waiving extradition to New York, was designated for trial as a spy amidst a blare of media publicity. After his arraignment, James B. Donovan, a distinguished member of the New York Bar, was appointed by the court as his defense attorney. Donovan, a World War II naval officer who had served with distinction in the Office of Strategic Services, noted at a press conference the difference between the Abel case and the trial of such individuals as the Rosenbergs and Alger Hiss. Donovan said, "If the allegations are true, it means that instead of dealing with Americans who have betrayed their country, we are dealing with a Russian citizen, in a quasi-military capacity, who has served his country on an extraordinarily dangerous mission." Donovan's comment set the tone of mutual professional respect between the lawyer and his client.

The Justice Department prosecuted "Colonel Rudolf Ivanovich Abel" on multiple counts of espionage in the United States District Court for the Eastern District of New York and on 25 October 1957 the jury found him guilty on three counts. His sentencing was scheduled for 15 November and Attorney Donovan argued against the death penalty by saying:

> It is my contention that the interest of justice and the national interests of the United States dictate that the death penalty should not be considered because:
>
> (1) No evidence was introduced by the government to show that the defendant actually gathered or transmitted any information pertaining to the national defense;
>
> (2) Normal justification of the death penalty is its possible effect as a deterrent; it is absurd to believe that the execution of this man would deter the Russian military;
>
> (3) The effect of imposing the death penalty upon a foreign national for a peacetime conspiracy to commit espionage should be weighed by the government with respect to the activities of our own citizens abroad;
>
> (4) To date the government has not received from the defendant what it would regard as cooperation; however, it of course remains possible that in the event of various contingencies this situation would be altered in the future and accordingly it would appear to be in the national interest to keep the man available for a reasonable period of time;

25

(5) It is possible that in the foreseeable future an American of equivalent rank will be captured by Soviet Russia or an ally; at such time an exchange of prisoners through diplomatic channels could be considered to be in the best interest of the United States.

Donovan also argued with respect to a term of imprisonment that, in similar circumstances dating from the 1920s, France had imposed an average sentence of three years. He pointed out that in Britain, prosecution under the Official Secrets Act (the sole statute dealing with such matters) the maximum sentence was 14 years. He closed his argument by saying, "The defendant Abel is a man 55 years old. He has faithfully served his country. Whether right or wrong, it is his country, and I ask only that the court consider that we are legally at peace with that country. I ask that the judgment of the court be based on logic, and justice tempered with mercy."

The court sentenced Abel to 30, 10, and 5 years on the respective counts as well as fines totaling $3,000. Thus, Abel was to serve 30 years, less time off for good behavior. Donovan appealed the case. The appeals were unsuccessful and Abel was sent to the Federal Penitentiary in Atlanta to serve his term. [5]

On 1 May 1960 Francis Gary Powers, piloting a U-2 aircraft over the Soviet Union, was shot down near Sverdlovsk. Powers was subsequently tried and convicted. After protracted and involved negotiations, Donovan arranged an exchange of Abel for Powers, and on 10 February 1962 at the Glienicker Bridge in Berlin, Abel was turned over to the Soviets and Powers accompanied Donovan back to freedom.

About the Man

William August Fisher, alias Rudolf Ivanovich Abel, survived a lengthy career in a clandestine service, successfully for the major part, largely because he left no footprints where he walked. Willy Fisher was impatient with his first boss, Alexander Orlov, because Fisher believed that Orlov was too careless and indifferent to basic tradecraft. The dissolute Hayhanen must have driven Fisher to distraction. James Donovan, his court-appointed (and unpaid) attorney, said, "For the Colonel's court-assigned lawyer, the long hours were more than compensated by the fascination of the case. Part of this was the nature of the legal issues and their challenge, but most of it was the man Abel." Many of the insights into the character of Fisher are found in the detailed diary Donovan kept. For example, his disciplined character is illustrated by detailed instructions for appeal given to his attorney. Donovan remarked, "Rudolf, I concluded, must have been a hard man to please when on the job." To have been a second lieutenant under Colonel Abel in his heyday must have required self-discipline and meticulous attention to every detail. Hayhanen had never made the grade.

---

[5] Abel was aggravated at the severity of his sentence because Master Sergeant Roy Adair Rhodes, USA, who had testified against him on a collateral matter, had received a sentence of only three years on a conviction of multiple counts of espionage. Rhodes had been compromised by the KGB while serving with the US Embassy in Moscow and later provided the Soviets with data from NSA and other sources in return for considerable sums of money.

26

Fisher/Abel

Fisher was demonstrably a man of many talents and adaptable to many situations. While detained in the Federal Detention Facility in New York, he noted many deficiencies in the prison and drew up a set of plans for rehabilitation of the facility by which better use could be made of space and cost savings could be realized. The warden, impressed by the drawings, sent them to the Federal Prisons Bureau in Washington where they were well received and approved. Unfortunately, there was no money to do the work. [6]

When Abel learned that Donovan was on the Board of an art museum in New York, he wrote an essay on modern art for him. On a more professional note, Abel read in the newspapers that Donovan, on a committee supporting the organization of the Central Intelligence Agency, had testified before Congress, made speeches to civic groups, and had written articles on the subject. Abel gave Donovan a critique of one of the speeches:

> I think you did a good job considering space limitations; I might quibble that some aspects were emphasized more than they need have been (i.e., Soviet lead in rocketry being due to overt intelligence . . .).

> The aspect that seems to me to be least developed relative to the others is that of evaluation. As a lawyer you know how difficult it is to obtain a true picture from evidence given by eyewitnesses to an occurrence. How much more difficult must it be to evaluate political situations when the sources are human beings, with their own political opinions coloring their statements. One of the dangers in the assessment of information lies in the possibility that the men responsible will themselves slant the evaluation in response to their own opinions and prejudices. This demand for objectiveness in evaluation, i.e., restraining the evaluation to the question of the factual correctness of the information, is paramount.

> The determination of policy is not the function of intelligence, although some—particularly the Germans during World Wars I and II—may try to influence policymaking by biasing their information. This is one of the greatest mistakes an intelligence organization can make.

Not long before his release from prison and the exchange, Fisher remarked to Donovan, "I am no longer of much use to my service. I can never again be used outside my country." This comment shows that Fisher had a realistic view of his future employment. Even so, he did expect to be received as befitted an officer with long and honorable service. (Trusting a returned spy is something that has never been a hallmark of the KGB.) In the case of Fisher, the treatment was downright shabby. When he returned to Moscow, he found that his family

---

[6] On another occasion, the warden received a complaint from the attorney of another prisoner who had been assigned to Abel's cell. The lawyer said, "It's cruel and unusual punishment, and downright un-American to compel my client to share a cell with a convicted Russian spy. People might say my client is a Commie." The client was Vincent J. Squillante, a Mafia king of the garbage hauling racket in New York. Abel calmed Squillante down by getting him to scrub the cell and clean it up. In return, Abel gave Squillante French lessons. Later, Abel was put out because Squillante was moved to another prison before he progressed beyond the regular verbs. When Squillante was released from prison in 1963, he was murdered in Connecticut by a rival gang.

27

no longer occupied their two-room apartment on the Second Lavrskiy Pereulok but had been moved to a smaller unit (27 square meters) on Prospekt Mira. He was further disappointed in not receiving the award, "Hero of the Soviet Union," particularly since this honor had been awarded to Ramon Mercader, Trotsky's assassin.

Fisher continued to work at the KGB headquarters in Moscow. Mainly, he gave lectures to trainees or visited East European capitals for ceremonies (such as dedication of a monument to Richard Sorge in East Berlin) or, on one occasion, meeting a high ranking Catholic Church dignitary in Budapest. "I'm just a museum exhibit," he told a friend.

After Fisher returned to Moscow from his American imprisonment, he confided to friends his dissatisfaction with the headquarters mentality as well as with the newer leadership in the KGB. This did not represent a sudden change in his outlook because of disappointment.

In 1955, when he was on home leave trying to rid himself of Hayhanen, he had spoken, according to one friend, about his confusion concerning organizational changes: Beria was now gone; Abakumov had been arrested and executed, and Molotov was headed for oblivion. Fisher had been particularly critical of changes in the First Main Administration as being vastly overstaffed. "It took two hundred people today," he said, "to do work that had been done by five people in the old days. The inclusion of a single paragraph in an enciphered message required the signature of a department chief." After his experiences in World War II, Willy Fisher expressed to a colleague the feelings of a field man who never had much esteem for his bosses in Moscow. In earlier years, he observed, the bosses had at least been individuals with lengthy personal experience and possessed of the revolutionary ideals that made them serve the cause. The new bosses, he said, "were an altogether different breed of self-centered careerists with no aims other than to advance themselves and move into privileged positions."

The final blow came during the summer of 1971. Fisher applied for leave, intending to continue some work on the dacha he had inherited from his parents. A secretary on the administrative staff asked him why he was going to take leave since she was typing his retirement papers. "Once you're retired, you can rest all you want," she said. After so many years of devoted service, to learn of a forced retirement from a secretary was a blow to Fisher's pride. His health failed and he died of cancer on 15 November 1971. His body lay in state for several days in a building behind the Lubyanka headquarters of the KGB, then, after cremation, his remains were buried in the Cemetery of the Monastery of the Don under a tombstone which identified him as Colonel Rudolf Ivanovich Abel. This was too much for the devoted Yelena Stepanovna. Enraged, she conducted a vigorous campaign for most of the next year. Finally successful, on the anniversary of his death, family and friends attended a dedication of a new tombstone correctly identifying him as William Genrikhovich Fisher (and in smaller letters, as Abel).

•   •   •

28

Fisher/Abel

Krasnaya Zvezda, Moscow, 17 November 1971

Colonel Rudolf Ivanovich Abel, one of the oldest Chekists, a well-known Soviet Intelligence officer, distinguished employee of the organs of State Security, and member of the CPSU since 1931, died after a serious illness in his 69th year.

R.I. Abel was assigned to work in the organs of the OGPU in accordance with a Komsomol levy in 1927. From then on, for a period of nearly 45 years, he faultlessly carried out complex tasks in the maintenance of our Motherland's security in various sectors of Chekist activity. Rudolf Ivanovich proved to be a daring, experienced intelligence officer and capable leader. He was always distinguished by love of the Motherland, a high sense of duty, party principle, impartiality, and honor.

Being abroad, working there in complicated and difficult circumstances, R.I. Abel displayed exceptional patriotism, tenacity, and steadfastness. His high moral character and manly conduct are widely known, evoking a deep response and arousing sympathy through-out the world.

The Communist Party and the Soviet government highly esteemed the services of R.I. Abel, conferring upon him the Order of Lenin, three Orders of the Red Banner, two Orders of the Red Banner of Labor, and the order of the Red Star, and many medals.

Rudolf Ivanovich remained at his combat post until the very last days. He contributed all his strength and knowledge to that honorable cause to which he had dedicated all his magnificent life. He devoted considerable attention to the training of a younger generation of Chekists, transmitting to them his rich experience and indicating the qualities inherent in the first Chekist-Leninist F.E. Dzerzhinski.

Great personal charm, modesty, simplicity, and a sympathetic nature won Rudolf Ivanovich universal esteem and well-deserved authority.

The bright memory of Rudolf Ivanovich will be preserved forever in our hearts.

A Group of Comrades

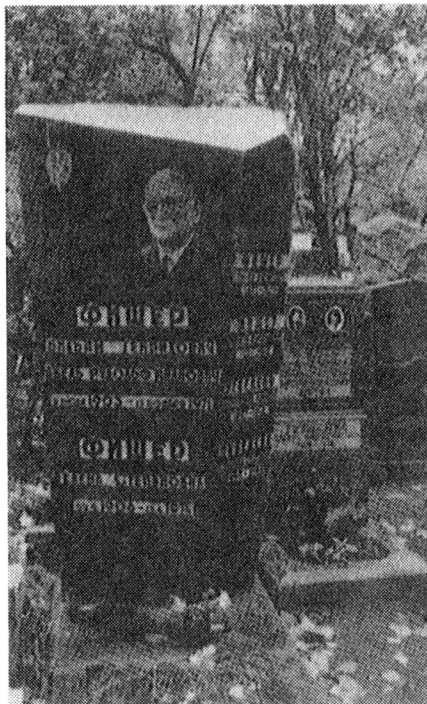

29

In 1960, James B. Donovan met with Director of Central Intelligence Allen W. Dulles and CIA General Counsel Lawrence Houston to discuss the implications of exchanging Abel for Powers. During their conversation, Donovan observed, "While I admire Rudolf as an individual, I don't forget that he's KGB. Bars and prison are not going to change his allegiance." Dulles puffed on his pipe and responded, "I wish we had three or four just like him inside Moscow, right now. . ." The Dulles comment would have been a suitable epitaph inscribed on the stone for Willy Fisher.

———————

For Further Reading

Strangers On A Bridge, James B. Donovan, Athenem House, New York (1964).

James Donovan kept a detailed diary from which this book was prepared. Together with his own notes, Donovan extracted items from court and other official records. The book gives characterizations and insights into Rudolf Abel's personality.

Okhotnik Verrkh Nogami (The Hunter, Hunted), Kyrill Khenkin, Kossev Verlag, Frankfurt a/M, (1979).

Khenkin, an emigre living in Germany, has written a comprehensive biography of Abel. Because Khenkin was personally acquainted with the subject for a long time, knew the family and had access to otherwise unavailable material, his book is useful. It is available only in the Russian language.

The Shadow Network-Espionage as an Instrument of Soviet Policy, Edward Van Der Rhoer, Scribner's, New York (1983).

In this rather ponderous tome which covers a broad view of Soviet espionage activities, Van Der Rhoer made use of much of Knenkin's book. The Shadow Network contains some detailed descriptions of Abel's life and work.

30

Cuban missile crisis

The San Cristobal Trapezoid

John T. Hughes with A. Denis Clift

Aerial photos give crisp, hard information, like the dawn after long darkness.

Arthur Lundahl

A courier stepped forward to meet me as I reached the Pentagon's River Entrance. I remember the moment: 7:30 a.m., 8 February 1963, a wintery morning brightness just emerging. "Mr. John Hughes?" "Yes," I said. "I've been asked to deliver this to you." He handed me a manila envelope, return address, "The White House," in block letters, and departed.

My office was nearby inside the Pentagon in the Joint Staff spaces next to the National Military Command Center, almost directly beneath the office of the Secretary of Defense. I opened the letter. It was from the President.

> Dear Mr. Hughes:
>
> I thought you did an excellent job on television in explaining our surveillance in Cuba. I understand it was done on short notice. I want you to know how much I appreciate your efforts. With best wishes.
>
> Sincerely,
> John Kennedy

Cuba. For the past seven months, the US Intelligence Community had riveted its attention on that island nation. Its topography, road network, cities, military garrisons, storage depots, deployed ground-force units, airports and airbases, seaports, merchant shipping and naval units had been photographed, categorized and studied. US reconnaissance also zeroed in on Soviet merchant ships, fighter aircraft, surface-to-air-missile (SAM) units, missile patrol boats, and rocket forces.

As photointerpreters, my colleagues and I could recall the key features of the intermediate-range (IRBM) and medium-range ballistic missile (MRBM) sites the Soviets had been rushing to complete in October 1962: the missile-servicing buildings, the nuclear warhead storage bunkers, the oxidizer vehicles, propellant vehicles, missile shelter tents, and the missiles. San Julian, Holguin, Nuevitas, Mariel, Sagua La Grande, Remedios and San Cristobal were names that took on a special meaning after the discovery of the missiles and bombers, the peaking of the crisis, Soviet withdrawal, and my briefing to the nation on network TV on 6 February 1963, two days before the President's letter arrived.

As Special Assistant to Lieutenant General Joseph F. Carroll, Director of the Defense Intelligence Agency (DIA), I was responsible for providing reconnaissance intelligence support during the crisis to Secretary of Defense Robert McNamara, Deputy Secretary Roswell Gilpatric, Chairman of the Joint Chiefs of Staff (JCS) General Maxwell Taylor, and the Joint Chiefs. There had been intensive coordination with Arthur Lundahl, Director of the National Photographic Interpretation Center (NPIC). In this capacity, he was responsible for providing critical national intelligence support to the President, Director of Central Intelligence (DCI) John McCone, and the Executive Committee of the National Security Council.

Building on the CIA's initial U-2 reconnaissance flights in the summer and early autumn of 1962, the Department of Defense would eventually fly more than 400 military reconnaissance missions over Cuba during the crisis. Targeting information for each photo mission had to be developed for the JCS Joint

Copyright © 1992 by John T. Hughes

41

1962 SAM Sites

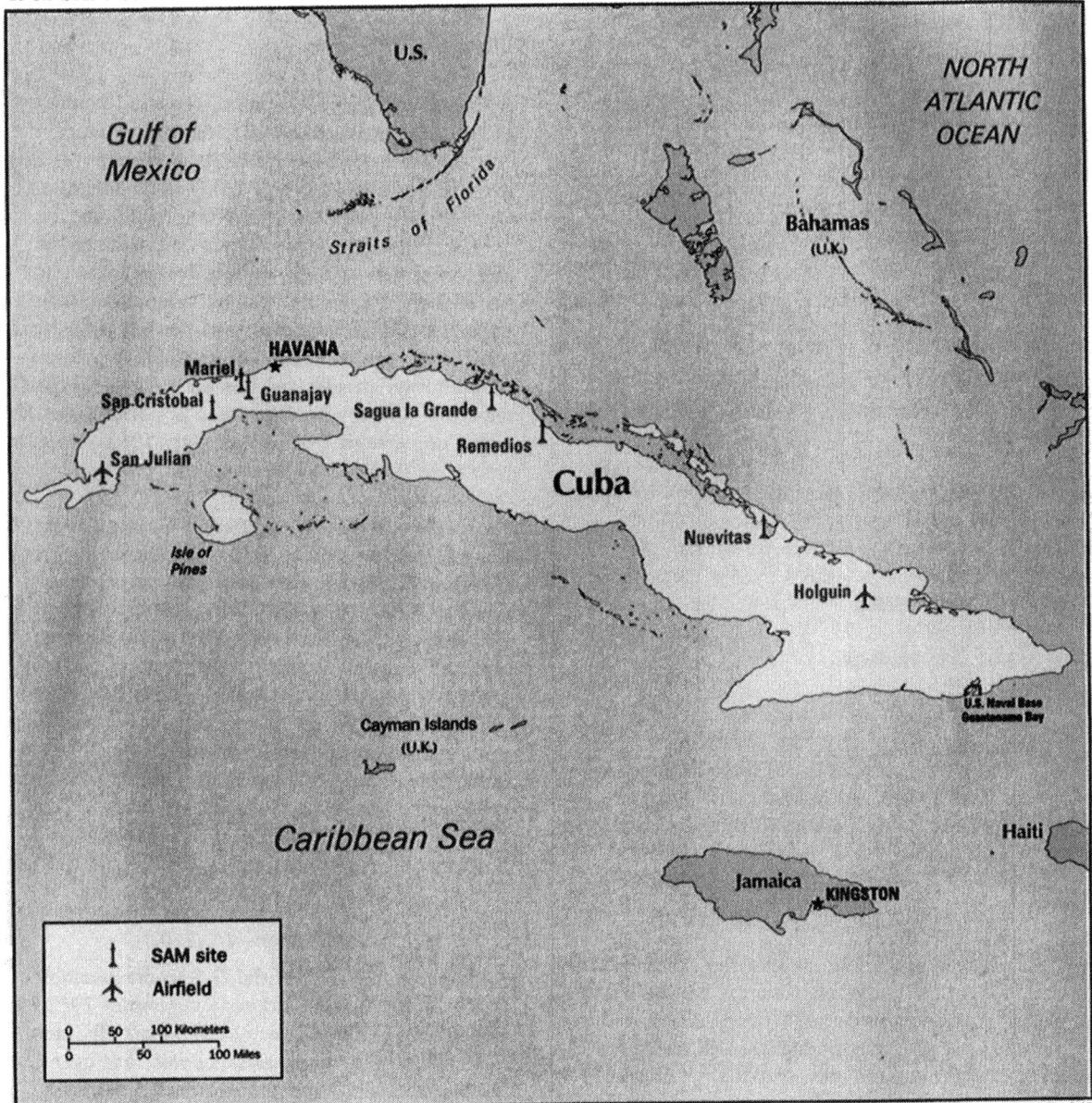

Gulf of Mexico

U.S.

NORTH ATLANTIC OCEAN

Straits of Florida

Bahamas (U.K.)

Mariel

HAVANA

San Cristobal

Guanajay

Sagua la Grande

San Julian

Remedios

Cuba

Isle of Pines

Nuevitas

Holguin

U.S. Naval Base Guantanamo Bay

Cayman Islands (U.K.)

Caribbean Sea

Haiti

Jamaica

KINGSTON

| | SAM site |
| | Airfield |

0   50   100 Kilometers
0   50   100 Miles

727945 (R00865) 3-93

Unclassified

40

Reconnaissance Center (JRC) to coordinate the operations and allow for policy review by the Secretary, the Deputy Secretary, and the White House, and then be delivered to the "recce" units that would fly the missions. The highest priority was to move that film from the returning aircraft through the photo labs, through analysis, to the policy level of government—a 24-hour-a-day operation, with intense time pressures, and a crucial need for accuracy.

In his introduction to Robert F. Kennedy's memoir of the Cuban missile crisis, *Thirteen Days*, McNamara wrote:

> The performance of the US Government during that critical period was more effective than at any other time during my seven years' service as Secretary of Defense. The agencies of government—the State Department, the civilian and military leaders of the Defense Department, the CIA, the White House Staff, and the UN Mission-worked together smoothly and harmoniously.[1]

The entire intelligence-operations team for US reconnaissance against Cuba demonstrated a sense of urgency and national mission that epitomized this effort.

Tactical Data

Intelligence did not perform flawlessly during the crisis. The Intelligence Community had not provided clear warning of the Soviet Union's intention to place offensive nuclear weapons in Cuba. Indeed, the debate over Khrushchev's motives and the USSR's strategic intentions continues. The community did, however, provide tactical intelligence on the USSR's rapid deployment of missile and bomber forces in Cuba. As the crisis mounted, tactical warning and targeting data were developed and steadily updated in support of strike options being developed by the JCS and the NSC Executive Committee. Targets included the MRBM and IRBM missile installations, the IL-28/BEAGLE bombers, the 24 SA-2 SAM sites, the MiG-21 fighters, and other ground, air, and naval targets.

The intelligence flowing from the reconnaissance missions provided the irrefutable evidence the US required to document to the world the basis for its response, as well as the targeting data that would have been needed if the crisis touched off an armed conflict. It tracked the surge of Soviet military personnel to some 22,000 by the end of October 1962, and then the ebb in those numbers to some 17,000 as the troops manning the offensive weapons departed.

Strategic Warning

Strategic warning is the most important component of effective intelligence. Perhaps the greatest barrier to developing effective strategic indications and warning for decisionmaking is the tendency of the human mind to assume that the *status quo* will continue. The Cuban missile crisis and many other conflicts of the postwar era, including the Arab-Israeli Yom Kippur War and the Falklands conflict, confirm that nations generally do not credit their potential opponents with the will to take unexpected acts. We did not believe the Soviets would do so in 1962.

I was part of a team assisting General Carroll in his responsibilities as a member of the US Intelligence Board (USIB), the top policy forum of the Intelligence Community, whose membership included the DCI and the Deputy Director of Central Intelligence, the Director of the DIA, the Department of State's Director of Intelligence and Research, the Director of Naval Intelligence, the Army and Air Force Assistant Chiefs of Staff for Intelligence, the Director of the National Security Agency, the Assistant General Manager for Administration of the Atomic Energy Commission, and the Assistant to the Director of the FBI. Each person brought the intelligence strengths of their respective organizations to the table. It was the Board's primary duty to produce the formal National Intelligence Estimates (NIEs) and Special National Intelligence Estimates (SNIEs) on key international issues and events for consideration by the NSC. With the memory of the Bay of

Pigs disaster still fresh and with the politically charged US concern over Fidel Castro's consolidation of communist power in Cuba and the growing Soviet military presence there, the USIB focused on Cuba in its estimates. At the same time, the Intelligence Community tracked and recorded the entry of Soviet weapons by type and capability.

Two NIEs

NIE 85-2-62, *The Situation and Prospects in Cuba*, was issued by the Board on 1 August 1962. It underlined Castro's political primacy, the loyalty of the Cuban armed forces to Castro and his brother Raul, the provision of Soviet Bloc military equipment and training to Cuban Forces, and the deepening commitment of the Soviet Union to preserve and strengthen the Castro regime.[2]

As of 1 July 1962, the monitoring of Soviet military deliveries indicated that there were 160 tanks, 770 field artillery and antitank guns, 560 antiaircraft guns, 35 jet fighters, 24 helicopters and 3,800 military vehicles of various types in Cuba.[3] On 27 July, Castro announced that Cuba would soon have new defenses against the US. On 29 August, as the weaponry continued to roll off Soviet ships in Cuban ports, a CIA U-2 photographed the first SA-2 SAMs. Human intelligence sources in Cuba were reporting the sightings of rockets on the island. We concluded that these rockets were not MRBMs/IRBMs.

On 19 September 1962, in NIE 85-3-62, *The Military Buildup in Cuba*, the Intelligence Community reiterated its belief that the USSR would not introduce offensive strategic weapons into Cuba. Its key conclusion stated:

> The USSR could derive considerable military advantage from the establishment of Soviet MRBMs and IRBMs in Cuba, or from the establishment of a submarine base there. As between these two, the establishment of a submarine base would be the more likely. Either development, however, would be incompatible with Soviet practice to date and with Soviet policy as we presently estimate it. It would indicate a far greater willingness to increase the

level of risk in US-Soviet relations than the USSR has displayed thus far, and consequently to other areas and other problems in East-West relations.[4]

DCI McCone personally was not persuaded that the Soviet buildup was essentially defensive. Fate, however, would have him in Europe on an extended honeymoon when the crisis began. His messages to the President from Europe in mid-September advising that the evidence pointed to Soviet preparations for introducing offensive weapons into Cuba could not compete with the contrary judgment of the formal NIEs that the missiles would be for defensive purposes.

Following the discovery of the defensive SAMs in late August, the President warned Khrushchev that the US would not permit the introduction of offensive weapons. The Soviet leader's responses through several channels from Moscow to Washington repeated the official Soviet position that only defensive weapons were being introduced into Cuba. In his news conference on 13 September 1962, the President delivered a clear statement of the US position on Cuba and on the possibility of Soviet offensive weapons being deployed there.

Soviet Buildup

The Intelligence Community continued to monitor the rapid buildup and assess its implications. From July to 1 November 1962, the number of tanks would grow from 160 to 345; the field artillery and antitank guns from 770 to 1,320; the antiaircraft guns from 560 to 710; the jet fighters from 35 to 101; the helicopters from 24 to 70 or more; the military vehicles from 3,800 to between 7,500 and 10,000. And through late August, September and early October we continued to identify new categories of weaponry: the construction of 24 SAM sites with 500 missiles by 1 November; the introduction of some 24 to 32 Free Rocket Over Ground (FROG) rockets; the installation of four cruise missile sites and 160 air defense radars; and the arrival of 12 Soviet KOMAR-class cruise-missile patrol boats at Cuban ports.[5]

43

U-2 Missions

From 1956 on, I had participated in the Intelligence Community's tasking of the U-2 by contributing the Army's and DIA's intelligence collection requirements to the flight planners of the operational missions. I had helped analyze the photographic intelligence from the U-2 flights over the Soviet Union from 1956 to 1960.

The extraordinary capabilities of the U-2 as an aircraft were complemented by its advanced photographic gear. The U-2 carried the HR-73B camera system, a big, high-technology camera with a 36-inch focal-length lens able to capture considerable detail from altitudes of 14 miles. The camera load was two 6,500-foot rolls of 9 1/2-inch film. Each mission could produce more than 4,000 frames of film, with vertical, single-frame ground coverage of 5.7 x 5.7 nautical miles.

Following the flight of 29 August 1962, CIA launched additional U-2 missions on 5, 17, 26, and 29 September and 5 and 7 October. Working through an interagency committee, collection requirements were formulated that would shape the flight profile of each mission. The work of reading the film from each mission took place in NPIC in an atmosphere of intense analytical debate throughout September and early October. These U-2 missions established an excellent baseline for judging the nature and pace of the Soviet military buildup.

The success of our efforts owed much to the brilliant leadership of Art Lundahl, who was internationally recognized for his contributions to photographic interpretation and photogrammetric engineering. His dedication to improving the nation's reconnaissance capabilities and his professional standards shaped the work of all who were a part of his crisis team.

SA-2 Controversy

One issue for the photointerpreters was the intended role of the Soviet SA-2 GUIDELINE SAM, which had been operational with Soviet air defense forces since the late 1950s. The 30-foot-long SA-2 had a solid-propellant booster and a kerosene-based second stage sustainer, and it could sprint to Mach 3 carrying a 280-pound high-explosive warhead with a proximity fuse to a range of 30 miles. Radio guidance from ground-based target acquisition radar fed steering commands to the missile's control fins. We assessed it as reliable and accurate.

The U-2 missions through 5 September revealed a disproportionate buildup of SA-2 launch sites in western Cuba. One school of thought contended that this deployment pattern was not particularly worrisome, given that Havana and the larger part of the Cuban population were in that region. Further, most of the sites were along Cuba's periphery, where one might expect such missiles arrayed in a national air-defense network.

Another line of analysis held that the disproportionate concentration of SA-2s in the west meant that the Soviets and the Cubans had important military equipment there requiring greater protection. The photointerpreters pushed on with their analysis, somewhat hampered by a policy-level decision following the 5 October mission to avoid the western sector on future U-2 missions because of administration concerns that an SA-2 might shoot down a U-2, thereby escalating the crisis.

Analysis was not based exclusively on photointerpretation. One of my DIA colleagues, Colonel John Wright, directed the work of a center in DIA that collated intelligence from all sources. The center evaluated the photography together with other sources, including reports from refugees and agents in Cuba. These reports continued to warn of large rockets, possibly missiles, arriving in Cuba and of suspicious military activity in western Cuba.

Focus on San Cristobal

Colonel Wright and his staff became increasingly interested in the SA-2 sites near San Cristobal, in the western part of the island. Most important, the U-2 photography indicated that these sites formed the outline of a trapezoid. This suggested that the sites

44

1990-1994

Trapezoid

were forming a "point defense" to protect some extremely important weapons emplacements or installations.

This deployment pattern was similar to those identified near ballistic-missile launch sites in the Soviet homeland. The stationing of these SA-2s, together with human-source reporting of missiles in western Cuba, strongly suggested that there were offensive Soviet ballistic missiles to be found within the San Cristobal trapezoid.

Shift In Responsibility

The President's advisers largely agreed that the new evidence warranted resuming U-2 missions over western Cuba. New requirements were issued for photographic reconnaissance of the San Cristobal area. Because of continuing concern over the international repercussions should one of the U-2s be shot down, it was decided that future U-2 missions should be flown by the Air Force. If any questions about the flights should arise, they would be acknowledged as military reconnaissance missions.

The 4080th Strategic Wing of the Strategic Air Command, based at Laughlin Air Force Base in Del Rio, Texas, was given the assignment. The next flight was set for 14 October, with Major Rudolph Anderson, USAF, as the pilot. The mission went flawlessly, and copies of the photography were sent by courier to NPIC, Navy analysts, the Strategic Air Command (SAC), and other key commands.

Evidence of MRBMs

Photointerpreters at NPIC called me at the Pentagon on 15 October. MRBMs had been found and confirmed. I called General Carroll to tell him what I had just heard and that I was on my way to NPIC. He asked me to give him another call as soon as I had personally reviewed the evidence.

After a quick look at three or four of the frames, I called General Carroll back and told him that the film showed ballistic-missile carriers, associated equipment, and support trucks. The U-2 camera had caught an MRBM convoy just as it was preparing to pull into the cover of a wooded area.

That evening General Carroll, my colleague John McLauchlin and I reported directly to Deputy Secretary Gilpatric. He asked me the same question that the President would ask Art Lundahl the following morning. It was the same question that would be asked by each of the select senior US officials being informed of the discovery as they looked at the tiny objects and patterns on our photographs of the Cuban countryside: "Are you sure that these are Soviet MRBMs?" I answered, "I am convinced they are." The next morning, Lundahl told the President he was "as sure of this as a photointerpreter can be sure of anything...."

Strategic Surveillance

The urgent work of the Executive Committee would begin on the morning of 16 October. While the world remained ignorant of the mounting crisis, those supporting the President and the Executive Committee were aware of the responsibility and trust that had been given us. The President needed absolute confirmation of the presence and numbers of MRBMs and any other offensive weapons that the Soviets had in place in Cuba. He needed time to marshal US ground, sea and air forces and to consider the options for their use should military action be required. He also needed time to decide how best to confront Khrushchev with the evidence, and he had to plan how to implement the US response. Secrecy was essential. More documentary evidence was required.

U-2s from SAC were moved to Florida. Between 15 and 22 October, they flew 20 missions over Cuba to search the entire island. These reconnaissance flights helped us to understand what the Soviets were up to and what stage of weapons deployment they had reached. This information enabled the Intelligence Community to give the President and his advisers its best judgment as to whether the missiles were operational and, if not, when they would most likely become operational.

As a result of highly classified and urgent work, the community would determine that the first of the MRBMs would become operational on 28 October.

45

154

While US intelligence had not provided strategic warning that the Soviets would introduce such weapons, intelligence had discovered the weapons before they became operational, giving the President an advantage in planning his response.

Analysis of U-2 photography went on around the clock, with few, even in the Intelligence Community, given access to the intelligence. As new photography became available, General Carroll and I would brief the Secretary and then take the same findings to the Chairman and the Joint Chiefs to prepare the Defense representatives for the continuing deliberations of the Executive Committee. Our photointerpreters poured over earlier U-2 photography of the geographic locations where we were now discovering the offensive weapons. These comparisons enabled us to determine when the Soviets had begun construction, a process which confirmed the clandestine and time-urgent design of the Soviet operation.

Seaborne Shipments

With the deployment of the missiles in Cuba now established, we began to re-examine earlier photointelligence to determine how they had arrived. From September to mid-October, the Navy had photographed several Soviet merchant ships en route to Cuba, including the *Poltava* and the *Omsk*, riding high in the water and with unusually long cargo hatches. It was apparent that these merchant vessels must have been transporting a high-volume cargo that was not particularly heavy. We then realized that they had, in fact, been delivering missiles that were to be offloaded at night.

SS-4s and SS-5s

The photography of the 17 October U-2 mission revealed a major new development: the construction of a fixed IRBM site at Guanajay, just west of Havana. While the mobile MRBM posed a serious threat, its range was limited to targets in the southern US.

We had studied the SS-4 MRBM since before its first appearance on parade in Moscow the year before. It had an overall length of just over 73 feet

with warhead attached. It a had a support crew of 24 men, and it was serviced by a dozen vehicles. The SS-4 had sufficient fuel and thrust to deliver a 1-megaton nuclear warhead on short notice up to 1,000 miles, a range that threatened the southeastern US in an arc extending from Savannah, Georgia, to New Orleans, Louisiana.

The SS-5 IRBM, by contrast, had a range of over 2,200 miles, and it could hit any target in the continental US except Seattle, Spokane, and other cities in Washington state. It was clear that we were not facing a temporary expeditionary force in Cuba. The SS-5 required complex permanent launch sites, with troop quarters, missile shelters, warhead bunkers and a large logistics train.

We had monitored the development and testing of the SS-5 SKEAN since the late 1950s. Operational in 1961, the SS-5 was the newest of the Soviet Union's IRBMs and the product of their intensive strategic rocket program. Its warhead yield also was estimated at 1 megaton, but it had better inertial guidance than the SS-4.

Four Key Sites

Continuing intelligence analysis provided irrefutable evidence that the Soviets were pushing ahead simultaneously with the installation of ballistic missiles at four separate locations: MRBMs at San Cristobal and Sagua La Grande, and IRBMs at Guanajay and Remedios. Soviet construction was progressing at a breakneck pace; photointelligence from successive U-2 missions indicated that sites were rapidly approaching operational status. Their construction workers were experiencing some difficulties as was evident from earth scarring and deep tire ruts produced by heavy transporters in the soft soil of the semitropical countryside.

The Soviets and Cubans were working almost continuously to set up 24 MRBM launchers plus 18 reserves for a total of 42 SS-4 MRBM nuclear missiles, as well as three fixed IRBM launch sites, each

46

Trapezoid

with four launchers. If these sites were completed, their missiles would significantly affect the strategic balance.

Cratology

The U-2 mission of 15 October discovered a third dimension to the impending nuclear threat. In late September, US maritime surveillance had spotted a merchant ship bound for Cuba carrying a number of large crates on its deck. To deduce their content, US photointerpreters had to resort to the fledgling "science" of cratology.

Unique dimensions, shapes, volumes and other features of the apparently innocuous-looking crates allowed the analysts to determine with some precision by mid-October that the crates contained disassembled IL-28/BEAGLE bomber aircraft.

The U-2 photographed 21 of these crates, one with the top open and the BEAGLE fuselage exposed, at San Julian Airfield on the 15th. This was our first sighting of part of the total force of 42 bombers the Soviet Union was delivering to the San Julian and Holguin Airfields.

Meeting With Gromyko

At the White House, the Executive Committee weighed the new evidence in its deliberations on the best course of action to recommend to the President. On 18 October, the President proceeded with an office call by Soviet Foreign Minister Gromyko, an appointment that had been made many weeks before. Without tipping his hand about the US discovery of the Soviet MRBMs, IRBMs and bombers in Cuba, President Kennedy underscored to Gromyko the unacceptability of Soviet offensive nuclear weapons on the island. Gromyko responded with assurances that the weapons being introduced were strictly defensive.

SNIE's Judgments

The Executive Committee soon narrowed the options to airstrikes against the missile sites and bomber bases versus a naval blockade of the island. On 20

October, the Intelligence Community published its views on the implications of the committee's options in SNIE 11-19-62, *"Major Consequences of Certain US Courses of Action on Cuba."*

SNIE 11-19-62 was cautious about the likely results of either a selective or a total blockade of Cuba. It argued that nuclear warheads could be delivered covertly aboard aircraft or submarines evading the blockade, that the Soviet missiles already in Cuba would still be poised to strike, that it would not weaken Castro's regime, and that either a selective or total blockade would give the Soviet Union time to mobilize world pressure against the US. The SNIE judged that neither type of blockade would necessarily escalate to war, either in Cuba or elsewhere, and that the Soviets would not be driven to immediate military retaliation.

The estimate also judged that whatever the nature of any US military action against Cuba, it would not be likely to provoke Khrushchev and his colleagues into launching all-out nuclear war. The authors wrote:

> We believe that there would probably be a difference between Soviet reaction to all-out invasion and Soviet reaction to more limited US use of force against selective objectives in Cuba. We believe that the Soviets would be somewhat less likely to retaliate with military force in areas outside of Cuba in response to speedy, effective invasion than in response to more limited forms of military action against Cuba. We recognize that such an estimate cannot be made with very great assurance and do not rule out the possibility of Soviet retaliation outside of Cuba in case of invasion. But we believe that a rapid occupation of Cuba would be more likely to make the Soviets pause in opening new theaters of conflict than limited action or action which drags out.[6]

The President's Decision

Proponents of the alternate options of US response continued to argue within the Executive Committee until the President authorized a selective blockade of

47

deliveries of offensive weapons to Cuba. The President had chosen a course which he had judged would not push Khrushchev beyond the brink. It would demonstrate US resolve, and it would provide the President and his advisers the time and the leverage they required in their communications with Khrushchev to demand that the USSR withdraw its missiles and bombers from Cuba.

President Kennedy's report to the American people on the Soviet missile and bomber buildup in Cuba was delivered from the White House Oval Office at 7:00 p.m., 22 October, one week after the discovery of the MRBMs at San Cristobal. I was with Navy photointerpreters in Suitland, Maryland. We listened to the President's somber, electrifying words. As stated in the second of his announced actions, the President had ordered low-level surveillance photo missions by Navy and Air Force tactical reconnaissance squadrons to begin the following morning.

Given the array of MiG-21 fighters, antiaircraft guns and SAM defenses that would confront our reconnaissance planes, tactical intelligence support was vital to their success. In turn, their success would be essential to the President's strategy. As we worked to prepare for the following day's briefing, there was a profound sense of urgency.

Low-Level Missions

Shortly after dawn on 23 October, Navy pilots of Light Photographic Squadron 62 and Air Force pilots of the 363rd Tactical Reconnaissance Wing took off on the first low-level photo missions over Cuba. Later that day, the President issued Proclamation 3504: *Interdiction of the Delivery of Offensive Weapons to Cuba*. It stated that as of 2:00 p.m., 24 October, forces under his command had instructions to intercept any vessel or craft proceeding toward Cuba and to interdict the delivery of surface-to-surface missiles; bombers; bombs; air-to-surface rockets and guided missiles; warheads; mechanical and electrical equipment for such weapons; and any other materials subsequently designated by the Secretary of Defense.

Our aerial reconnaissance of Cuba took a quantum leap both in volume and in precision of detail with the low-level missions. The Navy and Marine Corps pilots assigned to Light Photographic Squadron 62 were flying the single-engine reconnaissance RF-8A version of the F-8 Crusader fighter. It carried five cameras. The Air Force pilots of the 363rd Tactical Reconnaissance Wing were flying the RF-101 reconnaissance version of the F-101 Voodoo fighter.

The RF-101's reconnaissance eyes were the KA-53 aerial reconnaissance cameras with black-and-white and color emulsion 5-inch aerial roll film loaded in 250-foot film cassettes, cameras with shutter speeds up to 1/3000th of a second. The combination of planes and cameras in these Navy and Air Force tactical units was as remarkable in its sophistication as was the technology aboard the U-2s.

The RF-8As and RF-101s covered their targets 500 feet off the ground at speeds of 600 mph. With this speed and altitude, the Soviets and Cubans had no warning, only the sonic roar as the reconnaissance planes flew by on flight profiles that brought them in low over the Gulf of Mexico with a pop-up over the target. At the successful conclusion of each mission, the VP-62 pilots would paint another dead chicken on the fuselages of their Crusaders to symbolize Castro's chickens coming home to roost.[7]

The reconnaissance photography these pilots were delivering was spectacular. It was clear, large-scale documentation. It permitted us to gain full understanding of the MRBMs that would be operational by the 28th and to track the continuing intensive construction of the IRBM sites. The photography provided our combat-mission planners with the precise detail they required in the event the President were to order a strike against the island.

As soon as each low-level mission delivered its film to the squadron and wing photo labs, it was developed and flown to Washington and to other photographic analysis centers.

Trapezoid

The JRC

The nerve center for the US reconnaissance effort was the Joint Reconnaissance Center (JRC) in the Pentagon, under the direction of then Colonel Ralph D. Steakley, USAF. The JRC had been created to provide the JCS, the Office of the Secretary of Defense, the Department of State and the White House with a focal point for policy decisions on the US reconnaissance missions being undertaken worldwide long before the Cuban missile crisis. The Intelligence Community, the Unified and Specified Commands and others would identify reconnaissance requirements. The JRC would clear mission plans through the appropriate policy level of the government, and, with approval received, authorize the reconnaissance missions.

We fed our reconnaissance targeting requirements to Steakley. He had assigned liaison officers from the Center to the Tactical Air Command and SAC. The JRC and the operational planners of the Air Force and Navy drew up detailed flight plans to fulfill the latest intelligence requirements. The work proceeded around the clock. Steakley had a cot in his office, where he lived throughout the crisis. He was under relentless operational pressure. He had received a telephone call from President Kennedy's secretary with the message, "The President has directed that you not be away from your phone for more than three rings...." Secretary McNamara had made it clear that he personally wanted to be certain that each mission flown was in accordance with a determined plan and a predetermined approval cycle. Steakley was regularly summoned to the White House to brief the President on the planned flights.

The President and the Executive Committee were seeing explicit details of the Soviet nuclear offensive buildup. They were following the advances of the MRBMs and IRBMs toward operational status with each day's low-level recce take. The missions, as the President knew, were dangerous and might escalate the crisis beyond the control of either side.

A Bad Day

On 27 October, an Air Force RB-47 flying maritime surveillance missions against Soviet shipping crashed on takeoff from Bermuda with the loss of all four

crew members. That same day, of a Soviet SA-2 GUIDELINE missile brought down a U-2 over Cuba flown by Major Rudolf Anderson, the pilot of the U-2 flight on 14 October that had filmed the discovery of the Soviet MRBMs. Anderson was killed, and the pressure to retaliate intensified.

An Effective Cycle

We felt this pressure in our support to Secretary McNamara and the JCS. The work cycle began with the delivery of hundreds of feet of new photography in Washington, usually each evening, which had to be analyzed around the clock. I would arrive at either the Pentagon or NPIC early each morning to review the findings and to prepare to brief McNamara and the JCS, usually before the start of the morning Executive Committee sessions at the White House. Current intelligence for targeting of SAM sites was fed to the military planners for inclusion in the target folders. There was a growing consensus that the US would have to act.

The gravity of the situation was confirmed by the results of the low-level reconnaissance missions. The JRC worked with Air Force and Navy planners in drawing up the final flight plans. The pilots agreed that flight tracks for each missions were flyable, and that they were the best tracks to achieve coverage of the requested targets. This success was matched by the cycle we had developed of film processing, readout and feedback to both the national level and the operators. The results of each day's reconnaissance were available to feed into the following day's planning and execution.

White House Statement

O n 26 October, the President approved the release of a statement updating the American people on the status of the Soviet missile sites. It reported that development of the IRBM sites was continuing, with bulldozers and cranes observed clearing new areas within the sites. It noted that MRBMs had been observed, with cabling running from missile-ready tents

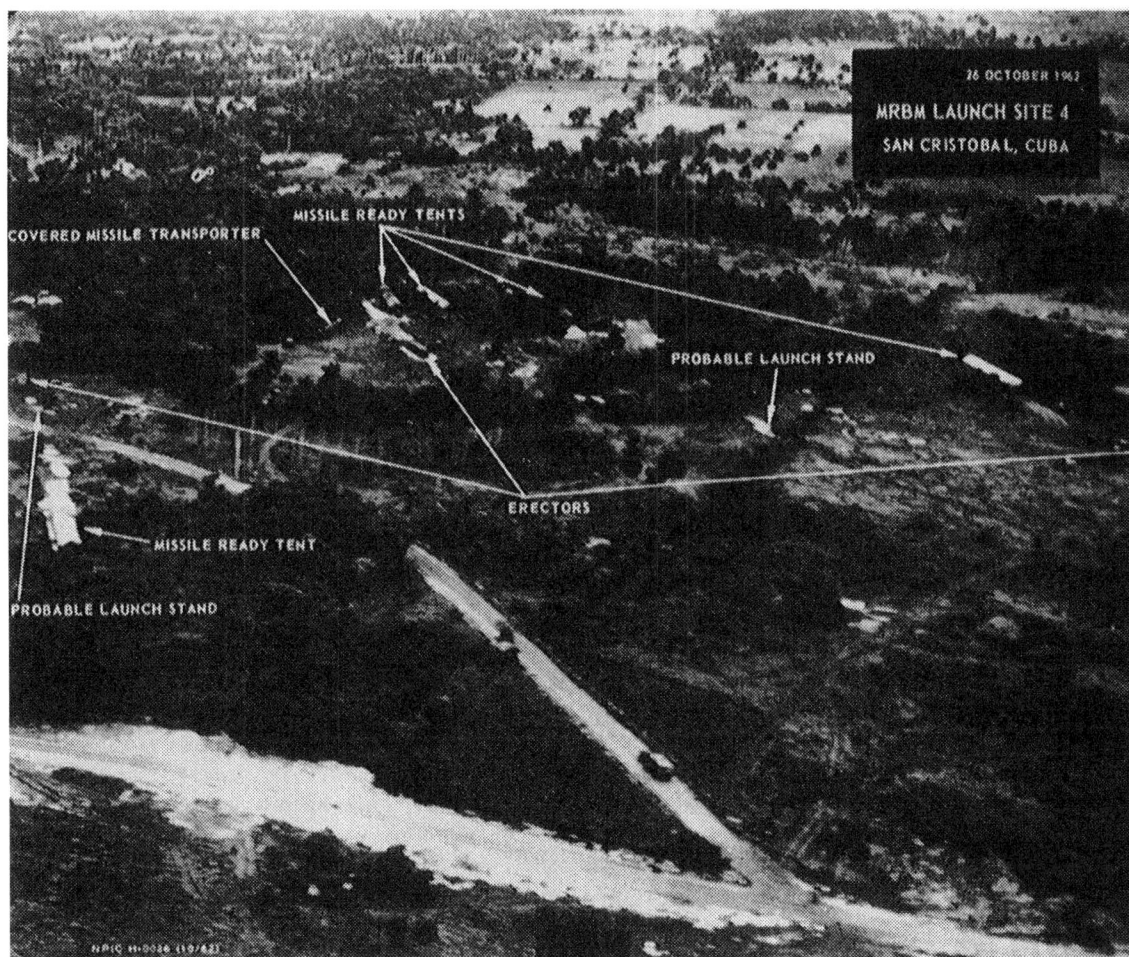

to nearby power generators. And it concluded that the Soviets were trying to camouflage their efforts at the sites.

The USSR's measured response to the quarantine was of critical importance to the President's restrained approach to the crisis. No ships with prohibited or even questionable cargoes had tried to run the blockade. The shootdown of Major Anderson had brought the US to the brink of a retaliatory strike against military targets in Cuba, but the President remained determined to force Soviet compliance with US demands on terms short of war. Intelligence had given him the information he needed to catch

Khrushchev red-handed. There could be no question of the validity of the US charges. But the President knew he was running out of time: the MRBMs would become operational on 28 October.

Messages from Khrushchev

On 26 October, Khrushchev sent President Kennedy first one message, then another. The first couched the Soviet Union's conditions for the withdrawal of its missiles and bombers from Cuba in terms of a requirement for an end to the US blockage and for a promise from the US that it would not invade Cuba. The second Khrushchev letter added another, far more difficult demand:

> You are worried over Cuba. You say that it worries you because it lies at a distance of 90 miles across the sea from the shores of the United States. However, Turkey lies next to us. Our sentinels are pacing up and down watching each other. Do you believe that you have the right to demand security for your country and the removal of such weapons that you qualify as offensive, while not recognizing this right for us?

> This is why I make this proposal: We agree to remove those weapons from Cuba which you regard as offensive weapons. We agree to do this and to state this commitment in the United Nations. Your representatives will make a statement to the effect that the United States, on its part, bearing in mind the anxiety and concern of the Soviet state, will evacuate its analogous weapons from Turkey. Let us reach an understanding on what time you and we need to put this into effect....[8]

The US Replies

While the US missiles would eventually be withdrawn from Turkey, at the peak of the Cuban missile crisis the President rejected including them or any mention of them in the terms that would be set for the withdrawal of the Soviet missiles from Cuba. In the midst of the Executive Committee meeting on 27 October on the next step to be taken by the US, Attorney General Robert Kennedy proposed that the US reply to Khrushchev's first letter and not to the second. He actually drafted the reply, stating the terms we were willing to accept, plucking them from several often disparate Soviet messages. They were the terms on which the settlement ultimately was based.[9]

The President's reply of 27 October opened on a positive note, welcoming Khrushchev's "desire to seek a prompt solution to the problem." The President then stressed that if there were to be a solution, work had to cease on the missile bases, and the offensive weapons in Cuba had to be rendered inoperable and removed, with supervision of the removal under appropriate UN arrangements. The US in turn would lift the quarantine and would assure the Soviet Union that it would not invade Cuba.

The President then hinted at future US willingness to consider the missiles in Turkey, without explicitly so stating. "The effect of such a settlement," he wrote, "on easing world tensions would enable us to work toward a more general arrangement regarding 'other armaments,' as proposed in your second letter which you made public." The President closed his reply by again stressing the imperative of an immediate Soviet halt to work on the MRBMs and IRBMs and rendering the weapons inoperable.[10]

Attorney General Kennedy handed over a copy of the President's reply to Soviet Ambassador Dobrynin, stressing the President's belief that the substance of the Soviet response to this message would dictate swiftly whether the two superpowers would resolve the crisis or escalate to war.

On 28 October 1962, Khrushchev agreed to President Kennedy's terms: work would stop on the missile sites, and the weapons would be dismantled and withdrawn. The word arrived quickly as we continued to support preparations for US military action. There was tremendous exhilaration. The Intelligence Community and the military shifted gears, moving to the responsibility of monitoring Soviet dismantlement and withdrawal.

Monitoring Withdrawal

New orders from Moscow to the Soviet missile and bomber forces in Cuba were dispatched immediately. As early as 29 October, low-level reconnaissance flights brought back evidence that the MRBM missile erectors were no longer in their missile-ready firing positions. We would monitor every step of the Soviet withdrawal through photography, reports from

51

human sources, ship-to-ship inspections, air-to-ship surveillance, and other sources and methods. Weather permitting, the Navy RF-8As and Air Force RF-101s flew across Cuba on daily missions collecting thousands of frames of up-to-the-minute evidence for examination by the photointerpreters, analysts, and the senior levels of government.

Early on, the Soviets started to break up the IRBM sites—sites which would never meet their planned 15 December operational date, which was chosen to coincide with Khrushchev's planned address to the UN. Bulldozers tore up the missiles' concrete launch pads and smashed through missile-support facilities. Each of the sites was systematically monitored. The status of the support equipment, propellant trailers, nuclear weapons-handling vans and communications vans was also an intelligence indicator. We tracked their withdrawal from the missile sites to the ports and onto a succession of Soviet merchant ships. The reconnaissance cameras documented Soviet personnel boarding ships for the voyage back across the Atlantic.

The Navy quarantine remained in effect, examining any inbound ships and, in a new phase, inspecting outbound ships to determine their cargoes. The Soviets complied with orders to strip away canvas covering each of the missiles in their canisters, with each clearly in the open, riding as deck cargo. They also complied with orders to break open the wooden crates containing the IL-28 bomber wings and fuselages, permitting us to count each and to confirm their departure.

Quarantine commander Admiral Ward reported that while the business was deadly serious and while the US forces insisted on full, precise compliance with all demands, there was no sign of Soviet hostility.

Status Reports

On 2 November, President Kennedy provided his first formal status report on the dismantling of the Soviet missile bases in Cuba in an address to the nation. He reported that careful examination of aerial photography and other information was confirming the destruction of the missile bases and preparation of the missiles for return to the USSR. He said that

US surveillance would continue to track the withdrawal closely and that this unilateral inspection and monitoring would continue until the US arranged for international inspection of the cargoes and overall withdrawal.

By the time of his news conference on 20 November, the President had received sufficient intelligence to be able to report that the missile sites had all been dismantled, that the missiles and associated equipment had departed Cuba aboard Soviet ships, that US inspection at sea had confirmed that the numbers departing included all known missiles, and that Khrushchev had informed him earlier that day that the IL-28 bombers would all be withdrawn from Cuba within 30 days. Following this Soviet compliance with US demands, the President announced that he had ordered the lifting of the quarantine. He went on to stress that close surveillance of Cuba would continue, bearing in mind that Castro had still not agreed to allow UN inspectors to verify the removal of all offensive weapons or to set safeguards in place to prevent their reintroduction.

In his news conference of 12 December, the President had to repeat his position of 20 November, stating that while the US continued to press for on-site inspection, he would take every step necessary through continuing close daily surveillance to ensure that no missiles or offensive weapons were reintroduced.

Paying Tribute

With the quarantine lifted, the President flew to Florida on 26 November to pay tribute to the reconnaissance wings and squadrons. At Homestead Air Force Base, the President presented Outstanding Unit Awards to the 4080th Strategic Reconnaissance Wing and the 363rd Tactical Reconnaissance Wing. He saluted the work of the pilots and their ground crews:

> I may say, gentleman, that you take excellent pictures, and I've seen a good many of them. And beginning with the photographs which

Trapezoid

were taken on the weekend in the middle of October, which first gave us conclusive proof of the buildup of offensive weapons in Cuba, through the days that have followed to the present time, the work of these two units has contributed as much to the security of the US as any units in our history, and any group of men in our history.[11]

He then flew to Key West, to Boca Chica Naval Air Station, to present Unit Citations to Navy Light Photographic Squadron 62 and Marine Light Photographic Squadron VMC-J2.

On 28 November, SAC Commander-in-Chief General Thomas Power awarded the Distinguished Flying Cross to 10 U-2 pilots of the 4080th. Admiral Robert Dennison, USN, presented the same decoration to 25 pilots of the Navy, Marine Corps, and Air Force tactical recce units. The next day the planes' cameras were again in action over Cuba.

Monitoring Continues

The reconnaissance missions of November enabled us to monitor the disassembly and crating of the Il-28 bombers at San Julian and Holguin Airfields and the departure of the crates from Cuba, just as we had earlier monitored the destruction of the IRBM sites at Guanajay and Remedios and the departure of the MRBM missiles from San Cristobal and Sagua La Grande. The first missions of 1963 also enabled us to continue to monitor the status of the Soviets' considerable remaining defensive installations, weaponry and personnel, ostensibly in place to protect against the threat of invasion.

The number of Soviet troops had swollen to between 22,000 and 23,000 on Cuba at the peak of the crisis. With the departure of the missile and bomber forces, we could now identify some 17,000 troops still on the island. Our order of battle in early 1963 showed that Soviet military equipment in Cuba included 24 SAM sites with 500 missiles; 104 MiG fighters, including 24 of the new MiG-21 jets capable of Mach 2 performance; 200 air defense radars; 12 KOMAR-class missile patrol boats; upwards of 100 helicopters; four cruise-missile sites with 150 cruise

missiles; more the 700 antiaircraft guns; 24 to 32 FROG rockets; 7,500 to 10,000 military support vehicles; more than 1,300 pieces of field artillery and antitank guns; and some 400 tanks.[12]

Taken together, this weaponry would have given the Soviets a layered set of ground, sea, and air defenses for their missile sites and bomber bases. And there could be little doubt that the remaining weapons were defensive in character. While the Intelligence Community assessed the MiG-21 as being capable of carrying a nuclear weapon, we knew that was not the fighter's intended mission. With a nuclear weapon aboard, the MiG-21 would have a combat radius of little more than 200 miles restricted to clear weather, daytime missions. Of prime importance, our analysis of each new batch of recce photography showed absolutely no evidence of the types of secure facilities that one could expect with confidence that the Soviets would have in place if there were still any nuclear weapons stored on the island.

We were confident of the complete withdrawal based on the comprehensive character of our reconnaissance and monitoring in late 1962 and early 1963.

Refuting Rumors

When the US Congress reconvened in late January 1963, our hard evidence on the defensive nature of the Soviet forces in Cuba remained largely classified. The public debate was feeding rumors that Soviet nuclear offensive capabilities remained in Cuba, that missiles were hidden in caves, and that the MiG-21s and KOMAR patrol boats could deliver nuclear weapons. Such rumors were pouring in from anti-Castro Cuban refugees, and they were fueled by those still angry that the President had not invaded the island and done away with the communist regime.

Following his Congressional testimony on 5 February, DCI McCone issued a formal unclassified statement in the name of the USIB reviewing the entire Soviet buildup and the departure of the missiles: "We are convinced beyond reasonable doubt, as has

53

been stated by the Department of Defense, that all offensive missiles and bombers known to be in Cuba were withdrawn soon thereafter. . . Reconnaissance has not detected the presence of offensive missiles or bombers in Cuba since that time." Referring to the alleged storage of missiles in caves, McCone said, "All statements alleging the presence of offensive weapons are meticulously checked. So far the findings have been negative. Absolute assurance on these matters, however, could only come from continuing, penetrating on-site inspection."[13] The statement still did not defuse the issue.

In my appearance with Secretary McNamara before the House Subcommittee on Defense Appropriations on 6 February, the Secretary reviewed each phase of the Soviet buildup since the spring of 1962. To set the stage for my classified presentation to the subcommittee of the most important photography, the Secretary described the role of reconnaissance in some detail. Immediately after my presentation, the President decided that the photographic evidence had to be declassified and shared with the American people.

Briefing the Nation

Shortly before noon, Secretary McNamara informed me that I was to present the briefing to the nation that evening on national TV from 5:00 to 7:00 p.m. I was to make the presentation in the State Department Auditorium to an audience of journalists and photographers assigned to the White House, State Department, and Defense Department. The briefing requested by the President included photos, charts, and tables that would document clearly the discovery of the Soviet ballistic missiles, their assembly and operational readiness, and their dismantlement and removal from the island. The photos were selected from among the best available and reflected the superb quality of the photography regularly provided by our reconnaissance jets.

Secretary McNamara told me that he would introduce the presentation and take the follow-on questions. He asked to see the text of my briefing and was surprised when I told him that there was no written text because I had committed the briefing to memory and that the sequence of the photographs and charts would shape and pace the presentation.

The Secretary directed his military assistant, Colonel George Brown, USAF, who would go on to become Chairman of the Joint Chiefs of Staff, to take me under his charge for the remainder of the day and ensure that I was at the State Department by 4:00 p.m.

By 3:30 p.m., we were ready. The graphics had been checked and rechecked, classifications removed or covered, and some descriptive annotations added. Colonel Brown and I arrived at the State Department at 4:00 p.m. The auditorium was larger than I had expected, and the viewing screen—at least 12 feet by 8 feet—towered above the stage. This screen would enhance and display the photographs to maximum advantage. To tell the story effectively, however, I had to be able to point to photographic details that would be well beyond reach. I contacted my special assistant, Captain Billy R. Cooper, USAF, at the Pentagon about the problem, and he was more than equal to the challenge. He grabbed a roll of tape, securely joined two long fishing poles, and rushed to his car. I had this tailor-made pointer in hand and was set and ready to go at 5:00 p.m.

The air was charged in the auditorium. The press was out in full force, and McNamara was to the point:

> Good afternoon, ladies and gentlemen. In recent days questions have been raised in the press and elsewhere regarding the presence of offensive weapons systems in Cuba. I believe beyond any reasonable doubt that all such weapons systems have been removed from the island and none have been reintroduced. It is our purpose to show you this afternoon the evidence on which we base that conclusion.

> Since 1 July, over 400 reconnaissance flights have been flown over the island of Cuba by US military aircraft. These reconnaissance flights provided the essential basis for the national decisions taken with respect to Cuba in October. They provided the basis for the military preparations necessary to support those decisions. They provided the evidence we were able to present to the world to document the basis and the rationale of our action.

54

Trapezoid

The reconnaissance flights recorded the removal of the offensive weapon systems from Cuba, and they continued to provide the foundation for our conclusion that such weapons systems have not been reintroduced into the island.

Mr. John Hughes, the Special Assistant to General Carroll, the Director of DIA, will present to you a detailed photographic review of the introduction of Soviet military personnel and equipment into Cuba, with particular emphasis on the introduction and removal of the offensive weapons systems.

After Mr. Hughes completes his review, I will summarize very briefly our current estimates of the Soviet military strength in Cuba.

Mr. Hughes.

I began my briefing.

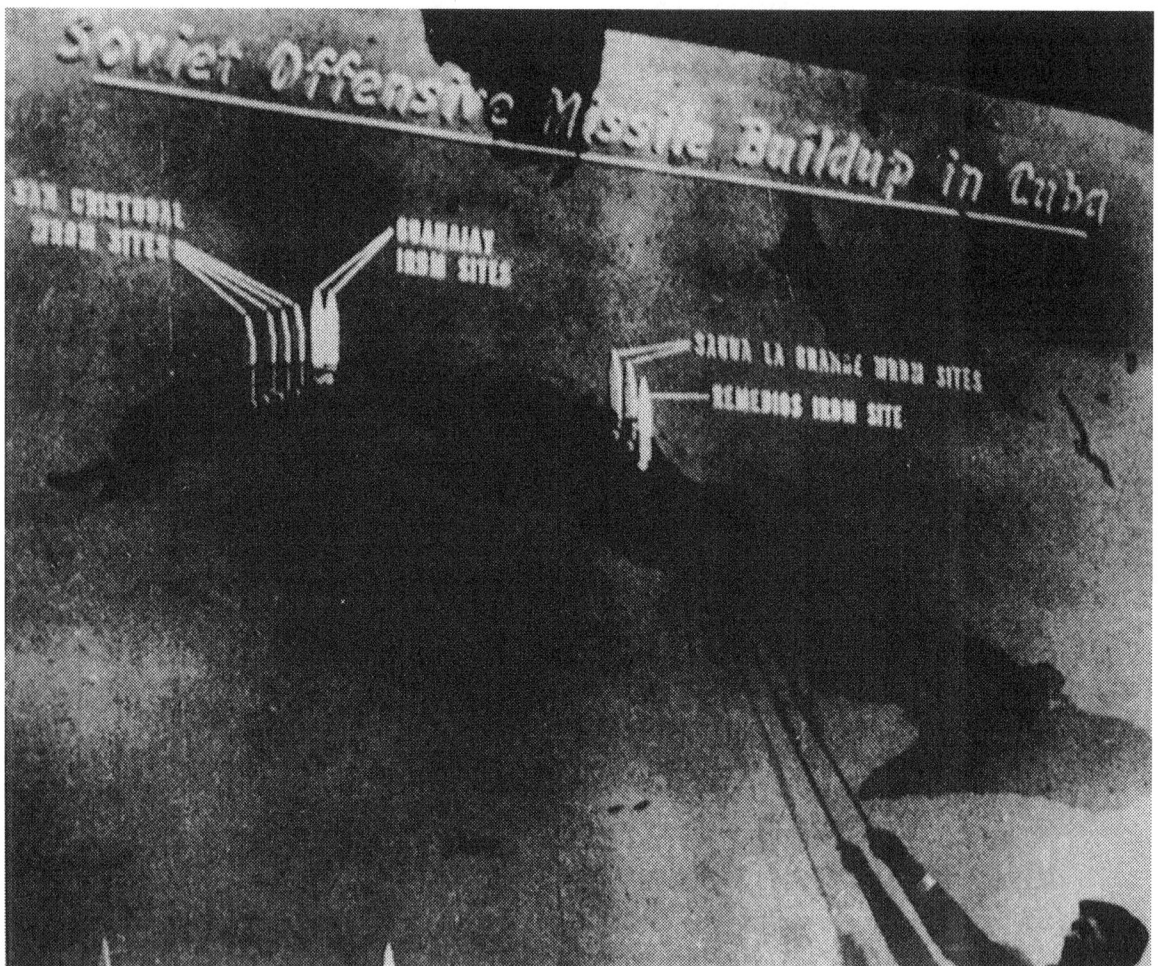

55

NOTES

1. Kennedy, Robert F., *Thirteen Days*, W.W. Norton & Company, Inc., New York, 1969, p. 14.

2. NIE 85-2-62, *The Situation and Prospects in Cuba*, 1 August 1962.

3. CIA Fact Sheet, *Soviet Forces in Cuba*, 5 February 1963.

4. SNIE 85-3-62, *The Military Buildup in Cuba*, 19 September 1962.

5. CIA Fact Sheet, *Soviet Forces in Cuba*, 5 February 1963.

6. SNIE 11-19-62, *Major Consequences of Certain US Courses of Action on Cuba*, 20 October 1962.

7. Newsletter, *Light Photographic Squadron Sixty-Two (VPF-62)*, February 1963.

8. Kennedy, Robert F., *op cit*, p. 198-199.

9. *Ibid*, pp 15-16.

10. *Ibid*, p. 203.

11. Public Papers of the Presidents of the United States, John F. Kennedy, 1962; US Government Printing Office, Washington, D.C.; 1963; pp. 832-833.

12. CIA Fact Sheet, *Soviet Forces in Cuba*, 5 February 1963.

13. Statement on Cuba by the DCI, 6 February 1963.

Held Hostage in Iran

A First Tour Like No Other

William J. Daugherty

> **It is not often that a newly minted case officer in the CIA's Directorate of Operations spends his first tour in jail.**

William J. Daugherty, Ph.D., served in the Directorate of Operations. He is now a faculty member at a university in the southern United States. In 1997 the Editorial Board of *Studies in Intelligence* chose him to receive the annual Sherman Kent Award for the most significant contribution to the literature of intelligence submitted for publication in *Studies*.

Copyright 1996 by William J. Daugherty

I do not recall now the exact circumstances in which I was finally and firmly offered Tehran for a first tour, nor even who made the offer. I do know, though, that I did not hesitate a second to say yes. For the most part, I have not regretted that decision, but at times it is only with a prodigious dose of hindsight that I have been able to keep it in perspective. After all, it is not often that a newly minted case officer in the CIA's Directorate of Operations (DO) spends his first tour in jail.

I was recruited into the Agency in 1978, during my last year of graduate school, and I entered on duty the next January. In my recruitment interviews, I was told about a special program managed by the DO's Career Management Staff that was designed to place a few selected first-tour officers overseas in a minimal period of time, without lengthy exposure to the Washington fishbowl or reliance on light cover. The program sounded fine to me, and so I joined the Agency and was rushed through the Career Training (CT) program by skipping the standard six months of interim assignments.

Something else that presented a problem initially—but later came to be a blessing in disguise—was that I enjoyed an astonishingly small amount of knowledge of the DO and how it did its business. Despite that innocent state, I managed to do well in training. I was particularly captivated by the stories told by the instructors from the DO's Near East (NE) Division, and by the challenging situations found in the Middle East; midway through the training course, I had decided I wanted to go

to NE Division. At that point, during a Saturday visit to Headquarters, the deputy chief of NE Division (DC/NE), knowing of my participation in the special program, raised the possibility of my being assigned to Tehran—even though I possessed absolutely no academic knowledge of, nor any practical experience whatsoever with, anything Iranian.

By the time of this conversation in spring 1979, Tehran station was in the midst of coping with postrevolutionary Iran. The Shah (ruling monarch) of Iran had fled the country on 16 January, and soon thereafter—on 2 February—Ayatollah Khomeini returned from exile in France to oversee a government founded on his perception of an Islamic state. Also of importance to later events, US Embassy and station personnel had already been taken hostage for several hours, on 14 February 1979, in what came to be called the St. Valentine's Day Open House.

This last event triggered an almost total drawdown of Embassy and station personnel, along with a reduction of active-duty American military forces in Iran from about 10,000 to a dozen or so, divided between the Defense Attaché's Office (DAO) and the Military Assistance Advisory Group (MAAG). It did not, however, generate much (if any) sentiment at the highest levels of the United States Government for disrupting or breaking diplomatic relations with Iran. In fact, it served mainly to strengthen American determination to reconcile with Iran's Provisional Revolutionary Government.

1

By March, Tehran station consisted of several case officers and communicators rotating in and out of Iran on a "temporary duty" basis. But NE Division was already looking ahead to the time when the station could again be staffed with permanently assigned personnel and functioning as a station should—recruiting agents and collecting intelligence. And that was the state of affairs when I met DC/NE in Langley on that spring day.

The Right Background

The deputy chief had fair reason to consider placing me in Tehran station. First, my special program had kept my cover clean: I had no visible affiliation with the US Government, much less with the Agency or any of its usual cover providers. I did have military service—eight years of active duty with the US Marine Corps. But between those years and my entry on duty with the Agency I had spent 5 1/2 years as a university student.

The nature of my military experience and education probably also helped prompt DC/NE to look at me for assignment to Tehran. During my eight years of Marine Corps service, I had first been an air traffic controller and, for more than half my service time, a designated Naval Flight Officer flying as a weapons system officer in high-performance jets. When my time for a tour in Vietnam rolled around, I was assigned to a fighter/attack squadron deployed aboard an aircraft carrier. I flew 76 missions over North Vietnam, South Vietnam, and Laos in the venerable F-4 Phantom. While no hero (indeed, I was the most junior and least experienced aviator in the squadron), I nonetheless had been subjected to the pressures of potential life-and-death

> ## "
> ## Tehran was a hostile environment in which contacts and agents were placing their lives at risk . . .
> ## "

situations and to high standards of performance. On returning to school, I earned a Ph.D. in Government, specializing in Executive-Congressional relations and Constitutional law associated with American foreign policy. This background seemed to nudge DC/NE toward selecting me for Tehran, and later it also was to serve me well in critical ways, in circumstances the nature of which I could have scarcely conceived.

Soon after my conversation with the DC/NE, however, I was told that the Tehran assignment was being withdrawn. When the acting chief of station (COS) was offered an inexperienced first-tour officer, he not unwisely rejected me. His position, which is difficult to rebut, was that Tehran was a hostile environment in which contacts and agents were placing their lives at risk by meeting in discreet circumstances with American Embassy officers (all of whom, of course, were considered by many Iranians to be CIA). Therefore, our Iranian assets deserved to be handled by experienced officers who knew what to do and how to do it. Further, any compromise whatsoever, for any reason, would unquestionably have severe repercussions for US-Iranian relations, which the Carter administration was trying to resurrect. Hence I was offered another station as an alternative.

It was sometime in late June or early July, while I was on the other country desk, that I was again offered Tehran. A permanent COS had finally arrived

in Tehran and, when my candidacy was raised with him, he did not hesitate to say yes. Later, he told me that given a choice between a well-trained, aggressive, and smart first-tour officer or a more experienced but reluctantly assigned officer who would rather have been somewhere else, he would take the first-tour officer. I thought then, and have thought ever since, that the COS made a courageous decision—one that, had I been in his place, I might have decided differently. He earned my respect right then and there, and it has never waned.

I accepted quickly. Shortly afterward, elated at the thought of going to a very-high-visibility post of great significance to policymakers, I was on the desk reading in. When the day came to depart for Tehran, I called on DC/NE. He ushered me into his office, chatted a minute or two about my itinerary, wished me well, and, shaking my hand, looked at me and said, "Don't [expletive] up." I wish he had been able to convey that message to a few other government officials downtown.

Historical Perspective

Iran (then known as Persia) at the turn of the century was a barren country barely existing as a grouping of tribal fiefdoms, more or less caught in the rivalry between Russia and Britain. The discovery of oil in Persia in 1908 changed things considerably for the Persian people and the two competing empires, particularly the British, but had little initial impact on US interests. With the events in revolutionary Russia in 1916 and 1917, that nation's ability to exercise power and influence in Persia diminished, and Persia quickly became fully incorporated into Britain's sphere of

> **CIA involvement in the overthrow of Prime Minister Mohammed Mossadeq in 1953 loomed extraordinarily large in the minds of Iranians.**

influence. Succeeding US presidents avoided any official contact or involvement, preferring instead to sidestep Persian entreaties and to recognize that the country was now within the British sphere.

In 1925 a Persian Army officer, Reza Pahlavi, became something of a national hero by halting a Communist-sponsored revolt in northern Persia. He parlayed that success into being elected Shah by the civilian Parliament, and then turned that semidemocratic position into a highly autocratic dictatorship. In short, he became just the latest in a centuries-long line of Persian masters who ruled by fiat and fear.

Officially calling his country Iran, Reza Shah began a reign that left him popular with virtually no one. Before World War II, he engaged in modernization of his country, although not necessarily for benevolent or public-spirited motives (one of many reasons he was detested by his subjects). During his reign, Iranian-US relations continued at a low ebb, with neither country understanding the other's culture and with much distrust existing on both sides.

It took World War II to create the Iranian-US ties that were eventually to become so seemingly invincible and permanent. The Soviet Union had been invaded by the Nazis in June 1941 with three field armies, one of which headed for the Transcaucasus region in southwestern Russia. With vital lines of transport and communication severed, there remained only two avenues of supply by which needed US lend-lease and other materials could reach the Soviets: the always dangerous Murmansk Run for ship convoys, and the Trans-Iranian Railroad reaching from the warm-water ports of the Persian Gulf

to the Soviet borders in northwestern Iran. The Transcaucasus thrust also threatened Iranian oil fields, for which Germany's need was desperate.

The outcome was the occupation of Iran in the north by Soviet troops and in the south by predominantly British forces. Reza Shah (whose army was completely undistinguished in its efforts to deter the arrival of foreign troops) was forced into exile on the island of Mauritius, and his teenage son, Muhammad Reza Pahlavi, was placed on the throne in a figurehead status. During this period, both Soviet and British troops earned Iranian antipathy as occupiers who were, in the eyes of most Iranians, looting their country while fighting a war in which Iran had no stake. (This enmity was not without some justification, although the British were never given the credit they deserved for significant and measurable assistance to the Iranian people throughout this period.) All of this, of course, deepened Iranian suspicions of foreigners and hostility toward outsiders who tried to or, in this instance, actually did control the country. The US Government's stake in Iran, as well as its diplomatic and military presence, concomitantly increased as a consequence of America's unyielding support to its wartime allies, Britain and the Soviet Union.

With the war over in 1945, the Soviets refused to leave Iran, as previously agreed to under a 1943 treaty.

Instead, relying on sympathizers in the local populace they had worked to cultivate during the war, the Soviets commenced a blatant attempt to annex the northern regions of Iran, coveting both the oil and access to a warm-water port. By the time American and British troops had departed from Iran in spring 1946, the Soviets were firmly ensconced in the province of Azerbaijan and were moving into Iran's Kurdish region.

Although George Kennan was still a year away from enshrining the geopolitical strategy of containment in his celebrated "Mr. X" article, the highest officials in the US Government had already recognized the true nature of Stalin's Soviet Union and the need to prevent, where possible and practical, the USSR's expansion beyond its own borders. Exerting strong diplomatic efforts, including mobilization of the nascent UN General Assembly, the US Government finally succeeded in getting the Soviets out of Iran and in having their puppet governments in Azerbaijan and Kurdistan disbanded.

Now, with Soviet and British influence over Iran greatly diminished, US-Iranian relations on all fronts gradually expanded, with the first arms sale by the United States to the Iranian military coming in June 1947. From then on, oil and "strategic imperatives" cemented and drove this unnatural relationship, despite continuing and increasing distrust and antipathy toward each other over the next decades.

CIA involvement in the overthrow of Prime Minister Mohammed Mossadeq in 1953 loomed extraordinarily large in the minds of Iranians. In April 1951 the then-popular but eccentric Mossadeq, a wealthy career civil servant and uncompromising

3

> ## " The United States, driven by the inexorable forces of the Cold War, increasingly assumed the role of chief protector for Iran and the Shah. "

nationalist, had been appointed by the Shah as prime minister to replace his assassinated predecessor. Shortly thereafter, the Shah, under pressure from Iran's political center and left, signed an order nationalizing the British-dominated, putatively "jointly owned" Anglo-Iranian Oil Company (AIOC); Mossadeq had earlier submitted, and the Majlis (parliament) had approved, legislation mandating AIOC's nationalization. The ultranationalist Mossadeq, who had advocated remaining aloof from both the Soviets and the Americans (rather than continuing the usual strategy of embracing both in order to play one off against the other), soon came to be seen by many in the West, including Washington, as de facto pro-Soviet.

The nationalization of AIOC touched off two years of political turmoil, during which Mossadeq's popular support eroded. This period culminated in August 1953 with the Shah's flight into a brief exile, CIA's stage-management (under explicit Presidential directive) of the coup against the Prime Minister, and the Shah's return (with US Government assistance) and consolidation of his power. Subsequently the United States, driven by the inexorable forces of the Cold War, increasingly assumed the role of chief protector for Iran and the Shah, leaving many Iranians more convinced than ever that the Shah and their country were simply a dominion of the United States, administered by or through the CIA. The seeds of the Iranian revolution of 1978-79 were being sown.

Fifty-Three Days

I arrived in Tehran on 12 September 1979 and began the first of what turned out to be only 53 days of actual operational work. If I knew

little about Iran, I knew even less about Iranians. My entire exposure to Iran, beyond the evening television news and a three-week area studies course at the State Department, consisted of what I had picked up during five weeks on the desk reading operational files.

Virtually all my insights into Persian minds and personalities came from a lengthy memo written by the recently reassigned political counselor, which described in detail (the accuracy of which I would have ample time to confirm) how Iranians viewed the world, and why and how they thought and believed as they did. It did not take much to see that even friendly and pro-Western Iranians could be difficult to deal or reason with, or to otherwise comprehend. The ability displayed by many Iranians to simultaneously avow antithetical beliefs or positions was just one of their quainter character traits.

One memorable introduction to all this was my first encounter with the Iranian elite several weeks after my arrival. In this instance, I met with an upper-class Iranian woman who was partnered with her husband in a successful construction company. This couple was wealthy and held degrees from European and American universities. They were well traveled. But, her exposure to the West and level of

education notwithstanding, this woman insisted that the Iranian Government was directly controlled by the CIA. She said that the chief of the Iranian desk at CIA Headquarters talked every day to the Shah by telephone to give the monarch his instructions for that particular day, and that the US Government had made a deliberate decision to rid Iran of the Shah. Since the US Government did not, in her scenario, have any idea whom it wanted to replace the Shah as ruler, it had decided to install Khomeini as the temporary puppet until the CIA selected a new Shah. I was both fascinated and stupefied by this explanation of the Shah's downfall.

The woman's unshakable theory did not encompass an explanation of why the United States would have permitted the bloody street riots in 1977 and 1978. Nor did it explain why, if the US Government (or the CIA) wanted the Shah to leave, he was not just ordered to go, thereby avoiding the enormous problems of revolutionary Iran.

My initial weeks in Tehran passed quickly. The Chargé, L. Bruce Laingen, was more than helpful, as was Maj. Gen. Phillip Gast, US Air Force, head of the MAAG, with both of them generously taking care to include me as a participant in substantive meetings at the Ministry of Foreign Affairs (MFA) and Iranian General Staff Headquarters. I worked essentially full-time during the day on cover duties, which I found much more interesting than onerous, dealing with issues of genuine import; in the evenings, I reverted to my true persona as a CIA case officer. I was 32 years old, at the top of my form both physically and mentally. Captivity was to change all that, and I have never since regained that same degree of mental acuity and agility. But during those 53 days on the streets of Tehran, I reveled in it all.

On 21 October, however, I came to realize that my euphoria would probably be short-lived. On that date, the other station case officer (as acting COS) shared a cable with me in which CIA Headquarters advised that the President had decided that day to admit the Shah, by then fatally ill with cancer, into the United States for medical treatment. I could not believe what I was reading. The Shah had left Iran in mid-January 1979 and had since led a peripatetic life; indeed, he had even rejected an offer of comfortable exile in America (to the relief of many US Government officials). Now, with US-Iranian relations still unstable and with an intense distrust of the United States permeating the new Iranian "revolutionary" government, the Shah and his doctors had decided the United States was the only place where he could find the medical care he needed.

The Shah Comes to America

Since February 1979, strong pressure on President Carter for the Shah to be admitted to the United States had been openly and unrelentingly applied by powerful people inside and outside the US Government, particularly by National Security Adviser Zbigniew Brzezinski and banking magnate David Rockefeller, with added support from former Secretary of State Henry Kissinger. Had the Shah come directly to the United States when he left Iran in January 1979, there probably would have been little or no problem—the Iranians themselves expected this to happen and were surprised when it did not. But, as the ousted monarch continued to roam the world, the US Government was

> **"**
>
> **Hundreds of thousands of Iranians were enraged by the decision to admit the Shah, seeing in him a despot who was anything but an adherent to humanitarian principles.**
>
> **"**

also working to build a productive relationship with the new revolutionary regime. Thus, as a practical working plan, the greater the American distance from the Shah, the better for the new relationship—and vice versa. The Shah's entry into the United States 10 months later, however, quickly unraveled all that had been achieved and rendered impossible all that might have been accomplished in the future.

When the Shah's doctors contacted the US Government on 20 October 1979 and requested that he be admitted immediately into the United States for emergency medical treatment, the President quickly convened a gathering of the National Security Council principals to decide the issue. Only Secretary of State Vance opposed the request; the others either strongly supported it or acquiesced. The CIA was represented by DDCI Frank Carlucci in the absence of DCI Stansfield Turner; it is instructive to note that Carlucci was not asked for CIA's assessment of the situation. The meeting concluded with President Carter, while harboring significant misgivings about letting the Shah in, nonetheless acceding to the majority vote and granting permission for the Shah to enter the United States for

"humanitarian" reasons. The President, familiar with warnings from Bruce Laingen about the danger to the Embassy if the Shah were to be admitted to the United States, asked what the advisers would recommend when the revolutionaries took the Embassy staff hostage. No one responded.

Hundreds of thousands of Iranians were enraged by the decision to admit the Shah, seeing in him a despot who was anything but an adherent to humanitarian principles. They also felt, not for the first time, a strong sense of betrayal by the US President.

Disillusionment

In 1976, Jimmy Carter had campaigned for the presidency on a platform that included a strongly stated position advocating human rights around the world. Friendly or allied nations exhibiting poor adherence to those criteria were not to be excluded from sanctions, one of which was the withholding of US military/security support and related assistance. Many Iranians heard this and took heart, believing that President Carter would cease US support to the Shah's government while also easing, or stopping completely, the abuses taking place in their country.

On 31 December 1977, while the President was making a state visit to Iran, he openly referred to the country as an "island of stability in a sea of turmoil," lauding the Shah for a commitment to democracy. All Iranians were keenly aware of the rioting that had broken out in their cities during the past year. Such disturbances were occurring ever more frequently, accompanied by a mounting death

5

toll at the hands of the Army and the internal security forces.

To many Iranians, this seeming unwillingness of President Carter to accept reality was a bitter sign that he had been dishonest and deceptive in his often-stated desire to promote human rights. Those few spoken words by the President generated an intense disillusionment within the Iranian populace—about which my militant captors frequently talked during the hundreds of hours of harangues, discussions, and debates I was to have with them.

Now the same President who had spoken fervently in support of human rights was letting the Shah into the United States for putatively humanitarian reasons. Again, a sense of betrayal flooded the Iranian people.

There was one notable irony in the decision to bring the Shah into the United States. After the Embassy was seized, President Carter publicly proclaimed that the lives and safety of the Embassy hostages were his first consideration. It was unfortunate that we did not occupy the same position in his hierarchy of priorities on 20 October; instead, the lives and safety of 66 Americans were secondary to the life of a man who was already dying. I have never understood that logic.

It is not accurate to say that the policies of and actions by President Carter and his advisers created the Iranian crisis; they in fact inherited and continued policies put in place by their predecessors. What is clear is that President Carter was not well served by several of his advisers in their unwillingness to face the possibility that the Shah's regime might not last the decade, much less to the end of the century.

> **To the ever-suspicious Iranian radicals, the admission of the Shah for medical treatment was a sham designed to hide a conspiracy aimed at overthrowing their revolutionary government.**

That said, I doubt that the United States would have been able to rejuvenate its relations with Iran even if the Shah had been denied admission to enter the United States. With hindsight, it is easily arguable that, if the militants had not used US admission of the Shah as a pretext to take the Embassy and break relations, some other unacceptable act would have occurred to sever the relationship. The Iranian revolutionary regime continued to engage in state-supported terrorism, murders of exiled dissidents, and attempts to acquire nuclear weapons. The country's new rulers also made an enormous (and at least partially successful) effort to export the revolution to other nations. The United States would not have been able to do business with such a hostile and outlaw government. Refusing the Shah would simply have prolonged what, in retrospect, was inevitable.

Feeding Xenophobia

To the ever-suspicious Iranian radicals, the admission of the Shah for medical treatment was a sham designed to hide a conspiracy aimed at overthrowing their revolutionary government. To add more fuel to the fire, Prime Minister Mehdi Bazargan and Foreign Minister Ibrahim Yazdi (a graduate of a US medical school who had practiced his profession in the United States, and who held a Permanent Resident Alien green card) met briefly with National Security Adviser Brzezinski in Algiers on 1 November 1979, during the celebration of Algeria's independence day. In this meeting, which was not publicized in Algiers, the Shah and the future of US-Iranian relations were discussed. When the radicals in Tehran learned of these talks, they used Radio Tehran to claim that nefarious motives lay behind the meeting.

In the eyes of the radicals, the prime minister and the foreign minister were meeting "secretly" and conspiring with a representative of the US President. The inevitable conclusion was that the United States was again planning to return the Shah to power in Iran. At a protest march in Tehran attended by anywhere from 1 million to 3 million demonstrators, the stage was set for actions against the American Embassy in Tehran and the actors were placed into motion.

Shaky Security

We all knew the Embassy was vulnerable, despite additional physical security measures taken to protect the chancery following the St. Valentine's Day Open House. But the building had not been rendered impervious to assault; rather, the structure had merely been "hardened" to provide protection from gunfire, increase the difficulty of forced entry, and establish an area of (relative) safety where the Embassy staff could hold out until help arrived. With news of the Shah's

6

admittance into the United States, there came a certain realization that it would now be just a matter of days before the Iranians reacted. The only question we had was whether they would repeat the 14 February take-over, with more serious consequences, or renew the terrorist attacks against US officials that had occurred early in the decade. But no new changes were made in the Embassy's security posture.

From all outward appearances, life seemed normal. The Embassy staff was being told that it was safe in Tehran, and employees were being encouraged to bring over their families, including preschool-age children; on the day of the takeover there were several dependent families of Embassy staff at the Frankfurt airport waiting to fly to Tehran.

The chief purveyor of this position was the State Department's office director for Iran, who was visiting the Embassy when the news of the Shah's admittance into the United States was announced to the staff. Bruce Laingen asked the office director to join him on the trip to the MFA to inform the Iranians and to ask for protection for the Embassy, which Foreign Minister Yazdi personally promised.

Unbeknownst to us, however, the same office director had, while in Washington before his trip, written a series of memos discussing in detail the lack of adequate security at the Embassy and the dangers the staff faced if the Shah came into the United States. He said nothing of this to the Embassy staff during his visit, preferring instead to repeat that it was now "perfectly safe" for us to be in Iran. (In a chance encounter with this officer following my return to the United States, I raised the issue.

Somewhat disingenuously, he replied only that he did not think it proper for "those of us in Washington to be second-guessing the assessments of those who are actually on the ground." I let the matter drop.)

One other sign that the State and Defense Departments were buying into the "perfectly safe" assessment was the presence of literally thousands of classified documents in the Embassy. Following the 14 February takeover, many Embassy safes and files had been flown to storage in Frankfurt, including over 30 safe drawers of materials from the Defense Attache Office. By mid-July, however, those files were back in Tehran, in anticipation of better relations with the new government and improved security measures at the Embassy. In addition to the DAO files, the political section had more than 24 safe drawers full of files, and the economic section had roughly the same number. Also on hand were all the personnel files for the Embassy staff of about 70. (The Iranian militants eventually published the documents taken from Embassy safes, along with translations into Farsi. As of around 1990, the Iranians had published more than 65 volumes of these documents.)

The political and economic section files included documents going back to the mid-1950s, useful only in a historical context, if that. These files provided the means to compile a list of all Iranians who had visited the Embassy officially during the past 25 years. As it turned out, "someone" did make a list, creating serious problems for hundreds of Iranians who found themselves accused of espionage and interrogated by militants demanding to know why they had visited the "spy den" two decades previously. When

visiting the DAO or the political offices, I had often seen safes with multiple drawers open. I had been dismayed by the amount of paper remaining in a building so vulnerable to another takeover.

Twice in the summer of 1979, Chargé Laingen had been queried by State as to when and whether the Shah should or could be admitted to the United States. Each time, he replied that this would eventually be feasible, but not before the US Government had fully signaled acceptance of the revolution and not before the Provisional Revolutionary Government had been replaced by a more stable and permanent government. To do otherwise, he warned, would place the Embassy and its staff in serious jeopardy. Neither criteria had been met before the Shah arrived in New York, nor was there any sign that officials in Washington were giving much thought or credence to Laingen's position.

Dubious Policies and Practices

It was only after our release in January 1981 that I came to understand fully why security precautions were ignored and our concerns unheeded. As background, it is useful to remember that the Carter administration, particularly in the person of Dr. Brzezinski, strongly desired to maintain friendly relations and a close military relationship with Iran. For Brzezinski, Iran was the cornerstone of his plan to thwart Soviet expansion in the region; it was also a key nation on which the United States would rely to maintain regional stability. To assist in making this strategic vision a reality, the Carter administration continued the program begun in the Nixon years to expand Iranian military capabilities substantially.

Iran

Iranian militants invade US Embassy, November 1979.

Beginning in the early 1970s with the sale of 72 advanced F-14 Tomcat fighter-interceptor aircraft to the Iranian Air Force, the United States steadily built up the Iranian military. Iran was the only country in the world to which the United States had sold the F-14. In the pipeline by 1979 was about $6 billion worth of military materials, including four technologically advanced Spruance-class destroyers. A side benefit of this largess was Iranian permission for the United States to establish and maintain two sensitive signals intelligence collection sites in the northern part of the country to intercept data link communications of Soviet missile tests.

But hundreds of thousands of Iranians who did not benefit from this official American aid or understand the reasons behind it viewed all this as a greedy, "imperialistic" America working with a greedy, corrupt Iranian Government to steal oil revenues

from the Iranian people to whom the monies truly belonged.

The Shah was the key to Dr. Brzezinski's strategic vision. The monarch had pushed the Iranians into the 20th century, modernizing the country as rapidly as he could spend the money necessary to do so—but not always wisely or productively. He especially kept pressing the United States to provide him with military equipment far too technical and complicated for his own military forces to maintain or use, as well as sufficient quantities of military supplies for him to maintain a standing force much larger than many American officials believed necessary. The Nixon administration acceded to the Shah's demands. In modernizing and enlarging his military, however, the Iranian monarch created a hollow force supplied with the latest in technological equipment but lacking in effective command leadership. He also came to depend heavily on SAVAK, the internal secu-

rity organization, to maintain his oppressive regime.

To ensure that the Shah remained in power, the US Government was required to turn essentially a blind eye to the harsh measures he employed to silence his critics. In an ill-considered policy early in the life of SAVAK, this force had been turned loose against opponents of the regime and against the general populace, even for minor civil infractions. Thus, large segments of the population came to suffer cruelly and often unjustly at SAVAK's hands.

Dr. Brzezinski, moreover, seemed to become unwilling to accept any possibility that the Shah's regime might be at risk from internal pressures that could lead to his overthrow. For Brzezinski's strategy to be successfully implemented, the Shah had to remain in power at least until the 1990s. Finally, in its efforts to please the Shah, the US Government for a

8

number of years had relied on information he provided on the stability of the country and the threat to his regime, eschewing any intelligence collection efforts against internal Iranian political targets.

As the populace became increasingly unhappy with the regime's oppressiveness and corruption and with the deterioration of the economy, resistance to secular authority by Iranian Islamic fundamentalists intensified and open displays of dissidence became more frequent. By 1977, street demonstrations were turning into open rioting, with a growing loss of life.

When the Embassy began reporting these events and citing growing indications that perhaps the Shah's grip was slipping, Dr. Brzezinski, and, by extension the President, became critical of the Embassy's reporting. The incumbent ambassador was replaced with William Sullivan, an experienced Foreign Service Officer (FSO) who had a reputation for dealing effectively with difficult situations. Sullivan's marching orders were to go to Tehran, put a lid on the unwelcome reporting, and get things back on track. But it soon became clear to him that Iran was in serious trouble, and with it the Shah's future. Dr. Brzezinski, meanwhile, seemed to be increasingly disregarding the information coming out of the Embassy because it did not conform to his strategic plans for Iran and the regional role the country was to play. During the summer of 1979, Brzezinski's and State's basic reactions were to listen to Bazargan and to ignore the radicals, even though Laingen—while noting that the situation was becoming calmer—continued to warn of dangers to US personnel.

> ❝
> **I looked out the window and saw young-looking Iranians swarming about the grounds surrounding the chancery.**
> ❞

The Ordeal Begins

Sunday 4 November 1979 was the first day of the normal workweek for the Embassy (in Muslim countries, the weekend consists of Friday—the holy day—and Saturday), and I was in the office by 0730. At about 0845, I heard the first stirrings of a crowd gathering in front of the Embassy for one of the frequent demonstrations we were subjected to, but it was nothing out of the ordinary. I paid it little heed. Absorbed in work, I was unaware of the time when the crowd noise became louder and closer, but it had to have been about 0930. I knew it was a different situation when I heard someone in the center hall call out that "they" were over the fence and into the compound. I looked out the window and saw young-looking Iranians swarming about the grounds surrounding the chancery.

The Embassy sat on a 27-acre compound surrounded by a high brick wall. The predominant structure was the chancery, a long, slender rectangular building with a basement, ground floor, and top floor. On each floor, a central hallway ran the length of the building, with offices opening on each side of the hall (hence, all the offices were directly entered from the hall and overlooked either the front lawn or rear parking lot and athletic field.) The ambassadorial suite was in the center of the top floor on the back

side, opposite the grand staircase rising up from the entrance. It consisted of the outer office occupied by the secretaries and the offices of the (nonexistent) ambassador and deputy chief of mission. Chargé Laingen was using the ambassadorial office.

The security drill required that all American and local employees in the chancery were to move up to the building's second floor. There, we were to be protected by a heavy-gauge steel door at the top of the winding staircase ascending from the main entrance, located in the middle-front of the building. The door was touted to be virtually impossible to breach. Thus protected, we were to sit tight and await the arrival of the Iranian police or military—the protection Foreign Minister Yazdi had promised to Laingen and the office director from Washington.

With the hallway full of local employees, most of us Americans stayed in or near our offices, looking out the windows to see what was transpiring. From the political counselor's office at the back of the chancery, we could see Embassy staffers who worked in the other buildings on the compound—administrative offices, a warehouse, and four bungalows used by TDY visitors—being marched across the compound toward the ambassador's residence, hands tied behind their backs and blindfolded. At about 1030, the Iranians broke into the chancery.

The intruders got in through windows in the basement and moved to the first floor. The personnel section offices were in the basement, and the DAO and economic section offices were on the first floor. In moving to the sanctuary of the top floor, the Embassy staff had to abandon the sensitive files in the DAO and

9

economic sections, and to give up the personnel files showing who was assigned to the Embassy, what our jobs were, and where we lived. All of this occurred without any resistance. At this point, a tear gas canister was accidentally set off in the central hallway upstairs, lending to the confusion and clamor.

When the Iranians first entered the compound, the station chief initiated destruction of the station's files, particularly the highly compartmented materials in the communications vault. After the Iranians came into the chancery itself, I returned to the vault in my office, where an operations support assistant (OSA) was rapidly removing files from our four safes.

Since early summer, when things began returning to normal, the station had been on a "three-month retain" basis. This meant that most cable traffic was destroyed after being read, but basic information necessary for doing our jobs could be retained in skeleton files for three months. An additional proviso was that the materials we did retain were not to exceed what could be destroyed in 30 minutes. The entrance to the station vault, a room about 12 feet by 12 feet with a most impressive-looking bank vault-type door, was in the office I was using temporarily—which created some problems for me later. In the vault was a device, shaped like an oversized barrel, for use in destroying classified material by shredding and then incinerating it. It was slow to work and temperamental in nature, subject to jamming at the least provocation. I went into the vault and began to feed documents into this "disintegrator."

Shutting out the wails of the Embassy locals in the hallway as well as the

> ## "
> ### The Embassy staff had to...give up the personnel files, showing who was assigned to the Embassy, what our jobs were, and where we lived.
> ## "

yells and shouts of the mob outside the door, I continued to feed the disintegrator, assisted by a member of the DAO contingent. Within a few minutes, the device went "ka-chonk" and shut down. Using a small commercial paper shredder, we continued to destroy what we could. As we made progress in our destruction, I noticed the growing pile of shreddings accumulating on the floor— rather than completely destroying each document, the machine cut the papers into strips. Around noon, just as the last of the papers were going through the shredder, someone appeared at the vault and exclaimed that we had to get out.

As I closed the vault door, I was struck by the sight of the large pile of shredded paper on the floor in the center of the vault and by a sign stating that the vault was secure against forced intrusion for 30 minutes. I thought about burning the shreddings, but reasoned—too optimistically—that the door would hold until authorities arrived and dispersed the mob in the next few hours.

Surrender

I left the office and made my way to the outer office of the Chargé's suite. There was a lingering, acrid mix of tear gas and burning wood—the Ira-

nians had tried to set the steel door afire, not realizing the wood was only a veneer. In the Chargé's outer office, a senior political officer was on one phone to State's Operations Center while Chuck Scott, an Army colonel who had replaced General Gast as head of the MAAG, was talking by phone to Chargé Laingen. The Charge had gone to the MFA that morning with one of our two security officers and the political counselor. From what I could gather of the latter conversation, the Chargé was still telling us that we should hang on and that Yazdi was trying to make good on his earlier promises of protection.

This went on for another 15 minutes or so while the Iranians outside the main door by the stairwell were yelling to us and to each other, and trying to force the door. And then one loud American voice was heard over the din: "Open this door right now!" Someone standing close to me yelled back that the Chargé was on the phone and that our instructions were to hold our ground. To which the voice on the other side of the door screamed back in panic, "You tell Laingen I said to open the goddamn door NOW!" I looked at Chuck Scott, telephone in his hand, and wondered if the pained look on his face was a reflection of the one on my own.

Earlier that morning, after the Embassy compound had been overrun, but before the Iranians had gained entry into the chancery itself, the second of our security officers announced that he was going to go out and "reason" with the mob. Having by then seen a number of our colleagues in the outer buildings marched away bound and blindfolded, none of us were surprised when, a few minutes later, we saw him, hands tied behind his back, being escorted to the Embassy's front entrance by several Iranians. It was that same security officer to whom the voice on the other side of the door belonged, now claiming that the Iranians would shoot him if the door was not opened immediately. (In response, one of his colleagues muttered, "Let 'em shoot, but keep the damn door closed.")

Chuck Scott relayed this information over the phone to the Chargé, listened a moment, and then informed us that we were to surrender. The door that would supposedly protect us for days was to be opened after only three hours. The classified material in the political section and MAAG safes on the top floor, the destruction of which the security officer could have been overseeing had he not walked out to certain capture, remained intact for the Iranians to recover. Just before the door opened and the Iranians began swarming about us, Bert Moore, the Administrative Counselor, looked at his watch and remarked, "Let the record show that the Embassy surrendered at 1220."

We were blindfolded and bound and escorted to the Ambassador's residence, where we were freed of the blindfolds only and placed in chairs and on sofas located anywhere on the first floor. We remained that way for the first night, but the next morning we were tied to our chairs and again blindfolded. The earlier arrivals had been taken to the living room and salon, where the chairs and sofas were oversized and plush. The last of us to surrender ended up in the dining room, seated around a long table on uncushioned, straight-backed and

> **66**
>
> **It was inconceivable to us that we could be held prisoner for as long as we had already been by . . . a gang of youths.**
>
> **99**

armless chairs matching the table. We had to endure what were surely the hardest seats in the Eastern Hemisphere, and we sat there for two days and nights.

Our bewilderment as to why we remained captives was worse than the physical discomfort. Once, in the middle of the second day, a helicopter landed and took off from the open area between the residence and the warehouse. Our hope was that some outside mediator had arrived and that our release was imminent. It was inconceivable to us that we could be held prisoner for as long as we had already been by nothing more than a gang of youths.

I overheard my colleagues several times asking the Iranians when we were going to be freed. "When you give back Shah," was the reply, in their fractured English, "when American people force 'the Carter' to give back Shah, then you go home. But not before." I knew that such an act by the US Government was unthinkable, and I began to wonder if the irresistible force had just met an immovable object.

"You Are Wanted In Your Office"

Shortly after dinner during the first night of captivity, a young Iranian

carrying a .38 came into the room calling my name, using pretty good pronunciation. The thought did not occur to me until much later—and was subsequently confirmed—that he had had some prior help from someone who did know the correct pronunciation. "You are wanted in your office," I was informed. I was again bound, blindfolded, and then assisted out of the residence. Considering my true professional affiliation, being singled out by name and separated from the others did not strike me as a positive development. It was a frightening walk through a dark night.

I was walked to the chancery and led into my office with its impressive-looking vault. Still bound and blindfolded, I was placed not ungently against the wall. I heard the escort leave, but, in the silence, I sensed another presence. I reminded myself that it was imperative to act like a genuine State Department Foreign Service Officer would act, and to say those things that a real FSO would say. During the past few hours, and in expectation of such a turn of events, I had given this subject some reflection. I had decided that, if I was interrogated, my actions and words would be guided by two principles. First, I would try to protect classified information; as part of this, I would talk about anything in order to appear as though I had nothing to hide. Second, I would do or say nothing that would or could bring harm to any of my colleagues. The exception to this second "rule" was that I would take advantage of any opportunity to escape, even though it might lead to retaliatory measures against the others.

11

Iran

> ## "
> ### I believe one is duty-bound to resist his captors. Each has to decide, alone, how and to what extent to resist.
> ## "

I had already decided that refusing to talk at all to any interrogators would be about the dumbest thing I could do. First, I did not think bona fide diplomats would clam up in this kind of situation. Silence would not only give off a signal that the interrogatee had been up to something nefarious; it also would run contrary to the personality of most legitimate diplomats, whose business it is to talk to people, to negotiate, and to reason.

The second problem with the "John Wayne I'll-never-say-anything-to-you-bastards" school of interrogation resistance is that it presents a challenge to the interrogators that most likely will not be ignored. While considering whether or to what degree to resist in such a baldly confrontational manner, it is not a bad idea for the prisoner to recognize that his captors hold absolute control over his health and welfare. That does not mean that he should not try to resist, only that there will almost certainly be consequences from doing so. When the prisoner refuses to say anything, acquiring information becomes a secondary objective for the bad guys. Their overriding objective will now be to break the prisoner; they cannot permit his obstinacy to threaten their control.

As was learned from the experiences of the American aviators who were POWs in the Vietnam war, additional problems accrue when a prisoner is finally broken. First, he no longer has the ability to withhold sensitive and secret information. Second, the "breaking" is likely to be both a physical and a mental process, thus rendering it harder for the prisoner to resist in general and harder to escape should the opportunity present

itself—and probably doing permanent damage to his health.

The broken prisoner also will be likely to carry permanent psychological scars, feeling that he is a coward or that he let down his country or comrades, even though he may have suffered terribly and endured the truly unendurable longer than anyone would have reasonably expected. The point is worth a moment's reflection: secrets and lives must be protected, and I believe one is duty-bound to resist his captors. Each has to decide, alone, how and to what extent to resist. In my mind, trying to tough out an interrogation by refusing to talk was not a good idea.

Interrogation

Following a brief silence, probably intended to intimidate me, an unseen interrogator began to speak. I remained standing against the wall for what I believe was several hours while this first interrogation ran on and on. My questioner spoke good English in a deep but surprisingly soft voice that he never raised, despite his growing frustration with me.

I was confused at first by the direction of the questioning, but it soon became clear that because of my large office, executive-style furniture, and especially the vault, the Iranians had

assumed that I was a senior official, someone who really mattered. They even went so far as to postulate that I was the "real" chief of the Embassy while the Chargé was merely a figurehead. As a GS-11 who was so new to the Agency that I would still get lost in the Headquarters building, this construct left me speechless for a moment.

As "proof" of Iranian conclusions about the scope of my work, the interrogator noted that the Chargé had only a small, two-drawer safe in his office while I had an entire vault. This suspicion was fed by the Iranians' penchant for conspiracy and their pervasive belief that the CIA controls the State Department (if not the whole US Government). Regardless of how ludicrous the Iranian accusation was, I still had to deal with it.

To the Iranians, it made perfect sense to have the CIA secretly running the Embassy in what they would consider the most important country in the Eastern Hemisphere. How, the interrogator continued, could I be only a junior officer when no other junior officer had such large office or a "personal vault"? Moreover, the real junior officers were all in their early- to mid-twenties, while I was clearly much older. So, he asked, why was I trying to deny the obvious? Why didn't I just tell them about all the spy operations I was running in their country? And would I mind opening the vault, too?

From my side, the discussion centered around explaining why I really was just a junior officer; why I had worked for the State Department for only three months; how I had completed graduate studies in January 1979 and then worked for a civilian

12

> ## "
> **Every time [the interrogator] raised the idea that I was the true head of the Embassy, I would laugh and remark what a preposterous idea that was.**
>
> ## "

"company" before joining State; and why I was only temporarily in that particular office. I tried to explain why I could not possibly have the combination to the vault and why I was not sure who did. My interrogator kept pushing on this subject, and I finally said that there was one guy who would come in and open the vault, but I maintained that I did not know him and that he was in the United States on R&R. I told the interrogator that, having recently arrived in Iran, I did not know many people at the Embassy.

I stayed with this story, which was not hard to do because much of it was true. But the interrogator returned repeatedly to the vault. It was evident that the vault would continue to be a problem until we were released or the Iranians opened it by force. During this interrogation session, I was directly threatened only a few times. More often, it was a subtle sort of warning, such as reminders of firing squads and SAVAK torture rooms. Also, the interrogator occasionally would work the action of an automatic pistol and pull the trigger, but I always could hear him playing with the weapon, so its sounds never came so suddenly as to make me flinch.

I concentrated on staying outwardly calm, answering his questions in as normal a tone of voice as I could muster. I emphasized that this was a breach of diplomatic practice, that I should immediately be returned to my colleagues, and that we should all be released forthwith. Every time he raised the idea that I was the true head of the Embassy, I would laugh and remark what a preposterous idea that was. Interestingly, the interrogator never became angry in return; he would just repeat his "evidence" and

continue. While I really did have trouble at that moment comprehending that the Iranians would actually believe something so farfetched, it did not take long before I learned enough about our captors' perspective to realize that they genuinely believed things that were much more absurd. This realization began to sink in later, when they started accusing me of being the head of all CIA operations in the Middle East.

In more than 100 hours of hostile interrogation, this particular man was the only interrogator I never saw. I also believe that he may have been someone who was accustomed to, possibly trained in, interrogation techniques. He certainly exercised abundant self-control and seemed at ease in this environment. That he was not harsher may have been due to the Iranians themselves thinking that the situation would be over soon, and thus they did not need to press hard for answers. Later, it would come out that the Iranians took the Embassy initially intending to hold us captive only for as long as it took the US Government to break diplomatic relations. The ultimate length of the hostage crisis surprised virtually all the participants, Iranian and American alike. Having unlimited opportunity to conduct interrogations of Embassy personnel was probably not an ele-

ment they considered in their initial planning. This bears some explaining.

In February 1979, to the chagrin of many Iranians, the Carter administration had elected to continue with a business-as-usual attitude following the St. Valentine's Day Open House rather than breaking diplomatic relations. Thus, in summer 1979, seeing the US Embassy staff grow steadily in size and the secular-oriented government of Prime Minister Bazargan move toward normalization of relations, militant Iranians had begun envisioning another takeover of the Embassy. This time, the militants would hold the Embassy staff captive for as long as it took for the United States to break relations. This was the only action, they believed, that could foreclose any opportunity for future US interference in their revolution. Always suspicious of US motives and sincerity, Iranians during this period were constantly looking for signs of US intentions to repeat the coup of 1953. These signs appeared with the admittance of the Shah to the United States and with the meeting in Algiers between Brzezinski and Bazargan.

The Vault

After what seemed like all night but probably was only a few hours, the interrogator left. I was moved by the student guards into the OSA's office, and my blindfold was removed. I found myself surrounded by a group of about a dozen Iranians, the oldest of whom could not have been more than 20. I was not pleased to see several youths who looked to be 15 or 16 waving Uzi assault weapons. The oldest looking, who was armed with a .38, which I suspected had not too

13

> 66
> ## I was not pleased to see several youths who looked to be 15 or 16 waving Uzi assault weapons.
> 99

many hours before been part of the Marine Security Guard weaponry, was also the leader. In good English and making a sweeping gesture about the room, he ordered me to open the vault. I replied that I could not.

We went back and forth on this for some time, with the atmosphere becoming increasingly hostile. The Iranian finally said, "All right, so you can't do it. Now tell me who used this office." I replied that it was just a secretary, to minimize her importance to the Iranians, and said that I had never seen her go near the vault, much less open it—as I had earlier told the interrogator numerous times. But this young Iranian looked right in my eyes and ordered the two youths standing beside him to "find the girl and bring her here." I had been afraid this might happen.

A number of things ran through my mind at that point. One determinant for me, in those days before "political correctness," was my belief that I was paid to take responsibility and risks but that secretaries and OSAs were not. I had no idea of the methods they might use with the OSA to get her to open the vault, nor did I know what would happen to her afterward if she did open it. I was aware that prospects for my immediate future would not be particularly brilliant if I now opened the vault after denying vigorously for some hours that I could not.

One probability was that the Iranians would be much less inclined to believe anything I said in future interrogations, thus making it harder to protect that which had to be protected. But that also assumed the Iranians were in fact believing what I had been telling them up to that

point. If not, then I was already in deep trouble. At the time I had no way of judging how effective my dissembling had been. Months later, however, I discovered that the Iranians had learned, with some assistance, that I was CIA within a few hours of surrender; in the end, it did not really matter what I had told them earlier. When they asked for the OSA's name, I told them to leave the woman alone, that she could not open the vault. I then said that because the guy who worked in the vault had left me the combination in case of emergency, I really could open it. And I did.

As the door opened I could not keep from laughing at the Iranians' reactions to what they saw inside. Or, rather, what they did not see. From the surrender to that moment, they had believed there were one or more persons actually inside the vault. This notion was based on two factors. First, the staff members in the communications vault at the other end of the hallway were among the last to surrender, if not the last. So it was not necessarily illogical for the Iranians to assume there were people inside this vault as well. Second, and supporting the first factor, was a steady, clearly audible clicking noise coming from inside the vault, a sound like that of a typewriter. I had told the interrogator earlier that the sound was the alarm, which had not been set properly—which was exactly the case. But, given the earlier discovery of Embassy staff in the

communications vault, there was no way this Iranian was going to believe that the vault was empty.

When the door swung open to reveal the worthless disintegrator, four empty safes, and a pile of shredded paper, but no humans, the Iranians who had crowded around the door did classic movie-quality double-takes, looking back and forth at each other, at me, and at the emptiness of the vault, as though they had just witnessed Houdini pull off the greatest escape trick of his life. I laughed aloud. All the while, the alarm box inside the vault was still emitting its typewriter sounds. And then the Iranians got angry.

I was barraged with shouted questions: who had been in the vault, what had happened to them, who had shredded the paper, and where was the stuff from the safes? I just shrugged. I was led to the chair behind the OSA's desk and, to my great surprise, left to sit unbound and with no blindfold.

I was then witness to a steady stream of Iranians who came to gaze into the vault and then leave. When this parade finally waned, and with no more "adults" around to supervise, the dozen young Iranians who had watched the opening of the vault and then vanished—reappeared. They seemed to take up where they had earlier left off, yelling and waving Uzis, pistols, and one USMC-issue riot gun. I was propelled out of the chair and shoved up against the wall by the door opening to the center corridor, next to a four-drawer safe. The Iranians now insisted that I open this safe, too.

But I did not know the combination, nor did anyone else in the station.

14

Iranian demonstrators burn American Flag on wall of US Embassy shortly after takeover by militants in November 1979.

AP/WIDE WORLD PHOTOS©

When I had first arrived, I asked the OSA about the safe, and she told me that it was thought to be empty, but no one really knew because the com-

bination had been lost. So it just stood in her office, serving as a stand for a house plant.

The more I denied knowing the combination, the angrier the Iranians became, until I found myself looking down at the muzzle of an Uzi about

15

Iran

> ❝
> **I was politely
> threatened with
> summary execution a
> couple of times . . .**
> ❞

two inches away from my navel. It was being held by a kid who had probably never before held such a weapon. It became even scarier when I noticed that the weapon's safety was off. With all the jostling and shoving, I thought there was a good chance I could end up, perhaps unintentionally, with some extra navels about nine millimeters in diameter. Suddenly, the commotion stopped, and I found myself out of energy, patience, and adrenaline, and I became very tired.

When I was told that, if I did not give them the combination, I would be shot at once, I told them to go ahead because there was no way I could open the safe. By then, I was so exhausted that I did not care. The Iranians appeared nonplussed, and the apparent leader said that they were going to have to ask the secretary to open the safe. Then I was led back to the ambassador's residence and the hard chair.

During the next two months, the Iranians forcibly opened all locked safes, and this safe was one of the last. Yet, that first night, they appeared to be so anxious to get into it that some of them were willing to kill me. Why this safe seemingly lost its priority status is beyond me. When it was finally forced open, it was indeed empty.

Solitary

During the third day, most of us were moved to the basement of the Embassy warehouse (quickly dubbed the Mushroom Inn by its inhabitants, for its lack of windows), and some were moved out of the Embassy compound altogether. I spent two more days as a guest in the Inn, with

about 40 of the Embassy staff, and then I was moved into one of the four TDY (temporary-duty visitors') bungalows with eight others, mostly members of the Marine Security Guard. We were no longer blindfolded, but our hands were continually bound, usually by strips of cloth. On occasion, and just for the hell of it, the Iranians would come in with handcuffs and take delight in using them. There was no reason for this, but it did underscore that we were essentially defenseless.

I stayed in the bungalow for eight days and nights. During that time I was taken back up to my office for one additional interrogation, which was similar to that of the first night. I was placed against a wall, blindfolded, and questioned by the same interrogator. I maintained my cover story, and this man, to my surprise, never pressed. I was politely threatened with summary execution a couple of times, but I did not take it seriously because the interrogator made it sound pro forma.

What was threatening were the huge crowds that gathered almost nightly outside the Embassy compound walls, frequently being driven to near-hysteria by the speakers. I think we were all afraid that the mobs, whipped into a frenzy, would break into the compound and slaughter the lot of us.

On the night of 22 November, I was taken back into the chancery and

placed in the COS's former office, which was now vacant save for a desk, a chair, and a foam-rubber pallet on the floor. The room, at the front of the chancery and overlooking the wide boulevard in front of the Embassy, was sufficiently close to the street to make the collective roar of several hundred thousand demonstrators a frightening experience for the first several nights it happened, and unsettling thereafter.

I was to be held alone in the chancery until the night of 24 April 1980, when we were moved out in the aftermath of the tragic events of Desert One—the attempt by US military forces to rescue us. In the meantime, I was moved to five other rooms in the chancery at varying intervals. The worst times were the six interrogation sessions I endured from 29 November to 13-14 December 1979. These sessions each began sometime after dinner and continued through the night until daybreak. My principal interrogator was Hossein Sheik-ol-eslam, a mid-thirties "student" who had previously studied at the University of California-Berkeley. (In the years since, Hossein has served as a deputy foreign minister and has played a major role in Iranian-sponsored terrorism.)

The first two of these interrogation sessions, and most of the third, were long recitations of my cover story and denials of any activity beyond normal diplomatic work. While frustrating and not a little frightening, these particular sessions did give me a chance to learn more about the students and why they took the Embassy, as well as to gauge the expertise of Hossein and two other Iranians as interrogators. On one level, the sessions were total-immersion lessons in the workings of the

16

> **"**
> **What the Iranians did not know was that, thanks to my years in the US Marine Corps, I knew much more about interrogation than they did. And that was the key to withstanding their efforts.**
> **"**

"Iranian mind" and the Iranian brand of revolutionary theory; in a detached, academic sense, I was highly intrigued and curious. I chafed over the confinement, even while (for the first three months or so) being held in thrall of my own psychological denial that such a thing was happening. But when I could mentally take myself out of the immediate circumstances, I often found the hours and hours of nonhostile discussions and conversations with the Iranians (interrogators and guards alike) to be interesting, occasionally useful, and not infrequently a source of true amazement. And it killed time.

In gauging the abilities of Hossein and friends as interrogators, I quickly came to realize that they had no training or experience as such, nor did they comprehend any of the underlying psychological factors used by professional interrogators. While these students all claimed to have been arrested and interrogated by SAVAK at one time or another, being victims of interrogation did not mean that they learned how to interrogate. What they did, at least in my case, was only an emulation of the surroundings and trappings of their interrogations by SAVAK (that is, times of day/night, room lighting, the good cop-bad cop routine, and so forth). But having an idea of what to do while not understanding the psychology of why it is done served to make them ineffectual questioners. As such, they often undermined their own progress and left me openings in which I could damage or deter their efforts.

This ineptitude enabled me to withhold successfully large amounts of classified information. It also allowed me to have the upper hand on occasion, when I was able temporarily to

manipulate or disrupt the proceedings. Instances such as these, while seemingly of little import, provided me with tremendous psychological victories when I most needed them. What the Iranians did not know was that, thanks to my years in the US Marine Corps, I knew much more about interrogation than they did. And that was the key to withstanding their efforts.

One Lucky Guy

Actually, it was military service combined with an excellent graduate education that enabled me to get through intensive interrogation sessions and to survive captivity in general and return to the United States in better psychological condition than many of my colleagues (despite having arguably been treated worse than anyone else, except the COS). There were several elements at play. First, as a Marine aviator in the early 1970s, my fighter/attack squadron had been deployed to Vietnam with a Navy carrier air wing. Before that deployment, in the process of earning my wings and then going through fleet training in the F-4, I had had two courses on survival in captivity, one ending with a stay in a

mock POW camp. In these courses, we learned the theory of interrogation and ways to resist interrogation techniques. While on the carrier in transit from Norfolk to Vietnam, we had another several days of survival in captivity, taught by a former POW from the Korean war and by Doug Hegdahl, a former Navy enlisted man who had been held in the "Hanoi Hilton." I never forgot these instructors, and seven years later I could recall their lectures, especially Hegdahl's, word for word with almost crystalline clarity.

The second element was that I was used to living routinely with a level of activity that most people would agree constitutes stress. I attended military school for high school; went through Marine Corps boot camp; trained and served as an air traffic controller; attended Officer Candidate School and took flight training; and subsequently flew F-4 combat missions over North Vietnam, South Vietnam, and Laos. After leaving the service, I earned a B.A. in two years and a Ph.D. in three-and-a-half years, and then entered the Agency's Career Training program. To me, life was fun, challenging, interesting, and occasionally exciting—but I never thought of it as stressful.

At the time of my captivity, I had already been shot at and had come close to death or serious injury several times. I was often as scared as anyone else in the Embassy, but the one important difference was that I had had experiences in dealing with fear created by different kinds of dangers and pressures, while almost all of my nonmilitary colleagues had not. Among the military officers captured in the Embassy were a number who had seen service in Vietnam, some as

17

> ## "
> **Both of the assistant interrogators had emotional buttons which, when pushed, would quickly turn a structured interrogation into a shambles of shouting and insults.**
> ## "

aviators. They had backgrounds similar to mine, and they too survived the experience in much better form than those without military experience.

Third, I had recently finished my graduate degree, and my mind was sharper than it ever had been before captivity (or since, for that matter). I had limitless mental nooks and crannies into which I could retreat to find stimulation, entertainment, comfort, and distance. Thus, mentally surviving solitary was in some ways not as difficult as it could have been.

Because of these life experiences, I could not have been better prepared to deal with the rigors, fears, and uncertainties of captivity. It was nothing that I deliberately planned for or trained to accomplish. Rather, it was only by great good luck that I had a background which allowed me to survive mentally and physically.

Uncovered

Toward the end of an interrogation during the night of 5-6 December, my cover went up in smoke. As with the session the night before, I adhered to my cover story while seizing or creating opportunities to digress into areas that had nothing to do with my real assignment in Tehran. My working theory—which was the opposite of the "name, rank, and serial number only" dicta of military service—was that the more time we spent talking about neutral or irrelevant subjects, the less time they had to talk about things which I hoped to avoid. I had discovered earlier that asking questions about the Shia brand of Islam, the Koran, the Iranian revolution, and why they continued holding us would often

generate long discussions with Hossein and his two cohorts, as well as occasional tidbits of news of outside events. So, I took every occasion to delve into these areas.

I also learned that both of the assistant interrogators had emotional buttons which, when pushed, would quickly turn a structured interrogation into a shambles of shouting and insults. For example, one assistant was a man, probably in his late twenties, who liked to brag about having spent a couple of years in Florida as a student. He also was highly sensitive about being viewed as a devout Muslim. I found that looking in his direction and asking if he had enjoyed doing unnatural acts with young girls on Florida beaches, or if he enjoyed drinking and gambling in beach-front bars, would make him go almost blind with instantaneous rage. By the time Hossein could get him calmed down and the interrogation back on track, at least 15 minutes or more would have passed and the subject being pursued just before the outburst would have been forgotten.

This tactic also undermined any progress the interrogators had made toward establishing a psychological mood that they could ultimately

exploit. I could not use this technique too frequently, but it generally worked exceedingly well. Usually, there was a physical price to pay for this because it often entailed insulting one of the interrogators. The penalty was never unbearable, however, and the ensuing disruption was always worth it.

I had also learned that I could ask for tea or fruit juice and that the Iranians would actually stop, bring in the refreshments, and for 15 minutes or so, we would sit around and chat like next-door neighbors. When the cups were empty, Hossein would say, "OK, back to work," and the questioning would resume. The level of intensity that had developed during the interrogations before the break was destroyed, leaving the interrogators to begin anew in their efforts to create a psychologically productive mood. These little time-outs were among a number of episodes that always seemed surrealistic. I never did understand why Hossein permitted me to control the sessions to such a degree; he obviously did not comprehend the effects of the interruptions.

On the night of 1-2 December 1979, we had gone on at length and, sometime well after midnight, I was becoming complacent and tired. I had successfully, it seemed, kept to my cover story while instigating or capitalizing on a half-dozen or so digressions of some length. To my mind, I was outwitting the interrogators, and I was smugly satisfied. Returning to the subject of my general duties (yet again!) after an interlude for tea, Hossein asked if I still denied I was CIA. When I responded yes, Hossein handed me a sheet of paper, and my heart seemed to stop dead in midbeat. In that moment, I thought my life was over.

> ## 66
> **I learned that I could ask for tea or fruit juice, and the Iranians would actually stop [the interrogation], bring in the refreshments, and for 15 minutes or so we would sit around and chat like next-door neighbors.**
> ## 99

The sheet of paper was a cable sent through special diplomatic channels that are used for certain sensitive matters. And the subject of this message was me! I could not believe what I was reading. The cable gave my true name and stated clearly that I was to be assigned to the station in Tehran. It also mentioned the special program under which I had come into the Agency 10 months previously. When I looked up at Hossein and his stooges, they were grinning like a trio of Cheshire cats. My astonishment quickly gave way to fright and despair.

I should note here that copies of the cable hit the world press corps on the morning of 2 December 1979, a few hours after the 1-2 December interrogation session ended. Hossein and a female student, dubbed "Tehran Mary" on American television, held a press conference in the Iranian capital attended by several hundred media people, and passed out copies of the cable to all present. The cable was subsequently reprinted in newspapers the world over. To my dismay, many American newspapers reprinted the cable again on 21 January 1981, immediately after our release.

It somehow got though to my addled mind that I had two options: try the "this is a fake document" accusation, or anything else. It was not clear to me at that precise moment what the "anything else" could be. I knew that the document was real and, more to the point, that it looked identical to other State Department traffic in terms of format, routing lists, appended comments, and so forth. Denying its provenance, which the Iranians were probably expecting, did not seem realistic. With my stunned brain generating no other brilliant ideas, I looked up at the gloating Ira-

nians and said, "OK, so what?" To my surprise, the three interrogators stopped laughing and, for a moment, they looked back and forth at each other, seemingly bemused. It dawned on me that they were not expecting this sort of reaction, and they did not know what to do. But that little respite lasted only a few seconds.

For the next few hours, the Iranians tried to confirm that their suspicions of my activities were correct. They said that I could have been a CIA officer disguised as a Marine for years and that my education was just for cover. They said they knew that I was the head of the CIA's entire Middle East spy network, that I had been planning Khomeini's assassination, and that I had been stirring up the Kurds to revolt against the Tehran government. They accused me of trying to destroy their country. Most of all, my interlocutors told me they did not believe anything I said. The Iranians ranted and screamed at times; I raged and yelled back.

We then engaged in mutual accusations of lying, which let to a semi-coherent digression about whether Iranians were bad Muslims, what the

Koran said, and so forth. Because I had never read the Koran and knew next to nothing about Islam, I wondered later how idiotic I would have sounded to a Muslim in a different situation. By the time the topic shifted from my being an evil person to their being good (or bad) Muslims, we all eventually ran out of steam.

We spent more time than I could fathom on why it was that I did not speak Farsi and was not an Iranian specialist. These Iranians found it inconceivable that the CIA would ever send to such a critical place as Iran someone who was so ignorant of the local culture and language. It was so inconceivable to them that weeks later, when they at last came to realize the truth, they were personally offended. It had been difficult enough for them to accept that the CIA would post an inexperienced officer in their country. But it was beyond insult for that officer not to speak the language or know the customs, culture, and history of their country.

I tried to string out this train of conversation as long as I could. Finally, seeking one more psychological victory, I said that there were many Iran specialists in my government who could come here, but none of them would, so I came instead. This deliberate insult took them aback. The younger Iranian, the one who was so easy to set off, asked why US Government officials who specialized in Iran would be so reluctant to come? Because they are afraid, I responded. Perplexed, he said, "What could they be afraid of?" I held up my bound wrists. "They are afraid of this," I said.

We spent the rest of the night in a calmer atmosphere, with the Iranians making some outlandish accusations, while I tried to refute some of the more reasonable charges with a mixture of the truth, when appropriate, and logic. The bizarre things I could only snort at or otherwise ridicule. Many of their charges were tossed on the table only once or twice, and it soon became possible to discern the ones about which they were really serious.

But there was one point that night that Hossein did make chillingly clear. "This is our country," he declared, looking into my eyes, "and we intend to find all the spies and foreign agents who have been disloyal and who are trying to stop the revolution." Hossein then went a step further without, I believe, realizing what he was saying. He stated emphatically that he did not care about anything I or the CIA had done outside of Iran, while re-emphasizing that he intended to find the spies inside his country.

I mention this because it occasioned some surprise in later interrogations. In three subsequent all-night grillings, Hossein would begin asking questions about my training and the identities of CIA officers elsewhere in the world. Each time he did this, I quickly reminded him of his statement about being interested only in events in Iran. And each time I was flabbergasted when he recalled his words and backed off. By then, I had learned that our captors were so completely untrustworthy, regardless of the issue, that I never expected Hossein to abide by his own words. But he did, much to my great relief. And I confess that I am still astonished by this today.

> ## "
> **During these interrogations, I continued to play the "new guy" card as often and as forcefully as I could, providing logical-sounding (to me) explanations as to why I could not have known or done whatever it was they were asking me about.**
> ## "

Protecting Secrets

There were three more all-night sessions in which Hossein and his comrades pressed hard to learn who I had been in contact with and what these Iranians had told me. In actuality, I had had only one agent who was providing sensitive material, but to the Iranian revolutionary mind simply meeting privately with an American Embassy official, much less a CIA officer, was grounds for severe punishment, including death. There were now a dozen or so Iranians in jeopardy merely because they had a dinner with me or had invited me into their homes. During these interrogations, I continued to play the "new guy" card as often and as forcefully as I could, providing logical-sounding (to me) explanations as to why I could not have known or done whatever it was they were asking me about.

I maintained that it had taken me several weeks after arrival to learn my way around just a part of the city and that, as a new, inexperienced officer, I was an unknown quantity to the station chief in terms of capabilities,

competence, and judgment. Given the serious security situation in Tehran, I told Hossein, this left the chief reluctant to give me any significant responsibilities so soon after arriving. Hence, I had been spending time familiarizing myself with the city and doing only some elementary work at finding possible meeting sites and so forth. I did not vary from this simple story, hoping that it sounded plausible, and that in its consistency it would also be convincing.

Unfortunately, the shredded documents that I had so casually left in the vault returned to make an even bigger liar out of me. The Iranian students had industriously set about reconstructing the shreddings; by early December, they had made sufficient progress to be able to read portions of most of the papers. They would eventually manage to piece back together virtually all of what we had tried to destroy. When Hossein and his pals began to ask me about specific nights or people, I knew with certainty they were no longer fishing for information and, whatever the source(s), were focusing on exact events, the answers to which they already had. When Hossein showed me one of my own cables—strips of paper carefully taped together—about a meeting I had had with a contact, everything became clear.

For the rest of that interrogation and the next two sessions, my goals were to limit the damage and to determine how much other information they had. I refused consistently to give accurate answers to any questions until, in a fit of pique, they would haul out a reconstructed document and show me they knew I was dissembling, and then we would go off again. While in the midst of intense questioning about one Iranian I had

> **The last two interrogations were, I believe, potentially the most dangerous period for me in terms of deliberate physical harm.**

met more than a few times, it became evident that this person had been arrested and interrogated, because Hossein gave out information which only that person could have known. (When I confronted Hossein with this, he did not hesitate to tell me that my surmise was correct; two months later, he told me that this unfortunate person had been executed.) Once I was proven again to be a liar, they would bring up another person or event, and we would go through the whole rigamarole again. And on and on we went, until they got tired of it and began to use physical means of persuasion, as much out of frustration as anything.

The final all-night interrogation, circa 13-14 December, was also the hardest. When I was returned to my room that morning, sore and tired, I was as despondent as I would ever be. The last two interrogations were, I believe, potentially the most dangerous period for me in terms of deliberate physical harm: the Iranians definitely knew I had been trying to recruit and run spies in their country, but they did not know how effective or successful that effort was. At that juncture, they had no reason to believe anything but the worst about my activities. Ironically, it was (I am convinced) the reconstructed documents, the shreddings I had neglected to destroy, that made further interrogation of me a waste of their time.

By mid-December, enough of these shredded cables and documents had been reconstructed to show that I had not done nearly as much as they had suspected. But I had done enough to justify being kept in solitary confinement throughout—as was the station chief. The third case officer, who had arrived in Iran a few days before the

takeover, apparently had not angered the Iranians to any great extent, at least in terms of being a "spy" in their country. He did provoke them frequently by trying to escape, assaulting the guards, and in general causing the Iranians more trouble than they liked. His reward was about 360 days or so in solitary, parceled out during the 15 months of the hostage crisis and based on his deportment. If resistance can be at least partially defined as making it difficult or unpleasant for your captors to hold you against your will, this officer was succeeding admirably. With the reconstruction of the station files, the Iranians had a fairly clear picture of my limited operational activities. After this point, they mostly left me alone and concentrated on the chief, who had no easy out.

The Daily Routine

My routine was to wake sometime after daylight, and then await the usual breakfast of Iranian bread or Afghan barbari bread with butter and jam or feta cheese, and tea. I would then prop my pallet against the wall and take my morning walk, beginning at one corner of the room and striding the eight to 10 paces to the opposite corner, then turning around and heading back. This would continue until I became tired or my feet

grew sore. I would then read until lunch, after which I would repeat the morning agenda until dinner. After dinner, I would again walk and read until I was sufficiently tired to sleep.

During the initial months when we were kept in the Embassy compound, and then later, when we were reunited in the summer of 1980 following our dispersal in the wake of the Desert One rescue attempt, our lunches and dinners consisted of American-style food prepared by Iranian students who were trained by the Chargé's cook. Most meals were adequately nourishing and palatable, with the food coming mainly from local US military commissary stocks seized by militants during the withdrawal of the 10,000 military personnel who had been in Iran as part of the MAAG. Toward the fall of 1980, however, some of the foodstuffs clearly were suffering from old age. Chicken, for example, began to show up in a marginally edible state, and eventually I had to abandon the powdered milk I occasionally received when it reached the point where there were too many worms to pick out.

It required some months before I was able to accept psychologically what was happening to us. It was a classic state of denial. I would go to bed each night thinking that it would all be over the next morning, and, when it did not end, I would have to deal with anger and disappointment until it was evening and I again convinced myself that the following day would bring release. It was months before I was able to accept that the next day would be another day of captivity.

During the first few months, I could not believe this was happening to me. I also could not believe that the American Government was unable to

21

Iran

gain the freedom of an entire Embassy staff held in contravention of international law by a motley band of revolutionary youths. And I could not believe that the President had made the decision he did concerning the Shah, when the potential damage to America's national security and the threats to our safety were manifest. The unanswered humiliation to the dignity and prestige of the United States was more intensely frustrating to me than any other aspect of captivity. I recalled an incident in Nicaragua in 1854, when a US diplomat received a small cut on his nose from a piece of glass thrown at him during a minor incident. In response, and to uphold the honor of the United States, a US Navy vessel shelled the small coastal town in which the incident occurred, completely destroying it. Now, nearly three-score US diplomats were being held by students and nothing seemed able to end the situation, much less restore the lost dignity.

What probably kept many of us from going nuts was a serendipitous supply of excellent books. Just before the Embassy takeover, the entire library of the Tehran-American School had been delivered to the Embassy warehouse for safekeeping. There was a large selection of novels, notably English mysteries, and thousands of nonfiction volumes. From the first days in the Mushroom Inn, the Iranians were good about keeping us supplied with books, although I suspect it had more to do with keeping us occupied (and, hence, less likely to cause trouble) than it was a matter of human kindness.

While in captivity, I read more than 500 books covering a wide range of subjects. I plowed through dozens of books I enjoyed and learned from, many of which I would have never

> ## " What probably kept many of us from going nuts was a serendipitous supply of excellent books. "

otherwise had the opportunity to read. I read most of Dickens's works, and lots of Agatha Christie and Ruth Rendell. I delighted in the adventures of Bertie Wooster and Jeeves. I devoured histories of Russia, Britain, World War I, early 20th-century America, and all of Barbara Tuchman's works up to that time. Some of the most enjoyable books I stumbled across were ones that I would never have even looked at in a normal life.

The Iranians with whom I had contact fit into two categories: the younger men, barely into their twenties (if that), who performed guard work; and the older men, in their thirties, who seemed to call the shots and did the interrogations. It was the younger Iranians who constituted my company for nearly 15 months. Unlike the older Iranians, who had no illusions about why they engineered the taking of the Embassy, the younger ones seemed to believe fervently that the only purpose of the takeover was to coerce the United States into returning the Shah. I never heard any of the young Iranians speak of ending the Iranian-US relationship, as did Hossein and his cohorts, nor frankly did the younger ones seem to want much of anything the older ones did. Virtually none of these youths, who were in fact real students at various universities, had ever traveled outside Iran. For many, the trip to Tehran to attend school was the first time they had ever left their villages. Their knowledge level seemed to be generally the equivalent of the average American ninth grader. But

they were as fanatically devoted to Khomeini as were their older leaders.

Over the months, we all came to know a number of the guards fairly well. Some were with us from Day One to Day 444. Others whom we saw frequently during the early days faded away after the first three or four months. Initially, the Guards were apprehensive of all of us, the first Americans many had ever met, and uncertain what to think because their elders, including the clergy, had clearly painted all of us as evil incarnate. As their contact with us increased, especially after we had been separated into smaller groups, they began to reevaluate their ideas of who and what Americans are. My Embassy colleagues, possessing the same American national characteristics which led many Japanese and Germans to like and respect Americans after World War II, soon were establishing friendly relationships with these young guards.

The Guards

After I was moved into solitary, there were guards in my room(s) 24 hours a day. I never discovered why or for what particular reason, if any, and at first I ignored them. I was angry over being held, angry at being in solitary, angry and frustrated at seeing them turn an American Embassy into graffiti-laden prison. I resented like hell having them in the same room with me, whether they spoke to me or not. I felt no impetus to make conversation, and did not. The Iranians were quiet at first, too. For almost their whole lives they had been told of how the CIA was responsible for many (or even all) of the world's problems, and especially the problems in Iran. And their perspective of the Shah's reign and their knowledge of the

22

Marching a prisoner around the occupied US Embassy in Tehran.

Alain Mingam—GAMMA/LIAISON

CIA-engineered coup in 1953 were certainly less than objective and by no means fully informed. Understandably, they approached me with some wariness, very much unsure about whether I was a real human being or the monstrous bogeyman of their imaginations.

For the first several days I was in solitary, some young Iranian would be sitting at a small desk just inside my door while I walked, read, slept, or ate, completely ignoring my existence, except when I needed to use the bathroom. The guard would then blindfold me, escort me down the hall and back, and resume his post. They would change at approximately two-hour intervals, and I neither bade

them good-bye nor welcomed the next shift.

But human nature has its way, and slowly and tentatively the young Iranians began to talk to me, as much out of curiosity as a desire to make me understand the evil of my ways. Inevitably, their first words spoken to me condemned various offenses, real or imagined, and were laced with quotations from the Koran and Khomeini's sermons. I would grunt back a word or two and go on with whatever I was doing. Soon, however, the guards became more talkative, asking more questions and making fewer accusations, impelled by a desire to convince me that the country I served and the government

I worked for were corrupt and evil. I would toss out a contradictory comment and then, in Socratic fashion, ask them a question intended to get them to justify or expand on their comments or ideas.

It was not long until all but two of my 10 or so guards had become fairly garrulous. From then on, until I no longer had them in the room with me, almost every time the guard changed, the new watcher would come in ready to talk. And so we began to have conversations that ranged from amusing to amazing to surrealistic.

There were a number of common denominators among these young

Iran

men. First and foremost, they were fanatically religious and totally obedient to the wishes (or what they perceived as the wishes) of the clergy, as personified in Khomeini. Literally hundreds of hours of talks with these kids distilled down to one basic tenet: Khomeini was infallible because he was the Imam, and he was the Imam because he was infallible. It was not necessary for any of them to really know firsthand anything about anything, or to be independently convinced of the correctness of any position or action. If Khomeini said it was so, or if he ordered it done, then that was all they needed to know. Not once did I ever hear one discuss anything, whether the subject was religion, human rights, politics, or social responsibilities, in which he felt obliged or even willing to question Khomeini's judgments or to decide facts, opinions, and actions for himself.

My Iranian captors contended that America was responsible for all the evils and wrongs in the world. One of them declared to me that Iran had been America's main enemy for over 400 years! Even after I mentioned that America had actually been a nation for only 203 years and had been populated only by Native Americans less than 300 years before that, I could not sway him.

I learned from these Iranians that America had created plagues and national disasters in its efforts to control the world ("hegemony" was a favorite criticism); that all the West European countries and NATO as an organization were controlled by the United States; that we had decided—apparently just for the hell of it—to beat up on the peace-loving Vietnamese people, creating and then maliciously prolonging our war in Southeast Asia; and that in general

> ## "
> ### These same Iranians who shouted "death to America," who condemned everything American as evil or decadent, and who would have killed us had it been ordered, would nonetheless ask my colleagues for help in obtaining visas to the United States.
> ## "

America had never done anything positive or good for the world. When I pointed out a few of the innumerable "nonpolitical" things Americans had done which benefited the world (the Salk polio vaccine and other medical discoveries), the Iranians would find ulterior motives underlying each accomplishment; world control was one of the all-time favorites, as were greed and profit. Or they would deny that the achievement was useful, or say they had not heard of it, in which case it could not be really important or true. I asked one premed student to compare the number of American Nobel prize winners to the number of Iranian Nobelists, and the student replied that America always fixed the voting so that no Iranian could win; it was just part of our war against Iran.

Most of my captors stubbornly asserted that they were always right and that everyone else was always wrong. If they broke any law, it was because they had a justification for doing so. One student related the story of how he had been in a car accident because, at 0200, he had run

a red light, and another car, which had the green, hit him broadside. Perfectly seriously, he said that the little traffic at that hour made it OK for him to ignore traffic signals (no point in waiting at a red light when no one is coming from the other side) and that it was the other driver who was at fault because he should have known someone might be running red lights and therefore should have been driving slowly while looking out for other drivers like him.

The corollary to never being wrong was that nothing was ever their fault. In the midst of our captivity, more than one of the guards complained to me that holding us hostage was ruining their lives: they could not go to school, they were not spending time with their families, they were not able to go home to their villages. In short, it was their lives which were on hold. And it was all our fault because we were there. The obvious solution of putting us on a plane and sending us home made no impression.

These same Iranians who shouted "death to America," who condemned everything American as evil or decadent, and who would have killed us had it been ordered, would nonetheless ask my colleagues for help in obtaining visas to the United States, and then could not understand why they were laughed at. If the reader by now suspects, too, that these Iranians, at least, seemed to have difficulty with the concept of cause and effect, he or she would be dead on.

The Education of Tehran Mary

In my discussions and debates with my Iranian captors, I was frequently numbed by their lack of knowledge about the world and about critical events which, they claimed, "proved" how right they were. I have never forgotten a conversation I overheard between Tehran Mary and Air Force Col. Tom Schaefer, the Embassy's Defense Attaché. For much of February and into March of 1980, Tom and I were kept in small adjoining rooms in the basement of the Embassy, for which there was a common air vent. By remaining still, I could often hear what was being said in Tom's little corner of paradise.

One day an unknown (to me) female voice—I had no idea who Tehran Mary was, until I came home—started berating Tom for the US decision to drop the atomic bomb on Japan, calling it barbaric, inhumane, and racist. Tom replied, "The Japanese started the war, and we ended it." That was obviously news to Mary, who asked in disbelief, "What do you mean, the Japanese started the war?" And Tom replied, "The Japanese bombed Pearl Harbor, and so we bombed Hiroshima." "Pearl Harbor? Where's Pearl Harbor?" asked Mary. "Hawaii," said Tom. A long pause occurred, and then, in a small voice pregnant with incredulity, Mary said, "The Japanese bombed Hawaii?" "Yep," stated Tom, "they started it, and we ended it." Mary's sense of astonishment was easily discernible, even through the wall. After another long pause, I heard her rush out of Tom's room. ("Mary" is now one of several vice-presidents in the government of President Mohammad Khatami.)

Small Victories

Even though conversations with the guards began to fill some of the solitary hours, I was still not happy with

> ❝
> ## I came to understand that, should they actually put us on trial, they would probably execute several of us and give the others long prison sentences.
> ❞

them being in the room at all hours. And so I undertook a covert action campaign to get them out. One lesson I remembered from Doug Hegdahl's talks on survival in captivity was that it is vitally important to resist your captors in whatever way you can; to make it difficult or uncomfortable for them to hold you; and to make them pay some sort of price, however small, for denying you your freedom.

One small way I tried to make it harder on selected Iranian guards was to make their time in my room as unpleasant as I could. Doing things like breaking wind as I walked by their desk, belching after meals, and wearing only skivvies (that "public" state of undress being offensive to the Muslim religion) were steps toward this end. When I had a cold, I made sure to breathe hard in their direction as I passed by the desk. And, when I heard a few days later a guard complaining that he was having to do double duty because a couple of his colleagues, who had previously stood watch in my room, had been taken ill with bad colds, I felt one of those psychological boosts that comes from those little victories that keep you going. Soon afterward, around New Year's Day of 1980, I was moved to a room on the ground floor in the back of the chancery, and from then on I lived without guards inside the room. It was a truly solitary existence, although the guards

would still drop in for conversations from time to time.

One threat Hossein would occasionally toss out was that of placing me on trial as a spy. It struck me that this was no idle threat. The Iranians were obviously feeling a need to convince the rest of the world that they were justified in holding American diplomatic personnel captive and in demanding redress from the United States. I figured that the COS, myself, and any of the five or six military officers were prime candidates for the defendants' dock, inasmuch as we were the ones being singled out for harsher treatment. I had memories of the *Life* magazine photos of Francis Gary Powers' show trial in Moscow, and it was not something I wanted to experience firsthand. Moreover, as time went by and I learned more about the Iranians, their revolution, and their goals, I came to understand that, should they actually put us on trial, they would probably execute several of us and give the others long prison sentences.

There was also much talk of adding "war crimes" to the indictments for those of us who had fought in Vietnam. To bring this home, the Iranians taped to my wall a propaganda poster showing several American soldiers grinning and holding the severed heads of two Vietnamese. I used the poster as part of my own propaganda war: when new guards came into my room I would walk to the poster, put my finger on one of the severed heads, and point out that when Americans went to war, they were serious about their business—and one *casus belli* might be something like the capture and incarceration of American diplomats. The poster was soon removed.

The exceptionally supportive mood of many if not most Iranians toward the Embassy takeover, together with the zealots' desire to tighten their grip on the reins of government, elevated the possibility of trial (and execution). One discomfiting experience in having a room in the front of the Embassy was that I could hear clearly the din of the huge crowds that would gather in front of the compound on Fridays. I learned later that some of these gatherings had more than 500,000 Iranians in attendance, and I was always worried that some speaker would whip the crowd into a frenzy, culminating in a storming of the Embassy by a mob bent on lynching the vile Americans. Hence, were we to be put on trial, the revolutionary government probably would feel compelled to execute at least a couple of us, if for no other reason than internal credibility. That prospect concentrated the mind exquisitely.

But after the first of the year in 1980, talk of a trial receded. The last time I heard it mentioned was on George Washington's birthday (I kept a homemade calendar in the back of a book I managed to retain for almost the entire time). Hossein had come to my room for one of his increasingly infrequent visits and, in the midst of our chat, tossed out the threat of a trial. By that time, even he seemed to find it difficult to take seriously. The Iranian Government, however, continued to threaten in the world media to convoke public "spy" trials through the fall of 1980, apparently as part of its propaganda war.

Life Improves

Roughly coincident with the apparent end of the threats to put us on trial was a welcome, albeit limited,

> ❝
> **I was always worried that some speaker would whip the crowd into a frenzy, culminating in a storming of the Embassy by a mob bent on lynching the vile Americans.**
> ❞

improvement in our treatment. For me, this included a shower every week or 10 days instead of the usual two weeks; several short periods actually outdoors just to enjoy the sun; and visitations to the library—the economic counselor's former office that now housed the books from the Tehran American School. I was given pen and paper for the first time, and I began to draw whenever I did not feel like reading.

I was also told I could write home, and from then on I wrote three letters a week to my mother. Midway through our captivity, however, I learned that the Iranians had never mailed any of my letters. In fact, I later learned that I had not been heard of, or from, since Christmas 1979, when I was allowed to send a couple of cards in mid-December. When the press irresponsibly reported that some hostages had been able to spirit out "secret messages" in those cards, the Iranians assumed I was one of the culprits and my mail privileges were ended. I believe in freedom of the press, but this was one occasion in which it would have been helpful if the press had acted with some self-imposed restraint.

Nor was I ever filmed with visiting clergy like the others were, so my well-being and even my continued

existence remained a mystery to my family, friends, and colleagues from December 1979 until the Algerian Ambassador paid me a visit the night of 23 December 1980. In the end, keeping me in solitary and putting my family through the agony of not knowing was nothing more than an attempt by the Iranians to punish the CIA, as an organization, for all the "bad" things that had happened to and in Iran since the 1953 coup. Because these students could not get their hands on any of the CIA personnel who had served there earlier to punish them, my COS and I served as their surrogates. It was that simple.

There were, I believe, several factors that combined to ameliorate our conditions, none of which I knew about until after we were released, plus one element that I learned of only in 1985. These factors were basically the Iranians' realization that it was the American people, as much as it was the White House, who posed a serious threat to them; a back-channel message from President Carter to the Iranians warning of dire consequences should we be put on trial; and the increasing and unwitting involvement of the 52 of us in Iranian domestic politics.

First, regarding the fear the Iranians came to have of the American people, it will be surprising to many in the US that our captors fervently believed all Americans would support their seizure of the Embassy. Many of the younger and more naive students believed the American people might even begin a revolution in the United States. The older ones merely expected that the support of the American populace would become strong and influential enough to induce the Carter administration to give in to Iranian demands, which in reality had little or nothing to do with the return of the Shah.

The reason for this belief was simple: most Iranians had no concept of a "people's government" in the sense of the populace having any influence over or participation in their governance. To a majority of them, there was an unbridgeable chasm between government and the people. One common characteristic among many Iranians is ethnocentricity, a belief that every other society in the world mirrors theirs— a state of mind that was amplified by our captors' lack of life experiences and limited education; nor were they encouraged by their religion to look beyond their own ken. In this instance, the Iranians seemed to me truly to believe that the American people were as alienated from the US Government as the Iranian people had been from their government.

Thus our captors were at first perplexed and then greatly disappointed when the American public condemned their taking of the Embassy. And this held true even for Hossein and his peers, who were older and better educated and had lived or traveled in the United States for some period of time. The Iranians did not understand why there was so much antagonism and hatred shown by the American people over our captivity and why Americans were rallying behind President Carter. One night in early December 1979, Hossein admitted to me that the reaction of the American on the street was the opposite of what the militants had fully expected, and he added that obviously the United States Government, through the exercise of an enormous (and improbably successful) censorship program, had prevented the "truth" from reaching

> ❝
> **[Our captors] came to realize that the one thing that would almost certainly compel the White House to abandon its self-imposed restraint would be if any of us were harmed, for any reason.**
> ❞

the American populace. The solution to that problem was a public relations campaign by the militants.

After I returned home and was able to read press accounts of our captivity, it became clear that the Iranians had indeed tried such a campaign. The starting point was probably the distribution to the world press of the special-channel message in early December 1979 (see section above entitled "Uncovered"), followed by a number of appearances by Tehran Mary in the media throughout that period. The culmination of this effort was the "Crimes of America" conference held in Tehran in June 1980. The Iranians induced several US citizens, notably former Attorney General Ramsey Clark, to come to Tehran and criticize American policies.

By January or early February 1980, it seemed to have finally sunk into the minds of our captors that nothing they could say to or produce for the media was going to generate any surge of sympathy (much less support) in the United States for the militants' actions. And with it came a realization that they had much more to fear from the American public than they did from the White House. They had

assumed from the beginning that it was the American people's affection for Iranians and support for the takeover that kept the White House from responding militarily. It was truly a shock to their collective ego finally to accept that the depth and intensity of dislike with which most Americans viewed Iran was genuine. They came to realize that the one thing that would almost certainly compel the White House to abandon its self-imposed restraint would be if any of us were harmed, for any reason. And this realization at least partially translated into better treatment for us and, probably to a lesser degree, the end to threats of a trial.

The second development that benefited us was a back-channel message from President Carter to the Iranian leadership, via the good offices of the Swiss Government (representing US interests in Tehran), which warned the Iranians of exceptionally serious consequences if any of us were placed on trial for any reason. To this day, I do not know the contents of that message, but it had to have been very credible and truly frightening. The Iranians had, from the beginning, been openly scornful and contemptuous of the Carter administration— feelings that were formed beginning with the New Year's Eve toast to the Shah in 1977. When no US military action was taken against Iran in the aftermath of the earlier Embassy takeover in February 1979, Iranians began to view the administration as weak and cowardly— beliefs that only deepened and hardened after we were captured. They had no fear whatsoever of US military action. That evidently changed, though, with the receipt of the President's back-channel message. While the Iranians might have talked openly about trials for propaganda purposes, by mid-

27

February 1980 this no longer appeared to be a viable threat.

The third element that affected the conditions (and duration) of our captivity was our increasing utility to each side in the Iranian domestic political struggle between the "moderates" under Iranian President Abdulhassan Bani-Sadr (elected with Khomeini's approval in February 1980) and the hardcore "radical" Islamic fundamentalists. In essence, whoever controlled the hostages controlled the Iranian Government. By spring 1980, the only Iranians who were talking about returning the Shah were the young guards, who kept hoping; the older Iranians, such as Hossein, now a rare visitor, quit discussing why we continued to be held. One point all the Iranians repeatedly made was that they were going to make sure President Carter was not re-elected, as "punishment" for his "crimes."

Departing the Embassy

From February to almost the end of April 1980, life was the same, day in and day out. There were no more interrogations, no more guards in my room, and few "drop-in" visits by Hossein or any of the older students. The monotony was broken only by an occasional trip to a shower in some other building and, on a good day, maybe 10 minutes outside in the sun. I was moved to five different rooms in the chancery during this period, never being told either that a move was coming or the reason why.

Easter Sunday passed quietly, but long after midnight that night I was awakened and taken upstairs to meet Archbishop Hilarion Capucci, the

> "[Another] element that affected the conditions (and duration) of our captivity was our increasing utility to each side in the Iranian domestic political struggle...."

former Archbishop of Jerusalem, who had once been imprisoned by the Israelis for gunrunning. This occurred in the ambassadorial office, which was crammed full with our captors, some of whom I had not seen in months. It was a non-event for me, however, and to this day I do not understand the purpose. My picture was not taken, and I was not given anything. The Archbishop, the first non-Iranian I had seen in months, said nothing memorable. After a few minutes, I was taken back to my room, befuddled as to why my sleep had been interrupted for something that was apparently meaningless.

One evening in late April 1980, the routine went awry, and it was quickly noticed. In late afternoon, there usually would be an increase in the sounds of life in the hall as the guards changed, as food carts were wheeled up and down the corridor, and as my colleagues were taken to and from the restroom. There were also numerous ambient noises; I was once again in a room in the chancery facing the street, and noises reached me from the street as well as from the compound just beyond my window, where some outside guard would work the action of whatever type of firearm he was carrying. And there was also an occasional gunshot, which would carry with it the sounds of

running feet down the hallway as the Iranians rushed outside, only to find a shaken guard who had accidentally discharged his weapon while playing with it—a wonderful source of amusement for us captives.

But in the afternoon of 24 April 1980, none of the usual noises were heard. In fact, as dinnertime approached, the chancery grew eerily quiet. I pounded on the door for a restroom call, but no guard appeared. Listening closely, I could hear a radio down the hall emitting what sounded like some sort of a newsbroadcast, judging from the intonations of the speaker. Continuing to bang on the door, I finally got a guard to come escort me down the hall to the bathroom; when I was finished, the Iranian, grim-faced, hurried me back to my room. I could by now easily hear the radio, just the voice, and nothing else. It was also quiet outside.

I realized that something major was happening. Long ago, I had learned that any unexpected shift in the routine was not because of our imminent release, but was probably because things were going to get worse. Dinner came late, and I was starving; in lieu of our usual weeknight fare of meat, vegetables, and bread, I was brought one bowl of a thin, chili-like soup. Much later, in the middle of the night, a heavy canvas hood was placed over my head and, in deathly quiet, I was taken from the chancery, seated in a van with perhaps five or six of my colleagues, and driven away.

Evin Prison

The ride lasted 30 minutes or so, with most of it uphill. The van stopped, and I was escorted through a large, possibly gymnasium-sized room, up several flights of metal stairs, and down a narrow corridor. Finally I was pushed into someplace small and told to remove my hood. When I saw my new quarters, I became instantly enraged, my emotions intensified by the adrenaline that had been flooding my body. My "room" was a prison cell, about six feet long on one side and about eight feet across the back. The opposite-side wall ran only four feet before angling in for another three feet (against which a stainless steel toilet was situated) and then angling back before joining the front "wall." This front wall was less than three feet in length and consisted almost entirely of a floor-to-ceiling steel door with a slot near the bottom for a food tray and a small closed window at face height. The ceiling was perhaps 15 feet above the floor, and one small transom-type window joined with a dim bulb to provide the only light. It was a scene out of Hollywood's worst B-grade movies. And I was furious.

I pounded on the door until my hands began to swell, but no one came. I paced angrily back and forth in the small area (three steps, turn; three steps, turn; three steps...) for what seemed like hours. Once, when the judas window opened and a strange face peered in, I rushed toward the door, whereupon the window was slammed shut. I let loose with a string of the foulest obscenities I could think of, insulting the unknown peeper, our captors, Khomeini, and Iranians in general. No reaction, no response. I had heard other doors slam down the cellblock, and at least I had the small reassurance that I was not alone. After enough time had passed for the adrenaline to begin wearing off and I

> **"**
> ## When I saw my new quarters [at Evin Prison], I became instantly enraged....
> **"**

had calmed down slightly, I had two thoughts: first, whatever had been on the newsbroadcast probably had also caused our relocation; second, this never happened to James Bond.

As dawn approached and I was running out of steam, one of the our student "guard supervisors" came to see me. While he would not tell me what was going on, he was at ease and friendly. I told him that putting us in prison was not a good move for him and his colleagues, and noted that it would no doubt create more antipathy toward him, his fellow students, and Iran. For once, the student made no attempt to justify the Embassy takeover or to condemn either the Shah or President Carter. He replied that the move was carried out only for our own safety and that we really were not in prison, we were only in a "prison-like place." I gaped at him and waved my arm to encompass the medieval-like surroundings. He smiled and left.

We were there 10 days. I left the cell three times for showers, followed by short stints in a 12-foot by 12-foot exercise pen with 15-foot brick walls and open only to the sky. For the rest of the time, it was pace, sleep, and try to read by the light of the bulb, which burned 24 hours a day. The food ranged from bad to abominable, and the only part of it I ever recognized was the rice. At least, I hoped it was rice. The only exception to this routine occurred the morning of the second day, when a fellow hostage was put in my cell.

While glad to see someone besides an Iranian, I was hoping the two of us were not going to have to live for an unknown period of time in the matchbox-sized cell.

After an awkward greeting (for I had not known him well), this non-CIA "colleague" asked me what I knew of the recent events, whether I had been able to communicate with anyone, and if I had any thoughts or ideas on what might be happening. We talked awhile, but I knew little to tell him, having been in solitary for so long and not having talked with any Iranian in weeks who could or would tell me anything. He also professed to know little. I thought it a bit strange that, after a short while, this individual wanted to quit talking and play cards. I also noticed that he had been able to keep his watch, which was odd; I and everyone with me in the dining room that first night had our watches and rings taken, never to be seen again. Nor did any of those who were with me in the Mushroom Inn or in the TDY bungalow before I was moved into solitary have their jewelry.

After we were all reunited at the Air Force Hospital in Wiesbaden, Germany, I learned than this individual was one of several who had collaborated with the Iranians. He had been able to receive uncensored letters from home and had even been allowed to talk to his family on the telephone, so he knew much that he did not share with me during our few hours together. Nor, as it turned out, did he share any information with his cellmates during all that time. I then understood why he had been put in my cell that day in Evin Prison.

I passed our 180th day in captivity (and my 161st day in solitary) in Evin. Then, in the middle of the 10th night, I was again subjected to the canvas hood and driven for several hours, along with a couple of others, to a new place. This time, it was an ostentatious villa that must have belonged to a wealthy person. After crossing an elaborate marbled grand foyer (although still hooded, I could see out of the bottom just enough to get a good sense of the surroundings) and ascending a wide and curving staircase carpeted with the deepest pile I have ever trod on, I ended up in a room about 10 feet by 12 feet, which had obviously been the bedroom of a small girl. The bedspread, sheets, and wallpaper had green and pink cartoon-type dinosaurs and other creatures, the windows were framed with lacy curtains, and there were Nancy Drew books in the bookcases. The bed was about two feet shorter than my 6-foot, 3-inch height. Although there was a bathroom adjoining it, I was never permitted to use it; instead, I was blindfolded and walked down a corridor to an incredibly sumptuous black-marbled bath with bright brass fixtures. Despite the luxury, I was still a prisoner, and there was always an armed guard outside my door. I was struck then, and remain so today, by the highly surrealistic sensation these circumstances evoked.

If It's Tuesday, It Must Be...?

Along with several colleagues who constituted our little tour group, I was moved four more times in a short period. The villa was home for only five days, followed by about nine days in a ratty, filthy, rundown third-floor apartment in an urban area. Then I was moved to a ratty, filthy, rundown ground-floor room in the same building for another eight days or so. By this time, I had become so inured

> ## "
> ## Along with several colleagues who constituted our little tour group, I was moved four more times in a short period.
> ## "

to moving that it no longer angered me to be awakened in midsleep and told to get ready to move out. Not that there was much to move out in the first place; my belongings consisted of a plastic shopping bag holding a change of clothes, a few toiletries, a towel, pencil and paper, and a couple of books.

My next move, with US Air Force Capt. Paul Needham and Marine Gunnery Sgt. Don Moeller, was to a fairly modern Holiday Inn–type hotel, situated several hours away. I was on about the fourth floor, in a room with two double beds, a bathroom, and a balcony fortified with steel plates about three inches thick and a foot wide. The plates were welded together to form a nearly solid wall from the floor to the ceiling of the balcony, making it impossible to see out.

We spent six weeks there. They were not particularly bad weeks, except for our meals, which were so unpalatable even our Iranian guards had trouble choking them down. Most of the time I had no idea what it was we were being served, but I do know that there was no meat. Beans I could distinguish, and rice was a no-brainer, but much too frequently neither taste nor appearance lent any clues to the origin or nature of the glop before us. Of the two dishes I could handle, one was marginally satisfactory, and in the other I just dug out the beans and left the rest.

I lost quite a bit of weight. When we arrived in Wiesbaden I tipped the scales at 133 pounds; I had weighed about 180 on 4 November 1979. If it were not for the pistachio nuts and dates that appeared fairly frequently during our stay at the hotel, plus the barbari bread at breakfast, I would have lost even more weight.

On the positive side, the weather was superb, with cool evenings and warm days. I could sit out in fresh air, even if I could not be in the sun. I had unlimited access to a real bathroom with a Western-type toilet, rather than the usual porcelain holes in the floor—which I had quickly dubbed "Khomeini Holes." I was kept supplied with books, and I had a real bed with sheets I knew were clean because I washed them myself in the shower. In terms of captivity, it did not get much better than this. If it were not for the cuisine, this stay might even have been almost bearable.

Komiteh Prison

It did not last, of course. On the night of 22-23 June 1980 we were moved to Komiteh Prison in Tehran, where I would reside for the next 15 weeks. While my cell was bigger than the one in Evin, perhaps eight feet by ten feet, there was no toilet. I was back to sleeping on a foam pallet on the floor and had only a small desk, chair, and lamp for furniture, plus one small window high up on the back (outside) wall that let in partial light during the day. It soon was the middle of summer, and to handle the heat I began sleeping during the day and staying up all night. There was an open ventilation grill over the solid steel door; by standing on my chair, I could look out into the cell block.

> ❝
> **Colleagues starting whispering ... across the cellblock. When I chipped in, there was a startled hush at first [because] some of those present thought I had already been executed.**
> ❞

Within a few days, I discovered that my cell was at one end of the block and that there were five colleagues, including Tom Schaefer, in the cell across from me and three of the Marine security guards next door. I soon deduced from a number of clues in the toilet room and shower room (located at the opposite end of the cellblock) that there were about 20 to 22 of us in the cellblock, split among five or six cells. As usual, I was the only one in solitary.

Late in August and again in September, two memorable events occurred. On one night around mid-August, at perhaps about 0200 hours, I was reading when I heard someone down the cellblock knock on the steel door, the usual sign that someone needed to visit the toilet. But I then heard no sound of the door opening. A minute or two later the knocking came again, only louder. Again no response, and again a louder knock, followed by the crashing sound of a fist really hammering the door. An amazed voice said, "Christ, he's sound asleep out there!" I pulled the chair up and looked out the ventilation grill (which someone else had also obviously done) and saw our guard, possibly the youngest—and smallest—of all the Iranians I had seen during the entire hostage crisis, head down on his table and dead to the world only a few feet from the door that had received all the pounding.

With that, colleagues starting whispering back and forth across the cellblock. When I chipped in, there was a startled hush at first, caused, I learned, by the fact that some of those present thought I had already been executed. Once over this news, the others remained quiet while Tom Schaefer brought me up to date on such things as the Desert One rescue

attempt that prompted our forced exodus from the Embassy in April; the release of Rich Queen, who was sent home in July with multiple sclerosis; and other information on who was where and what others had heard, seen, or suffered. (Originally, 66 Embassy staff were captured on 4 November 1979. Two weeks later, most of the minorities and women were released, bringing our number down to 53. With the release of Rich, the rest of us would remain until the end.) This little over-the-garden-fence chat with Tom was wondrously rejuvenating.

The other momentous evening was on 23 September, when all the lights suddenly went out, not just in my cell but also on the cellblock and around the prison. This was followed a few minutes later by a warning siren going off outside my cell. On the heels of the siren came the somewhat distant but unmistakable whump, whump of exploding ordnance—my first clues that all the ruckus was an air raid. It took a minute for my bemusement to evaporate and then my spirits soared, thinking that President Carter had finally unleashed US military might against the Iranians in another rescue attempt. But common sense and reasoning quickly returned, and I realized that this scenario was very problematical.

It was too dark to read, so I sat on the floor watching the flashing light of shell bursts somewhere outside my little window and tried to figure out who the perpetrators might be. The only conclusion I could draw was that it was the Iraqis. I could not imagine why Iraq might be bombing Iran, but I did recall that the two countries had not always been the best of neighbors; nor did I doubt that it was in the Iraqis' character to attack Iran on any pretext if they perceived the Iranians to be in a weakened position.

I was not at all unhappy to see someone, anyone, dropping bombs on Iran. I felt reasonably sure a prison would not be a prime target. While a stray round could always drop in, I was feeling safe sitting in a room with three-foot-thick reinforced walls. So bomb away, I mentally told whoever it was, and damn good luck to you. The muzzle blasts of several antiaircraft guns in close proximity to the prison kept the noise level high, but it was not greatly disconcerting. I was also intrigued, having flown dozens of missions in Vietnam—the primary purpose of which was to drop bombs on people—by the unique sensation of being on the receiving end of an air assault.

Meanwhile, my Iranian guards kept popping in every five minutes, most of them gripped in something akin to an acute state of goggle-eyed panic, apparently to see if I were sharing the same fear—or perhaps to see if I was using some secret gizmo to guide the bombers; anything was possible to these kids, whose knowledge of the espionage business came from movie characters. One reason I had not been permitted to keep a watch was that at least some of the Iranians believed I might be able to use it to "talk to

> ## "
> ## Khomeini, when asked what to do next with the hostages, is reported to have replied, "We have squeezed them like lemons, and they are no longer of any use to us. Send them back."
> ## "

Washington." On the plane out of Tehran following our release, one colleague told the story of visiting the toilet room in Komiteh Prison, which was monitored by a video camera. While standing by the window, he continually looked back and forth between the sky and his watch, which he had been able to talk the Iranians into returning to him, mimicking someone checking the expected time of arrival of something, say a particular satellite. A minute or two later, he gave a nod of satisfaction and began alternately talking to his watch and then holding the watch up to his ear. After a minute of that, the guards burst into the room. That was the end of that watch. Now, with bombs going off in the vicinity of the prison, the guards did not know what to think when they found me sitting serenely on the floor cheering each explosion.

Evin Redux

We were in Komiteh only two more weeks before being moved back to Evin Prison, this time into a bungalow-sized house on the prison grounds that had been turned into a makeshift jail. From its hillside perch, I could continue to sneak peeks through a less than perfectly blacked-out window at the night air raids on Tehran. The room was only about four feet wide but possibly 15 feet long; it was actually half of a larger room, partitioned by a wall constructed of acoustic tile nailed to a framework of 2x4s.

This divide was not too substantial, and soon I was having short, whispered conversations with the adjoining occupant. Dave Roeder was an Air Force lieutenant colonel who had arrived in Tehran just days before the takeover to serve as the Air

Attaché. I had talked with him briefly before we were captured, but now we began a short-distance relationship that became a strong friendship. The dividing wall ended at the rear of the room against a window, leaving about a 1/4-inch gap between the wall and the windowpane. Dave and I soon began sliding notes back and forth between our respective cells; we communicated about many things, especially our prospects for release.

Dave had flown two tours in Vietnam, the first in B-52s and later in F-105 fighter-attack aircraft. Thanks, no doubt, to those experiences plus nearly a year in captivity, he had become thin, gray-haired, rather haggard-looking, and possessed of a scraggly beard. He looked like something between a kindly grandfather and a homeless person. We were again seeing a number of our old guards whom we had not seen since "the old days" back in the Embassy, and some were actually happy to see us. There were also some new students who did not seem to have the initial dread of us our guards had exhibited right after the takeover. Most of the guards soon came to consider Dave a pleasantly benign person, possibly something of a substitute father-figure, and they would often stop to chat with him. Dave

passed along to me whatever he was told, and I reciprocated, although the students were not nearly as forthcoming with me.

I would think about whatever news Dave would obtain from the guards and reach some general conclusions, which generated more questions in my mind. I would send a note back to him giving my thoughts and a list of questions, answers to which he should try to elicit from the students. The next time he was visited by these guards, he would work the questions into the conversation and, when alone, would send the answers back to me. Thus, the classic intelligence cycle: a recognized need for particular information was followed by tasking to a collector, who acquired information from sources and then reported it back to the requirements originator, where it was collated, analyzed, and disseminated, along with new requirements. By the time we were split up in late December, Dave and I had an efficient intelligence cycle working for us!

Other sources of "intelligence" were *Time, Newsweek,* and *Der Spiegel* magazines, which the Iranians began giving to us, albeit with information about our own situation carefully excised. Keenly interested in the coming US elections because one of the goals of our captors was the unseating of President Carter, the Iranians took great glee in showing us stories of the political campaign and nominating conventions that indicated former Governor Reagan held a significant lead over the President in the polls.

Fortunately, the Iranians did not always catch things they did not want us to see in these periodicals. In an issue of *Der Spiegel,* for example, our captors completely missed a story

32

about the Desert One rescue attempt, complete with maps and diagrams of the mission plan, as well as the photos of the burned wreckage of the C-130 in the desert. Although I did not read or speak German, the photos provided a clear picture of what the mission was to have been and, to a somewhat lesser degree, what had gone wrong. All this "open-source" information was factored into my disseminated "intelligence" to Dave Roeder.

Many conclusions Dave and I reached as a result of this collection program were right on the mark or nearly so. For example, from student comments about the elections and their much more cheerful attitudes, we hypothesized that those of us who were going to be returned to America would probably be released no later than the presidential inauguration on 20 January 1981; those who were not released by then (and we counted ourselves, plus Tom Schaefer, the COS, and one or two other military officers as potential members of this select group) would probably be kept in Iranian jails for at least several more years. Other possible, but not likely, release dates were soon after—but not before—the 4 November 1980 presidential election, and Christmas. We also concluded that the Algerians' offer to serve in an intermediary role was a positive step. Finally, from observing the changing attitudes of the students who guarded us, we decided that the shooting war with Iraq was now probably much more of a pressing problem to Iran than its diplomatic war with the United States.

Standing Tall

Our Iranian captors' hatred of President Carter was so deep and strong

> ❝
> **The Iranian Government finally began negotiating seriously with the American Government, with the help of the Algerians.**
> ❞

that they never focused on what his defeat might mean to Iran and to our situation. They believed Mr. Reagan would be their friend, someone who understood all the injustices America had perpetrated on their innocent country for so many years. Our captors were certain Reagan would understand their point of view and why they came to the Embassy that November day. Dave and I told them differently, but our words did not resonate. Imagine, then, the Iranians' utter befuddlement when, several days after the election, President-elect Reagan called the Iranians "barbarians" and noted that he did not bargain with such people.

Being labeled as barbarians was highly offensive to many Iranians, who believed their country and culture to be sophisticated and refined. Several students came to talk to Dave Roeder about this, and Dave would ask, in effect, "What did you expect? You capture the American Embassy, hold American citizens prisoner for over a year, claim that America is your number-one enemy, claim that you hate Americans, desecrate the American flag by burning it and hauling garbage in it before the world press, and maintain that you are at war with America. And now you think that Ronald Reagan is going to be your friend? He will not be your friend. You have brought this on yourselves, and that is the way the

world works." The overnight change in the Iranians' attitude was palpable. Their delight in a Carter defeat was replaced by a growing fear of the new administration.

The students knew that serious negotiations between the United States and Iran were finally in progress, spurred by two crucial facts: dealing with Iraqi aggression was almost a life-and-death matter for their country, from which the Iranian Government needed no superfluous distractions (such as the care and feeding of 52 prisoners of the state), and the hardcore Islamic fundamentalists had finally seized control of the government from the Bani-Sadr "moderates." In the midst of this, Khomeini, when asked what to do next with the hostages, is reported to have replied, "We have squeezed them like lemons, and they are no longer of any use to us. Send them back."

There was one additional element that had some bearing on our ultimate release. In October 1980, the new Iranian prime minister came to the UN in New York to seek support for his country in the war with Iraq and condemnation of Iraq as an aggressor. What he found was that no one wanted to talk to him about Iraq. Everywhere he turned, he was confronted with demands to release the American diplomats, with Iran—and not Iraq—the object of general condemnation. In a private conversation with the wife of one of our colleagues who was an effective leader in the family support organization, the prime minister offered the immediate release of her husband, only to be told in blunt terms that her husband was not to be released unless and until all hostages were released. The all-or-nothing policy had been voiced by the State Department and the White

33

House from the beginning, but the prime minister was surprised to learn that the families felt the same way.

So it was that the Iranian Government finally began negotiating seriously with the American Government, with the help of the Algerians. The task was not an easy one for the US negotiating team, headed by then Deputy Secretary of State Warren Christopher. To the Iranians, negotiating "seriously" did not necessarily mean negotiating in good faith; they looked at the beginning of talks as the opening of the bazaar.

The Iranians wanted a number of issues settled in their favor—particularly the freeing of several billion US dollars that had been frozen in their European and American bank accounts; the delivery of US military equipment on order, and, in some instances, paid for under the Shah's regime; and apologies for "previous wrongs" done to Iran by the United States. In bazaar-market fashion, the Iranians bargained for everything, soon frustrating not only the Americans but also the Algerians by apparently agreeing on certain points or amounts, only to renege several days later.

We could tell by the Iranians' attitudes and moods that things on the diplomatic front were, at last, moving along. Our move back to Evin was, at least in my mind, more than routine. In Komiteh, we were all together, in circumstances which made it easy for the Iranians to take care of us; and we were as safe from external dangers as we could probably ever be. For the Iranians to go to the trouble of moving us again to new quarters, which only increased their workload, seemed a positive development. The guards became

> ## "
> ## We could tell by the Iranians' attitudes and moods that things on the diplomatic front were, at last, moving along.
> ## "

more open and willing to talk (especially, and thankfully, to Dave Roeder). They began to talk more about us "going home," and there was an upswing in their collective mood, despite their disappointment with President-elect Reagan. And our quality of life marginally improved: I was able to shower more frequently (although there was no hot water, the shower room unheated, the window permanently cracked open—and it was getting damn cold in the mountains where Evin is situated). We continued to receive American-style food, and we were regularly given newsmagazines, minus stories about us and the negotiations.

As November 1980 moved into December, there was anticipation that Christmas would bring good news, perhaps even freedom. Dave hoped for a Christmas release. I too thought that was possible, considering that President Carter had been unseated and that Iraq was now Iran's biggest problem. To my mind there did not appear to be any substantive reason for holding us longer, although that did not rule out keeping us for spite or for leverage in trying to obtain more in the negotiations. I grew cautiously optimistic.

The Final Weeks

My positive attitude was dashed and replaced by an angry outburst on

23 December, when we were moved again. After a short ride from Evin, I was led into a building and down several flights of stairs. Just before entering my new quarters, we walked across the marble floor of what seemed to be a large, unfurnished room. When I heard one of the guards plink at a piano somewhere in the room, the first impression was that of a ballroom or other similarly large area.

When the blindfold was removed, I looked around. I thought that I had been magically transported to one of the men's restrooms at the Kennedy Center. I was standing in a room that resembled a small parlor; it was nicely carpeted and wallpapered, and furnished with an easy chair, a table, lamp, and the ubiquitous foam sleeping pad on the floor. Additional light was provided by sconces. On one side was a short hallway leading (I soon learned) to the toilet area. There was just one window in the "parlor," near the high ceiling on the wall opposite the double-entry door. (After release, I learned that we were being held at the Foreign Ministry's guesthouse. The source of this information was a colleague who had been living in one of the luxurious guest rooms upstairs, while I languished in what was a basement bathroom).

While I had a better living area than I had had in most of my previous abodes, I was still furious at being there, to the point of lashing out verbally at the guards, even trying to pick a fight with them. In earlier days, an episode like this would have resulted in some form of punishment, probably either shackling or loss of book privileges. Now the guards just shrugged, told me not to turn on the light, and left.

34

1995-1999

Iran

As I stewed in the dark (and in the cold, there being no heat coming from the radiator), a flak cannon opened up just outside the room's only window, and I could again hear the whump, whump of ordnance exploding in the distance. From the light from the muzzle flashes, I confirmed that I was in a basement (looking up and out the window, I could see that I was at least eight feet below ground level). I set about pacing across the room, full of anger and adrenaline, the way lighted by the flashes and a modest amount of ambient light. Finally, the gun silent, I walked until fatigued and called it a day.

Still in a funk the next morning, I ignored the guards when they brought me breakfast and again when they returned to fix the heat and jerryrig a shower in the toilet area. By day's end, after having taken long, hot showers following each of my two exercise periods, I was in a much better frame of mind. But I continued to ignore the guards, just to be perverse and to remind them of my intense dislike of being treated like a commodity. I had again been made aware of the utter lack of control I had over my life. That never failed to anger and frustrate me, not only while in captivity but also for years afterward.

Several hours after dinner on this Christmas Eve, the door opened and in walked three Arab men in suits and ties, accompanied by a contingent of our guards. I was then introduced to the Algerian Ambassador to Iran. He asked how I was faring and told me that if I wanted to write a letter home, he would personally carry it to United States Government officials. I quickly accepted the offer and then, speaking softly but quickly, outlined to the diplomat in terribly fractured French

> **When the Algerian Ambassador was able to report to US officials that he had personally seen and talked with me, that was the first news in a year that I was still alive.**

my previous treatment, including the 400-plus days in solitary. When the guards started to react to this discussion, which they could not follow, I switched back to English and thanked the Ambassador for his time.

I was in much better spirits following the visit, but was still surprised when someone collected the just-written letters. And I was even more surprised when I learned on release that the letter had made it to my mother (the Iranians had by then long destroyed any trust I placed in their word). When the Algerian Ambassador was able to report to US officials that he had personally seen and talked with me, that was the first news in a year that I was still alive; but it was good to have the letter as confirmation. The letter was hand-delivered to my mother by an Agency officer, who then sat with her and went over the letter, asking her to confirm that it was my handwriting and that it reflected my personality. With that, my name was apparently checked off on the "still with us" list.

Along with Christmas breakfast, I received a real present from home (the only package from home the Iranians let me have, out of many sent to me): a shoebox stuffed with goodies, including a crossword puzzle book, a deck of cards, and real Kleenex. It

struck me then that release was probably close, if not in the next day or two, then around 20 January (the symbolism of a release on inauguration day was not lost on me).

I tried not to be too optimistic by reminding myself that it was possible I would not be freed then or anytime soon. If nothing happened during the week of the 20th, then I should accept that I was in for a long term of incarceration and be grateful that things were not worse. (To put our situation in perspective, it is a fair comparison to say that our treatment was worse than that received by American aviators at the hands of the Germans in the World War II stalags, but unquestionably much better than the treatment Japan gave to its POWs during that same conflict or that meted out by the North Vietnamese to the POWs in the Hanoi Hilton.)

During this time, there reappeared one of the first guards I had had in the Embassy during the eternity before our dispersal around the country. Mehdi was perhaps 20 or 21, and he had consistently been kind to me while I was in his charge. We had spent hours talking on many topics, often with each trying to educate or explain things to the other. I was pleased to see him again, and he confessed to being pleased as well. It was interesting to note a change or two in him, particularly an improvement in his English, an ancillary benefit many of our guards obtained as their months with us passed. None of Mehdi's previous occasional dourness was in evidence and, although not giving away any secrets, he spoke more openly and frankly.

Mehdi's optimistic attitude and those tidbits he did let drop (or I elicited) in our chats served as additional

35

201

> 66
> **Nineteen January
> [1981] lasted forever. I
> could not sleep, read,
> or close my mind.**
> 99

indexes of possibly imminent release. Unlike any of the other guards with whom I spoke during those last few months, he had begun to engage in some objective reflection of what it was that he and his cohorts had done and what their actions might have meant in terms of his country's long-term stability. For example, although most of our captors seemed to have trouble grasping "cause and effect" relationships, Mehdi had independently concluded that Iran's loss of US friendship and protection had helped allow the Soviets to invade Afghanistan and later encouraged the Iraqis to initiate the recently begun hostilities with Iran. No other Iranian I talked with ever gave any sign of understanding this.

The End in Sight

With something positive finally in the offing, the days seemed to pass more slowly as we went from December 1980 into January 1981, with the only noticeable change being less contact with the guards. By early January, the only Iranians who came to my room, other than Mehdi, who still dropped by occasionally, were those who brought my meals. I did not mind this reduction in contact and was thus irritated when, several hours after dinner on 18 January, there was a knock on my door. I was startled by this unusual act of courtesy, and it did not occur to me to reply. The door opened, and a guard ushered in a young male dressed in a white jacket and carrying some sort of tray, only to find me standing perplexed in the middle of the room. Viewing the white jacket, I assumed that the guard had brought the cook down for a culinary review of that night's dinner. Then I took a good look at the tray and saw that it was a

medic's blood kit. With sleeve rolled up and fist clenched, I watched with no small amount of trepidation as this youth approached my arm with a huge hypodermic syringe, fully intent on draining a few gallons of blood.

My fears notwithstanding, the experience left me unharmed and for the first time almost free of pessimism: I had been seen by the Algerian Ambassador, permitted to write a letter home which enjoyed some real prospect of being delivered, and had blood taken, almost certainly as part of a medical examination. Looking at this evidence, I could not talk myself out of believing that the end was really coming.

Nineteen January lasted forever. I could not sleep, read, or close my mind. I spent most of that day pacing the room and waiting for another knock. Dinner came and went, while time dragged on and I grew more and more despondent. I had miscalculated, I thought; if I was not released now, then it would probably be a long time before I enjoyed any kind of freedom again.

But it did happen. Well after midnight, I was blindfolded and walked outside to another building. When I could see again, I was in a large institutional-type kitchen, and in the room beyond I could see some of my colleagues. I was taken to a smaller room, where there were three medical examining tables set up, two occupied by colleagues I had not seen in

over a year. A smiling Algerian doctor gave me a rudimentary physical exam and finished by telling me I was fine. While pleased to hear that, what was really exciting to me was the thought that the Iranians, now having had outsiders verify that I was alive and in acceptable health, could not very well claim I had been shot trying to escape or had died in captivity. Moreover, knowing that the Algerians had played a significant role in the negotiations between Iran and the United States, I thought it highly unlikely that they would certify we were alive and healthy, and then walk away and leave us. I knew then for sure that we were going home.

There were two other interesting events that night. First, I had to appear before Tehran Mary and a film crew. Mary and her friends were smiling and acting as though this was the social event of the season. In front of the camera, I was asked how I was doing, and I replied, "Fine." She then asked if I had been treated well while I had been a guest of Iran. I burst out laughing, and replied that I had been held against my will in solitary for more than a year, had not been able to tell my family that I was even alive, had been interrogated, was physically abused more than once, and had been threatened with trial and execution. And now I was being asked if I had been treated well. So the answer was, "No!" There were no follow-up questions.

As for the second event, I had not been back in my basement bathroom long when, near daybreak, Hossein came to say good-by. He sat on the floor against the side wall, looking tired and more than a bit haggard, but happy. Almost gloating, in fact. He began by telling me that it was all over, that we were all going home, and that Iran was finally going to be free from outside interference so Iranians could have the kind of country they wanted. I responded that it sounded good, but that I was sure it was not going to happen because, in my view, Iranians lacked the necessary self-discipline to keep the past from repeating itself.

Hossein said he did not understand. I noted that governing a nation and permitting at least some degree of freedom (which Hossein and his cohorts always maintained would be the case in Iran) required great tolerance on the part of the authorities. I said that the government of such a country could not lock someone away or execute them just because someone with the power to do so did not like something the person said or did. I told him that rules and laws had to be applied to all citizens equally and that it took governmental and personal self-discipline to make this work. Looking him directly in the eyes, I told him that nothing I had seen, heard, or experienced in my time in Iran gave me any indication he and his fellow Iranians had any understanding of this. The revolutionary government was unwilling to grant its citizens any measurable degree of true freedom, and there was not, in my opinion, a snowball's chance in hell that it would.

Hossein rebutted my comments, using the same idealistic revolutionary rhetoric that I had heard so many times, from so many Iranians. He ended by repeating that all Iran's problems had been caused by outsiders, most notably by America, and that now everything was going to be good in Iran. I did not carry the debate further. He tried to chitchat for a few minutes, but, when he realized that I had no interest in a

> ##
> **The last sounds I heard before tearing loose from the crowd at the bottom of the stairs and sprinting into the [aircraft] cabin were, "Hey, wait! Can you help get me a visa to America?"**
> ""

congenial farewell, he said he had many things to do. He then stood and wished me good luck. I shrugged, and he left.

After sundown on 20 January, I was blindfolded for the last time and walked out of the building, minus the little bundle of possessions that I had managed to retain over the months. The Iranians had taken everything we had and sent us out of the country with only the clothes on our backs. I was helped onto a bus and pushed toward the back, able to see from underneath my blindfold that all the seats were filled with Americans. I was the last one on. Standing at the rear, I glimpsed my COS sitting in the seat in front of me. This was the first time I had seen him in nearly 15 months.

As we slowed on the airport apron, we could hear a crowd yelling; the sounds were almost deafening as the bus stopped and the door opened. Each of us was walked to the door of the bus, where the blindfold was removed. We were then more or less pushed off and propelled through a gauntlet of screaming Iranians toward the rear stairs of a Boeing 727. As I was moved along to the airplane, I recognized some of our former guards. The last sounds I heard before tearing loose from the crowd at the

bottom of the stairs and sprinting into the cabin were, "Hey, wait! Can you help get me a visa to America?"

Epilogue

I want to record here some vignettes that did not make the evening news and were not of any great import to what happened to the 52 of us as a group. But these brief moments almost without exception hold indescribable meaning to me. Not coincidentally, whenever I have been privileged to speak to various audiences, these were also the stories that seemed to touch the individual listeners the most. Yet these stories, which put a human face on those events, are the least likely material to survive over time. And I do not want that to happen. Too many Americans gave too much of themselves during that time to allow these memories to fade.

It may seem odd that the 14-plus months I spent as a captive of the Iranians have endowed my life with memories actually worth safeguarding. Even some events that were not and are not things I like to dwell on had their uplifting and sometimes humorous aspects. My fondest memories are those of our return to freedom; one colleague likened it to being "bathed in love," which says it all. I should also add that this was all a tremendous surprise to me, and it was some time before I came to accept psychologically the great good fortune that befell us.

Confined in a solitary state for all but the first 19 days of our captivity and generally deprived of news from the outside, I had no idea of what awaited us when the time came for our return. Some of my colleagues

37

> ## We have many reasons to be eternally grateful to the Algerians.

who received changes of roommates more frequently than I received chances to shower had, through various sources, been able to glean some general idea of the public reception in the offing. I was clueless.

The above notwithstanding, I did have infrequent glimmers of the extent to which the American public supported us because the Iranians would, on rare occasion, give me one or two of the thousands of cards and letters sent to us by caring Americans throughout our captivity. These short missives would without fail inform us that we were in their prayers, urge us to be strong, and end with a hope for a speedy conclusion to our ordeal. Many thanked us for our sacrifice and for bringing the country together, even at such a cost to us and to our government.

The Iranians had waged a psychological war against all of us, its intensity varying only with the degree to which each of us was viewed by them as an "enemy of the revolution." A measurable element in that war was the unrelenting effort to convince us that we had been abandoned by the American people, that Americans everywhere wanted to see us "justly" held in prison for "crimes" against the Iranian nation and people, and that on return to the United States we would face only shame and humiliation. Permitting us to read those wonderful cards, which spoke just the opposite to our hearts, undermined their efforts to reduce our will to resist. These letters meant so much to all of us, and I am still amazed that the Iranians ever gave any of them to us. Nonetheless, even with the joy and strength those cards brought me, I never envisioned anything like what awaited us in Germany and back home.

It was only by happenstance that I even knew we would be heading to Germany. Tom Schaefer had shared this tidbit with me through an air vent one February day, when we were next door to each other in makeshift cells in the chancery basement. Beyond that one specific piece of intelligence, I was left with my imagination when it came to dreaming about and planning for my return home. And I will humbly note right now that for every single image, idea, or dream I had about our return, I was dead wrong on each of them.

The Captain

We left Tehran on an Air Algerie 727, and it all seemed surrealistic. It still does. But it was the best plane ride I have ever had. In celebration, we hoisted small glasses of champagne when we left Iranian airspace and, when dinner was served, bottles of Algerian wine surfaced, though not many; when they were emptied, no more appeared. (Some years later, I remarked that I thought the wine was excellent, only to have a skeptical friend point out that my taste buds at that particular moment might not have been in top working order.) Moreover, the feast of delicacies, which I had assured myself would certainly be ours, did not appear either. Our first meal in freedom was hard rolls and butter. Four or five of us were thus milling around in the aisle, somewhat perplexed at what was passing for our "welcome to freedom" dinner, when the plane's captain stopped by.

A remarkable man, the Algerian captain had a marvelous sense of humor and loads of charisma. The looks of disappointment, which must have filled our faces as we contemplated the rolls and butter, drew his concern. He inquired if everything was OK, and one of us managed to stammer out with some embarrassment that, while we did not mean to appear ungrateful, we had been looking forward to a meal that was a bit more substantial. The captain made a small joke, but then turned serious and apologized for the meager fare.

The reason, he explained, is that the plane had left for Tehran several days ago, unsure of exactly when, or even whether, our release would take place. He described landing in Ankara to top off the fuel tanks and to stock the larder, noting that the only food that would keep on the plane more than a day or so without spoiling were the rolls and butter. "So you see," he said softly, "we did not know how long we would be in Tehran, and we would not allow the Iranians to cater your food."

The Air Algerie 727 was configured in three sections, with first-class seating at the front and two economy seating areas behind. The VIPs on board were up front, and my colleagues and I were in the middle section. At Mehrabad Airport, we boarded in such a rush that I hardly noticed the occupants in the rear of the plane. Later, heading back to the restroom, I did notice a number of large, tough-looking chaps sitting in seats that were too small for their bulk. Later, I learned that they were Algerian commandos. On landing in Tehran, the commandos had set up a protective perimeter around the plane so that no could get within several hundred feet of the aircraft.

Actually, there were two Air Algerie aircraft that came for us. Identical 727s were used, not only to carry everyone connected with our release (negotiators, the Algerian doctors who examined us, Red Cross personnel, commandos, and so forth), but also for an added layer of protection. At departure time, the two planes taxied away from the lighted apron together and, by the time they had reached the runway, no one watching could be certain which plane held the former hostages. The two planes took off within a minute of each other and, once airborne, changed position a time or two. If the Iranians were of a mind to attempt a downing our aircraft, they would have been confused as to which plane was ours.

We have many reasons to be eternally grateful to the Algerians. They truly cared.

Warm Welcome

After we landed in Algiers for the formal turnover from Algerian custody to the US Government (as negotiated by the Algerians with the Iranians and our government), we were ushered into the VIP suite at the terminal. Some months later, I was watching a video of TV coverage of the event and, when the 727 came to a stop, I eagerly awaited my appearance. The opportunity to see myself on worldwide TV was more than just a novelty. So, I waited. And waited. A half-hour passed before the aircraft's door opened, and then more time elapsed before Bruce Laingen walked down the stairs toward the terminal. Watching the video, I was astonished at the time lapse. I still am. To this day, I have no idea where the time

> ## " On arrival in Frankfurt, it seemed as though most of the American population of Europe [was there to greet us]. "

went or what we did in the plane while we were waiting.

The walk to the terminal served as a modest introduction to the welcomes we were to experience in the days and weeks to come. The first thing I noticed was a VIP version of the Boeing 707 from the US Air Force Special Missions unit at Andrews Air Force Base parked about 50 yards away from our 727. There was a crew member hanging about halfway out the co-pilot's window, his face one huge grin, wildly waving a small but very visible American flag. We were as happy to see him as he was to see us. The first of what could be called our "cheering crowds," several hundred happy and smiling members of the American business community and Embassy in Algiers, were ecstatically waving more American flags.

The scene inside the VIP lounge could have been easily mistaken for a routine diplomatic cocktail party. We strolled in, accepted a small tumbler of tea or fruit juice, and then stood around making polite conversation with people we had never seen before and, at least in my case, have not seen since. It was clear, though, that these strangers were delighted to see us.

I do remember Algerian Foreign Minister Benyahia officially transferring custody of us to the State Department representatives. Other than shaking his hand before we left, we had no chance to meet him or talk with him; still, I know we were all

saddened when he died in a plane crash in 1982. He was a man who had devoted the better part of a year's energy and patience to gaining our freedom.

By 0300, we were aboard two US Air Force C-9 Nightingale medevac aircraft heading for Rhein-Main Airbase at Frankfurt, Germany. I was sitting in the jump seat on the flight deck, between the pilots, having something of a normal conversation in abnormal circumstances. The two pilots seemed as pleased to have been chosen to fly us as we were pleased to be in their charge—almost. In the midst of this conversation, the Italian air traffic control service handed off our flight to French controllers as we entered France's airspace.

After the check-in calls, the French controller departed from established radio procedure in his signoff message to the pilot. "I am sure all of your special passengers must be asleep in the back," (which was decidedly not true: all the interior lights were on, and my colleagues were all bustling about and acting as though it was an airborne New Year's Eve bash), "but when they awake before landing, please tell them that all France is happy their ordeal has ended and that French citizens everywhere wish them the best as they return to freedom." The pilot rogered his thanks and we flew on. Only much later did I realize I should have asked the pilot for the microphone to thank the controller personally for his wishes. I have always regretted not thinking faster.

On arrival in Frankfurt, it seemed as though most of the American population of Europe watched us leave the aircraft, walk across the ramp, and disappear into blue Air Force buses

> ## "
> **It is impossible for any of us to express our gratitude adequately to the staff of the Wiesbaden Air Force Hospital. … I cannot begin to describe the genuine kindness and expert care we received from these folks.**
> ## "

for the short trip over to the USAF hospital at Wiesbaden. A good number of my colleagues had the presence of mind to wave to the crowd that met us; I did not. I felt indescribably awkward and out of place. Later, I realized I was experiencing a species of culture shock; I did not know what to do or what was expected of me. I was self-conscious, did not know what was happening, and was overwhelmed.

I soon learned that these wonderful Americans were from the Rhein-Main Airbase and surrounding area, and that they had been waiting for hours during the coldest part of that January night to welcome us. They had a huge American flag hanging from the control tower, and almost everyone present was also waving small American flags while cheering without restraint. It was the warmest welcome anyone could ever dream of receiving.

There was also a sea of yellow ribbons, bows, and garlands fluttering around. No other colors, just yellow. There was even a huge yellow bow tied around the control tower. I mentally chalked up these displays of yellow to some quaint local German custom, and headed for the bus.

The short walk from the buses up the hospital's main entrance was through a corridor full of beaming faces and more flags and yellow ribbons. As I went to my room, it was impossible not to notice the wall decorations. Lots of art work by youngsters in grammar and middle schools led me to conclude that the Air Force had cleared out a pediatrics ward for us. And we were afloat on a sea of yellow ribbons. Later, when I had the time to look at each one, I saw that the drawings were letters of welcome

from children of American military personnel. At the time, however, the only sensation was that of being nearly overwhelmed by color and smiling faces.

I was looking forward to the medical exam, certain I had come through captivity in fine shape, save for the loss of a couple of pounds and a slight decrease in cardiovascular endurance. The examination went well; the doctor was wonderful, as was everyone connected with the hospital. But when I learned the outcome, I thought at first I had gotten someone else's results. I was flabbergasted to discover I had lost 47 pounds. My surprise was even greater when I saw my physical state described as "general wastage," because I certainly did not feel that way. Fortunately, "wasted" was a temporary condition remedied by a lot of eating.

When we arrived back home, many people—family, friends, neighbors, any groups we spoke to, as well as the folks who stopped us on the subway, in airports, and at the neighborhood tavern—were naturally highly curious about our first days in freedom, especially at Wiesbaden and, later,

West Point. That was because the State Department took great care to isolate us and our immediate families, and news organizations were not allowed near us. I will try to satisfy some of that curiosity.

I confess that I cannot remember what my first real meal was after we were released. What I was especially looking forward to was pizza and Heineken beer, and, as a good Oklahoma boy, a thick T-bone. But the first meals in Wiesbaden were not memorable. The doctors were doing a seemingly endless series of laboratory tests, requiring donations of about half the blood supply in our bodies; for accurate test results, our diets had to be restricted. Thus, we came to realize belatedly why we had only one cup each of Algerian champagne and wine on the flight to Algiers, and why we were kept on limited diets during our first days at the hospital. On our last night in Wiesbaden, however, we enjoyed Maine lobsters sent to us by a generous (and imaginative) American. What certainly had to be the best cooks in the Air Force prepared the lobsters and served them with an incredible array of side dishes. This delicious meal was truly a feast and a most memorable event.

It is impossible for any of us to express our gratitude adequately to the staff of the Wiesbaden Air Force Hospital. The people working at the hospital, including US military personnel and American and German civilians, were as happy to have us there as we were to be there. I cannot begin to describe the genuine kindness and expert care we received from these folks.

In the middle of the second day, Tom Schaefer and I were talking with the ward's head nurse, Maj. Toni

Carner. We were trying to tell her how much we appreciated everything her staff was doing for us and how grateful we were to be in their care. Recognizing what we were trying to say, Maj. Carner stopped us by taking our hands, looked up at us, and softly said, "We've been waiting for you for 444 days."

After the lobster feast, we were invited to a party in the enlisted barracks. A bar had been set up and music was playing, and many of the medics we had seen during our three days were there in casual clothes. I think about nine of the Tehran bunch showed up, to be welcomed with a large traditional German stein and beverages of our choice. With no dietary restrictions now, we could enjoy the world's greatest beer. I took special care to make sure the stein made it back home with me, and it now sits in my home office where I see it everyday.

We were given a lot of things while we were in Germany, including collector-type plates from several German cities depicting a local landmark, usually a cathedral or the city hall. We were given coffee-table books for these cities, a yearbook of the Wiesbaden Air Force Hospital, a crystal Christmas tree ornament, and a porcelain bell compliments of German Chancellor Schmidt. We received flowers by the truckload. On the day of our departure, about eight of us loaded up shopping carts and rolled through the hospital wards giving the still-beautiful flowers to real patients. But when it comes to gifts, what I remember most of all is the "klepto table."

Our ward was L-shaped, with the long side running along the center front of the hospital and the shorter

side heading off to who knew where. (Well, I knew where, actually, and so did several of the others—it led to a small men's restroom room and lounge in which several of us shared some contraband beers on our second day, smuggled in by a kind soul who shall remain nameless but who earned our eternal gratitude.) At the angle of the L was a large open area where a long, wide table had been set up before our arrival. And on that table were stacked many of the gifts, along with the myriad floral arrangements, that had been sent to us from people all over the world.

Two items on the table stood out: an amazing number of T-shirts (once back home, it was years before I had to buy another one) with mostly patriotic designs, and an enormous Hershey's chocolate bar. This slab of chocolate was probably close to four feet in length and an inch or two thick. Someone had tossed a wicked-looking knife on the table next to it so that we could hack off whatever amount we wanted. We ate so much chocolate that it is a wonder we did not all get off the plane at Newburgh resembling a bunch of ambulatory pimples.

It soon became second nature, whenever passing the gift table, to look it over for the latest arrivals, take one each of whatever there was, and then hew off a chunk of chocolate before heading off. It amuses me now to recall how quickly we got used to the table and how accustomed we became to getting unsolicited gifts. (Several months after we returned, seven of us were guests of Radio City Music Hall in New York City at opening night of a special production with a patriotic theme. We were staying in the exclusive Towers section of the Sheraton, and I had already entered an elevator

when, just as the doors started to close, one of my Tehran colleagues jumped in. As we began the ride up, he looked at me and said, "Nice tie. Did you have to pay for it?") By the time we left Wiesbaden, I felt like a latent kleptomaniac and fervently hoped this instinct would not manifest itself the next time I was in Sears.

A German orderly at the hospital was assigned to us, and he was always there whenever we needed anything. Herr Gottfried Pfeiffer had been at the hospital since at least World War II days, when the hospital served the German Army, and we all became indebted to him for his many kindnesses. Herr Pfeiffer even serenaded us on his accordion at the lobster feast, beaming with pride as he played.

Two years later, almost to the day, I was in Wiesbaden as a tourist. I made it a point to go to the hospital to look up old friends. Many of those who had waited for 444 days to care for us were gone; I saw no one I recognized as I walked up the main staircase. There were no yellow ribbons on the walls and no crayon drawings by school children. I walked past the room Don Cook and I had shared and into the central part of the ward. There was no klepto table, no wall of flowers. And then Herr Pfeiffer came around the corner. He recognized me immediately, and we greeted each other with joy. He then took my arm and led me to a wood plaque on the wall. This lovely tribute informed all readers that they were standing in "Freedom Hall" and encased a group photo of the 52 of us, taken minutes before we left the hospital for Rhein Main Air Base and the flight home. If there had been a "before" photo to go with the "after" photo, the viewer would have no trouble in noticing the difference. And much of that differ-

41

ence was due to the wonderful people at the hospital who cared so much for and about us.

VIP Visitors

We had two special visitors at the hospital—former President Carter and former Secretary of State Vance. Their receptions could not have been more different. We all gathered in our ward's lounge area to meet Mr. Carter, who arrived with former Vice-President Mondale, Secretaries Edmund Muskie of State and G. William Miller of Treasury, and several key members of the White House staff. None of my colleagues with whom I talked beforehand had much interest, if any, in seeing Mr. Carter. In fact, the atmosphere in the room as we were waiting for him to arrive was so chilly that Tom Schaefer felt obliged to remind everyone that Mr. Carter had been our President and Commander in Chief, and, as such, was due respect, regardless of our personal feelings. When he entered, the former President appeared to me to be ill at ease, uncertain of his reception.

Mr. Carter was introduced to us one by one, giving us each a hug. Few embraces were returned with any enthusiasm. He spoke to us for about 10 minutes, relating some background on why he had made the decision to admit the Shah and what had been done since to obtain our release. He then asked if there were any questions.

There were several soft questions posed out of politeness, and then a colleague stepped forward. He stated that he did not have a question but wanted to remind the former President that the Embassy had provided plenty of advance warning of what would happen if the Shah were

admitted to the United States. Mr. Carter looked down at the floor for a moment, then raised his head, smiled, and said he wanted his picture taken with each of us. End of meeting. (I still have the photo stashed away somewhere; the former President looks awkward, and I look like an unsmiling cadaver.)

I do not deny that President Carter's handling of the crisis after the Iranians took over the Embassy was the primary reason we all returned alive and together from Iran. Although hindsight shows that some mistakes were made, Mr. Carter's efforts were ultimately successful. But I believe he has to bear the responsibility for creating the circumstances that brought about the crisis in the first place. The Embassy, in my view, probably would have been left alone had the Shah gone directly to the United States from Tehran in January 1979; it had been a mistake to allow him into the United States after he had roamed the world for 10 months.

Our session with Mr. Vance was the opposite. He had opposed the rescue attempt and had resigned his office in protest, but only after the attempt had taken place, so as not to jeopardize the security of the operation or undermine the President's authority as Commander in Chief to conduct it. We received him with admiration and respect. He related honestly and forthrightly how and why various decisions were made, and what was done after the Embassy was taken.

Among the 52 of us, opinions were definitely mixed as to whether it had been wise to try a military rescue operation, but that diversity did not lessen the esteem we felt for Mr. Vance. He answered a great many questions with frankness. When he had finished, we gave him a standing

ovation. I doubt that any of us left his presence without feeling that we had been well served by an American of great dignity and honor.

The Prime Minister's Mug

On the flight home, we stopped to refuel in Shannon, Ireland, and were turned loose in the terminal for about an hour. Having an Irish name, I was selected, along with one other, to receive on behalf of the group a gift of one bottle of Irish Mist from the company that makes it. There was a nice little ceremony, after which I ended up talking to one of the company managers. We were soon joined by a friendly guy, who, when I mentioned in passing that I occasionally enjoyed a Guinness stout, suggested we repair to the bar for a glass or two.

The Irish Mist representative, this other chap, and I spent 30 minutes or so at the bar, where we each had several glasses of Guinness. Midway through a glass, this nice man asked to see the Waterford crystal Christmas bell, which had also been given to us at Shannon. While he was appreciating it, I mentioned to him that I had been given a Waterford beer mug as a gift before I had left Washington a lifetime ago, and I lamented its loss to the Iranians. A minute later, when the Irish Mist representative was talking, I almost did not notice when the other gent turned to a couple of big fellows who seemed to be just hanging around in background and whispered something.

A few minutes later, the hangers-on returned and handed him a box. He in turn handed it to me—it held a lovely Galway crystal beer mug. It is not Waterford, the man stated, but he hoped that I would enjoy it and think

42

of Shannon and true Irish hospitality whenever I drank from it. And I do. Because that is how Irish Prime Minister Charles Haughey came to present me with a Galway beer mug over a few glasses of Guinness stout at the Shannon Airport bar.

West Point

The reception in America is still difficult for me to describe. It could not have been any warmer or more memorable. I was—and remain so today—immensely grateful for the homecoming our fellow Americans showered on us. We landed at Stewart Airport near Newburgh, New York, and, after having cheerful and tearful reunions with our families, we boarded buses for the ride to West Point, where we were to have a sheltered two days with our families before going to Washington for our official welcome home. It took more than two hours to cover the 18 miles from the airport to West Point; the way was lined with well-wishers who carried all types of signs expressing their happiness to see us back and their feelings toward the Iranians who had held us captive.

One of the more common signs we saw used different cartoon characters or caricatures of famous people, all of whom were depicted condemning Iranians in general or Khomeini in particular. One frequent expression of disapproval was the blatant presentation of a hand with the middle digit extended, in the universal symbol which decidedly does not convey a "We're number one" meaning. We loved each and every one of those posters.

Around every turn, there were still more people waiting, with more signs and posters. There were masses of American flags and yellow ribbons

> **I was—and remain so today—immensely grateful for the homecoming our fellow Americans showered on us.**

everywhere. From the buses, we all waved until our arms grew tired, and then we waved some more. All of us were deeply touched by this parade.

The US Army and the entire staff at West Point were as caring, giving, and gracious as the Air Force personnel had been at the hospital in Wiesbaden. I was always amazed at the number of people in both institutions who would thank us for coming to be with them. But we were the ones who were really grateful, and we were extremely proud to have met all those who were involved in some way with our care.

About an hour before dinner that first night at West Point's historic Thayer Hotel, I was making the rounds of the hotel lobby and meeting room, looking at more pictures and letters sent by area grade-school children, surrounded as always by yards of yellow ribbon. Like those in the hospital at Wiesbaden, these missives all expressed happiness at our return. I wish I had had the foresight to have collected these on our departure and ensured that they ended up somewhere where the public could see them. To me, these works of hundreds of young Americans were priceless.

If the West Point faculty and staff were wonderful to us, they almost paled in comparison to the welcome we received from the Corps of Cadets. During the second day, we and our families were invited by the

Corps to dinner that night in the cadet dining hall. Although I found out later that many cadets expected a low turnout (anticipating that we would want to spend time alone with the families), almost all of us did accept. And of all the heartwarming and exciting events we experienced, this dinner with the Corps ranks at the top. As our buses neared the front of the dining hall we could a distant roar, almost like thunder, intruding into the quiet of the evening. The closer we got, the louder the roar. By the time we stepped out of the buses, it had become deafening.

The din, coming from inside the dining hall, was our greeting from the Corps. Walking into the building we witnessed the most extraordinary spectacle, as cadets of all ranks and classes were cheering and yelling at the top of their lungs, many standing on their chairs while creating this mind-numbing noise. This welcome home was the most touching of all to me, and it was all I could do to hold back the tears. I do remember being seated at a large table with perhaps 10 cadets, including several of the first women to enter the Academy, and being so pleased to be with these young Americans and future leaders. I do not think I have ever met a more impressive, motivated, and intelligent group of people. Today, I cannot adequately relate the pride I felt in being an American while in the company of these outstanding men and women.

The White House

On the morning of our third day, we retraced our route back to Stewart and boarded planes for the flight to Andrews Air Force Base, where we were greeted by more family and by close friends and colleagues. We were

> ## The First Lady laughed and gave me a warm hug and a kiss on the cheek. Holding my hands in hers, she smiled and welcomed me home.

then driven in another bus caravan past thousands of people through the Maryland suburbs and the streets of Washington, DC, to 1600 Pennsylvania Avenue. We were separated from our families and escorted to the Blue Room, where we were introduced to President and Mrs. Reagan and to Vice-President Bush. President Reagan welcomed us home in a short speech and gave each of us a silk American flag in a personalized rosewood presentation box.

I embarrassed myself somewhat in this simple ceremony. A presidential aide would call a name, and that person would walk up to the President and Mrs. Reagan, shake hands, and receive his flag. I was busy chatting with two colleagues as the others were called, however, so I did not quite follow everything. When my name was called I went up to the President, shook his hand, shook Vice-President Bush's hand, and walked directly back to where I had been standing. Only then did I notice that I was receiving a strange look from Mrs. Reagan, as well as a few pointed comments from my friends.

What I had not noticed before was that each person, after shaking hands with the men, had received a kiss and a hug from Mrs. Reagan. I was chagrined when I realized I had walked right by the First Lady. So, after the last name was called, I went quickly up to her and, apologizing profusely, asked if it was too late for me to get a kiss. The First Lady laughed and gave me a warm hug and a kiss on the cheek. Holding my hands in hers, she smiled and welcomed me home. We then followed the President out through the diplomatic reception entrance onto the south lawn.

Keeping Promises

As we sat in an unseasonably warm January sun, I tried to assimilate mentally all that had happened to us in this short period of time. It was almost incomprehensible. We were all heartened and cheered, though, by President Reagan's words, especially when he promised "swift retribution" against terrorists who might try to repeat such acts against Americans. When I heard these words, my mind flashed back to Evin Prison and the change in our captors' attitudes after the President-elect referred to them as barbarians, and the fear these Iranians had come to have of the Reagan administration. Good, I thought. What Mr. Reagan could only imply as President-elect, he could now state openly and authoritatively as administration policy.

But if I had to finger one single disappointment from that time, it is that President Reagan did not live up to his own words. The next horrific terrorist act against the United States came in April 1983, when 63 people, 17 of them American citizens, lost their lives in a car bombing of the US Embassy in Beirut. The US Government soon learned who perpetrated the act and where their headquarters was situated in Lebanon's Ba'aka Valley. But, because of Defense Secretary Weinberger's concern for possible civilian casualties, there was no US retaliation, no swift retribution.

Escaping without penalty for its awful deed, the same faction would, in October of the same year, kill nearly 250 US Marines in Lebanon with another car bomb. The next spring they would again bomb the US Embassy annex in East Beirut, with the loss of more lives.

When there was still no retaliation, the terrorists began attacks on Americans in Beirut, killing several and kidnapping others, including Bill Buckley, a man I respected greatly. The kidnapped victims were held in horrid conditions for as long as five years before their ordeals finally ended. Whenever I recall President Reagan's speech on that beautiful afternoon, I wonder whether there would have been any further attacks against Americans in Lebanon had we indeed meted out swift retribution for the first bombing of our Beirut Embassy. The failure to do so, in my view, only served to prompt more attacks and more loss of American life—and to institutionalize hostage-taking for the better part of a decade.

But all this was in the future on that wonderful January day. After the ceremony, we went back inside for a reception and reunion in the East Room, where the atmosphere was like New Year's Day and the Fourth of July rolled into one. In the midst of this, Anita Schaefer, Tom's wife, pulled me aside and said there were some special people she wanted me to meet. As we walked down the wide corridor leading from the East Room into the mansion, Anita told me that she was going to introduce me to the families of the eight servicemen killed during Desert One. I almost stopped dead in my tracks, overtaken by a complete evaporation of coherent thought. What, I asked myself, do you say—what can you say—to total strangers whose husbands and fathers

44

died trying to save your life and return you to freedom? How can you tell them you understand and share their sorrow? How can you tell them you are more grateful that you could ever possibly express? And how can you ever thank them enough for what their men tried to do for you?

While all this was running through my mind, Anita had been moving us down the hall and into another room, and suddenly I was in the middle of this group. It was the most moving and emotional experience of my life. The wives and children of these heroic men were elated with our release and so very happy that we were all safely reunited with our families. Their smiles were as big as those worn by our own family members, if not more so. If they had any regret or sorrow, there was absolutely no sign of it. They missed their men, I am sure, but on that day they were proud that their husbands and fathers had participated in such a noble cause, even though at terrible cost. I was immensely thankful to Anita for making it possible for me to have spent this brief time with those magnificent women and children.

> **"**
>
> **Suddenly I was in the middle of this group [of family members of the eight US servicemen killed in the rescue attempt]. They were elated with our release … and proud that their husbands and fathers had participated in such a noble cause, even though at terrible cost.**
>
> **"**

The day of celebration ended, and we soon went our separate ways, back to our careers and families and to a normal life. We went from being "hostages" to "former hostages," until, with the passage of years, we were not even that. That much has changed over the years is clear to me through at least one marker. For many years, when I spoke to groups about my experience, I was often speaking to people who were teenagers or young adults during the time of the hostage crisis. They had a clear memory of the events and had, in many instances, participated in letter-writing campaigns or in school projects, or simply followed national and international affairs, often for the first time.

As an audience, these folks were greatly interested in all aspects of the event. They were seeking to learn and understand more about something that had perhaps influenced their lives. But by the 1990s, there were few people in the audiences who were much over five or six years old when Iran and the United States were involved in this struggle of national wills. Now, when I speak to them of the Iranian crisis, they look at it as a historical, academic event remote from, or even unrelated to, their own lives.

And, interestingly enough, so do I.

All opinions expressed in this article are those of the author. They do not necessarily reflect the views of the CIA or any other US Government entity.

www.ingramcontent.com/pod-product-compliance
Lightning Source LLC
Chambersburg PA
CBHW082354270326
41935CB00013B/1620